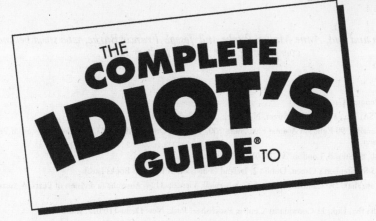

THE COMPLETE IDIOT'S GUIDE® TO

Discovering Your Perfect Career

by Rene Carew, Ed.D., with the American Writers and Artists Institute

ALPHA

A member of Penguin Group (USA) Inc.

For my mom and dad, Anne Malloy Burke and Joseph Francis Burke, who stood behind me in everything I ever wanted to do or to be.

ALPHA BOOKS

Published by the Penguin Group

Penguin Group (USA) Inc., 375 Hudson Street, New York, New York 10014, USA

Penguin Group (Canada), 90 Eglinton Avenue East, Suite 700, Toronto, Ontario M4P 2Y3, Canada (a division of Pearson Penguin Canada Inc.)

Penguin Books Ltd., 80 Strand, London WC2R 0RL, England

Penguin Ireland, 25 St. Stephen's Green, Dublin 2, Ireland (a division of Penguin Books Ltd.)

Penguin Group (Australia), 250 Camberwell Road, Camberwell, Victoria 3124, Australia (a division of Pearson Australia Group Pty. Ltd.)

Penguin Books India Pvt. Ltd., 11 Community Centre, Panchsheel Park, New Delhi-110 017, India

Penguin Group (NZ), 67 Apollo Drive, Rosedale, North Shore, Auckland 1311, New Zealand (a division of Pearson New Zealand Ltd.)

Penguin Books (South Africa) (Pty.) Ltd., 24 Sturdee Avenue, Rosebank, Johannesburg 2196, South Africa

Penguin Books Ltd., Registered Offices: 80 Strand, London WC2R 0RL, England

International Standard Book Number: 978-1-59257-297-7
Library of Congress Catalog Card Number: 2005926954

12   11   10   8   7

Interpretation of the printing code: The rightmost number of the first series of numbers is the year of the book's printing; the rightmost number of the second series of numbers is the number of the book's printing. For example, a printing code of 05-1 shows that the first printing occurred in 2005.

Printed in the United States of America

Note: This publication contains the opinions and ideas of its authors. It is intended to provide helpful and informative material on the subject matter covered. It is sold with the understanding that the authors and publisher are not engaged in rendering professional services in the book. If the reader requires personal assistance or advice, a competent professional should be consulted.

The authors and publisher specifically disclaim any responsibility for any liability, loss, or risk, personal or otherwise, which is incurred as a consequence, directly or indirectly, of the use and application of any of the contents of this book.

Most Alpha books are available at special quantity discounts for bulk purchases for sales promotions, premiums, fund-raising, or educational use. Special books, or book excerpts, can also be created to fit specific needs.

For details, write: Special Markets, Alpha Books, 375 Hudson Street, New York, NY 10014.

Publisher: *Marie Butler-Knight*
Product Manager: *Phil Kitchel*
Senior Managing Editor: *Jennifer Bowles*
Editorial Director: *Mike Sanders*
Development Editor: *Nancy D. Lewis*
Production Editor: *Janette Lynn*

Copy Editor: *Kelly D. Henthorne*
Cartoonist: *Shannon Wheeler*
Cover/Book Designer: *Trina Wurst*
Indexer: *Angela Bess*
Layout: *Ayanna Lacey*
Proofreading: *Mary Hunt*

Contents at a Glance

Contents

Foreword

Okay, first a confession. As an "outside of the box" career expert and dedicated "self-bosser," I had reservations about writing a preface to a book about careers and jobs. Despite spending ten years in the corporate world (or *maybe* because of it) my orientation to the world of work is different from the typical career change formula. Nearly every career change book ever published will tell you to take the same tired steps. Take inventory of your skills and interests, write a winning resume, do a job search, ace the interview, negotiate your salary, then make a merry dash for the corporate ladder. B-o-r-i-n-g.

While this one size fits all approach to career planning worked in simpler times, today we live in a fast-paced, information age. We are a multicultural, multicareer world where at the push of a button a museum staffer in Manhattan, Kansas, can easily apply for position at a museum job in the borough of Manhattan.

But that's not all that's changed. People are no longer satisfied with just getting a job. They want something more ... like a life! Rather than looking to simply land a job they want to create a livelihood and live the lifestyle that matters to them. Instead of focusing on what they've done (their resume) or what they can do (their skills) they yearn to work at something they love to do.

When you base your future career choice on skills alone you may wind up doing something you're good at, but will you love doing it? I knew an accountant named Tom who, true to his skills profile, excelled at crunching numbers. Do you know what he longed to do? He wanted to be an activities director on a cruise ship. Tom could have worked at any accounting firm in the country. But he wanted more. An interviewee in Pulitzer Prize winning author Studs Terkel's book *Working*, got it right when she said, "I think most of us are looking for a calling, not a job. Most of us, like the assembly line worker, have jobs that are too small for our spirit."

If you're looking for a calling, not a job, for a career that not only pays the bills but feeds your spirit, you need to broaden your horizons. This means widening your career planning lens. And that's where *The Complete Idiot's Guide to Discovering Your Perfect Career* can help. This easy to read, resource-rich manual takes you by the hand and walks you through the exciting process of discovering your perfect career. No career clue stone is left unturned. You'll be guided step by step to explore your unique gifts and interests, your values and how to use them to direct your career choices, your motivations, your personality, your work style, the skills you actually *enjoy* using—and perhaps most importantly, your dreams.

The Complete Idiot's Guide to Discovering Your Perfect Career is all about finding the right career fit for you. No matter whether you are looking for a full-time job in an organization or ideas for starting your own business, you will see how your unique profile matches all kinds of jobs and opportunities. In addition, you can find: the best places to work for people with disabilities, older people, people of color, gays and lesbians, and women; how to set up your own home-based business; and, discover the power of creating multiple streams of income. You get the information, insight, advice, tools, resources, tips, and support you need to dream big career dreams—and make them happen.

Scared to change careers? Lots of people say they want to change course and go after their dream job but few do it. Why? Frankly it's easier to be comfortably miserable. Making a major work-life change can be daunting—especially when you're already feeling caught between a "clock and a hard place." And yet as Tom Peter's reminds us, "Unless you walk out into the unknown, the odds of making a profound difference in your life are pretty low."

If you're drawn to discover your perfect career but feel overwhelmed at the prospect of actually making the change, heed the words of football legend Lou Holtz who said, "You can't accomplish anything big without doing the little things." *The Complete Idiot's Guide to Discovering Your Perfect Career* makes the process of pursing your true calling simple and fun. And as Katherine Graham once said, "To love what you do and feel that it matters—how could anything be more fun?"

Valerie Young
Dreamer-in-Residence at ChangingCourse.com

Introduction

You are about to take a journey that will lead to enormous satisfaction and well being in your life. The fact that you picked up this book is your first milestone on your way to successfully identifying your perfect career. Many more milestones are to come, and each section of this book will help you to learn what to do in order to reach your final goal.

Most of you probably haven't had the opportunity to focus on the work that is the most satisfying to you or the lifestyle that suites you best. Although many books, workshops, and even a few courses on career development are out there, most people either don't take advantage of them or don't have the stamina to stay with it. So, this is our caution: get yourself in position to stay the course, finish the book, do the work, put your supports in place that will make you accountable to someone besides yourself, and see this as your job for the next few weeks.

How This Book Is Organized

This book is presented in four sections:

Part 1, "What Do You Really Want to Do with Your Life?", warms you up to this whole career exploration thing. It identifies the myths about going after your career dreams, which get in our way and stop us from a life of happiness and job satisfaction. Then you get a chance to think about all the things you don't want in a job! You go on to open up your dreams about a perfect career and what some of the guidelines for choosing your career might contain—such as determining what are your values and what you do best. You also prepare for success by choosing how you will approach this career exploration—on your own, in a support group, with a coach, and so on, and learn what it will take to sustain your momentum.

Part 2, "Assess Yourself: Uncovering the Real You," is all about taking assessments in the areas of values, temperament and personality, motivation, interests, skills, and lifestyle preferences. You are going to create a Career Profile Map (compiled in Appendix A) that will build a picture of who you are and what is important to you in your career and life. This will be the foundation and guidance for choosing careers that are a good match for who you are and what you want. This section will also help you look back at your early career dreams and look forward to your vision of your career five years down the road.

Part 3, "Discovering the Perfect Career Fit," begins with an overview of the job market to help you look at the careers that are most in demand, most popular, and most profitable. Then you get to identify your ideal work environment to make sure that you are tuning into the location, type of environment, and type of people you like to work with on a day-to-day basis. The heart of this section is looking at the job lists that match your temperament, your interests, and your skills. At the end of this section, you will be able to narrow your own list of possible career areas to two or three occupations. For those of you who are considering further education or training, there is a chapter full of resources to aid in your decision-making.

Part 4, "Learn More About Your Dream Career," is all about taking those two or three choice careers from Part 3 and finding out more about them from selected resources: using the Internet, interviewing job holders, and working with a coach or a mentor to help you learn more about your top choices. Additional resources for the multicultural workforce are included as well as how part-time work through moonlighting can be an excellent transition step to your perfect career. For those of you who are interested in being in your own business, there are tips and resources for getting started and why multiple streams of business might appeal to many of you. It wouldn't be fitting, if we didn't end this book with a beginning: creating your own mission and goal statement with a practical action plan for continuing your journey to attain your perfect career

Things to Help You Out Along the Way

You will notice that throughout the chapters there are some special messages along the way.

Insider Tips

These tips will give you some steps or easy-to-remember ideas. They break down the content into straightforward ways of approaching the work you need to do.

Stop-Look-Listen

These are warnings to help you avoid stepping in the quick sand or going down the wrong path—give them due consideration!

Coach Wisdom

These are fun sidebars because they may be new information to you, things we have picked up along the way, and some additional goodies to use in understanding different aspects of the career journey.

Career Lingo

Most of the words used in career exploration are probably pretty common to you. I have highlighted those that might be new to you and some that stand out as key concepts for you to pay attention to.

Acknowledgments

I would like to thank Susan Clark who prepared the original chapter outlines and wrote Chapter 4: Thanks Susan and AWAI for getting this book off the ground! My partner in crime, Vince Wood from Advisor Team, was instrumental in bringing our readers the excellent assessments and information provided in Chapters 7 and 15 on David Keirsey's work on temperament. We worked together to create an opportunity for people who read this book to also take the real deal Keirsey Temperament Sorter and the Campbell Interest and Skill Survey at a discount, using the Bundle Discount on the last page of this book.

In addition to my colleagues, I would also like to acknowledge my family and friends who have encouraged me, put up with me, and understood why I needed to keep the creative juices flowing at times when they would rather have gone out to dinner! So, thank you so much to my sisters, Judy Burke and Geri Burke; my son and daughter-in-law, Scott and Carrie Carew; my good friend and coach, Ange DiBenedetto; my mentor and buddy, Valerie Young; and my Jupiter Consulting Group colleague, collaborator, and good friend, Moira Garvey.

Trademarks

All terms mentioned in this book that are known to be or are suspected of being trademarks or service marks have been appropriately capitalized. Alpha Books and Penguin Group (USA) Inc. cannot attest to the accuracy of this information. Use of a term in this book should not be regarded as affecting the validity of any trademark or service mark.

Part 1

What Do You Really Want to Do with Your Life?

Life is too short not to do what you really love. Most of us have to work for a living, so why not go after the perfect career for you? In this section, we will uncover the myths that stop you from going after your dream career. It's not too late or too early, and this book makes it pretty easy, so no excuses on that front. You will also have some fun thinking about your jobs from hell and what you do not want to do. Then you will start to dream and do an early identification of some of the key factors that guide you in making career and life decisions. You will also receive some guidance on what to do to make this career exploration journey successful.

Discovering Your True Purpose

In This Chapter

♦ Uncover the myths about finding your true purpose

♦ Real stories of people who are following their dreams

♦ Figure out what your success obstacles and drivers are

Are you dissatisfied with the work you are currently doing? Do you daydream about what life could be like if you were happy and fulfilled in your work? Perhaps you just graduated from high school or college and you can't stop that mantra in your head: "What am I going to do for the rest of my life?" Or perhaps you are one of many people today who is forced to think about different careers. You have been laid off, your position eliminated, or given early retirement. The challenge is the ability to see the opportunity in all these types of situations; to risk sticking your hand out there to grab the brass ring; to look beyond today to a future of your own making—to follow your dreams.

Job dissatisfaction is on the rise. A Conference Board 2003 study shows that there has been a steady decline in job satisfaction since 1995. Less than half of Americans say they are satisfied with their jobs. So many of us are not happy with the work we do, which means that at least eight hours of our days are spent doing something or being in a place we can't wait to get away from—now that doesn't make good sense, does it? Never mind satisfaction, CareerBuilder.com found that 75 percent of the workforce is still in search of their dream job!

Your career is a part of the landscape of your entire life. Discovering your perfect career means you need to pay attention to all those other aspects of your life, too. Relationships, health/fitness, spirituality, and recreation are all important aspects of our lives that affect our career choices and satisfaction. Although different aspects of our lives might take center stage at various times, it's important to know what our ideals are—what is really important to us.

Why We Don't Pursue Our Dreams

We know whether or not we are happy with our work. We take the time to complain about it and worry about it. How about taking the time to do something about it? Easier said than done, you say. Yes, we might have many reasons to avoid taking our career interests seriously.

The myths we tell ourselves can keep us from discovering our perfect careers. Pay attention to the myths you are saying to yourself. Do you find yourself in any of the following?

- "I'm too young to start thinking about my career."

- "I'm too old and jaded to pursue my dreams."

- "I made my choices, can't change my mind now."

- "Not a good idea to change jobs too often—doesn't look good on the resume."

- "I don't have the energy—this work is too difficult."

Each of these myths is dispelled in the sections that follow.

CAUTION

Stop-Look-Listen

Once you have identified your own personal myth, change the message. Stop the myth and start saying, "I deserve to find work that I love." "I deserve to be happy in my work."

Myth #1: Too Young to Start

"It's much too early for me to start thinking about my career"—coming from a high school junior.

It's never too early to introduce young people to different career alternatives—to take them to work, to give them books on people who love their careers, to organize a career a week in their classrooms, to give them feedback on skills, behaviors, talents, and attributes that you see them using well. It's a long life, but it's never too early to begin to pay attention to what you are good at and what you are interested in doing. Self-discovery is always occurring—whether or not we pay attention to what we are learning about ourselves is the issue.

Matt was a junior in high school, and his parents had the foresight to get him a career coach. Matt wanted some help in exploring what he was really interested in getting out of a college education so he could apply to the right colleges. In going through a series of exercises and discussions with his coach about his values, interests, talents, and dreams—as well as likes and dislikes in curricular and extra-curricular areas—he was able to say that any college he went to must have strong programs in both music and communication.

At this stage in Matt's life he didn't have to choose a career. But he did want to choose a college experience that would give him options in areas he already knew he loved and wanted to know more about. And hopefully this experience introduced Matt to a process he could continue to use throughout his life. A *career check-up* is key to a happily running life. Another thing Matt learned was that not everyone "knows what they want to do" early in life. His brother had his career and major picked out in a snap. Matt's career coach was able to help him to understand that people are different—and that is a good thing.

Career Lingo

A **career check-up** is similar to a yearly physical. It involves making an appointment with yourself to check your levels of satisfaction with your career. Are you satisfied with the goals you set for yourself? Is your career consistent with your values and interests? Are you using and learning desired skills and competencies? It also gives you the chance to set goals for the coming year.

Myth #2: Too Old to Change

"It's too late for me—I'm too old, too far into my career"—coming from anyone who has started into their career (10 to 15 years) or is over the age of 50.

It's easy to say that it's never too late, but Louise knew the feeling. When she was 50 she was not happy with what she was doing everyday. She felt the stress of trying to still be a generalist who could tackle any new situation. Louise longed to focus on a few things she could be an expert in. She wished she could be in business for herself and do only those things she loved to do. This would reduce her stress levels and bring the satisfaction she wanted. As she contemplated the future, she also reviewed her fears:

- not knowing how to run her own business
- dependence on a big salary and a retirement plan
- feeling the tip of the scale toward retirement versus going in a new career direction
- seeing the retirement age moving further and further away

Louise decided to put into place a plan that would move her toward her perfect career. For the last three years Louise was with her company, she took the time to do a career check-up and decided to specialize in the work she loved to do. Then she decided to reduce her commitment to her company to half time. In the remaining half of her work time she started to build her own business. She also attended marketing seminars and built a support network of people who specialized in her areas of focus. After a year, she took the plunge and was on her own. Two years later, her business was going well, and she was happier than she had ever been.

As a side note, Louise's mother-in-law was in her 70s when she went back to school for a degree in English. She was a life-long learner and wrote poetry until her passing at the age of 98. It's never too late to live a life of joy and meaning for YOU.

Myth #3: Limited by Choices

"My path is set. My choices are limited now. I majored in business, so I have to find a job in the corporate world"—coming from a graduating senior in college.

College is a wonderful place to develop our love of learning, our curiosity, our ability to think through problems, and our interpersonal and team skills. It is also a place that "some" of us learn the knowledge and skills we will use directly in our careers. For others of us, it's a starting place—although the learning you received in your major is never wasted, you go on to develop other skills in the career you chose.

Scott came home to his parent's house one weekend and slumped down on the couch. He started complaining about the job search he was going to have to embark on when he graduated from college with his degree in business. "Now I'll have to get up early in the morning, get dressed in a business suit, work until all hours, and come home and go to bed because I'll be so exhausted. I won't have any time to work out, to socialize with my friends—I'll just be part of the corporate grind." Well, this wasn't quite what Scott's parents envisioned he would be doing.

Scott loved health and fitness, loved combining work and social relationships. He wanted to make money and be his own boss—an entrepreneur they thought! So his parents reminded him of what he said he loved to do—and with a big sigh of relief, Scott started on his perfect career path. At the age of 25, he bought a health and fitness center in Boulder, Colorado. He created a business with values and an atmosphere that was a reflection of what's important to him in his life—people, and excellent service at www.MountainsEdge.net.

Myth #4: Too Many Job Changes

"I can't keep changing jobs; it won't look good on my resume"—coming from a woman who changed jobs within her nursing profession many, many times!

Even for those of us who don't want to change jobs, the world of work is forcing us to consider this option much more today. Companies are seeking employees who have up-to-date skills. And employees want to work for companies that can provide training and development to keep their skills current. Then there are those people who get bored and need to make a change. Sometimes you can change within one organization, and other times you need to move to another organization. Whatever the reasons for changing jobs—you have the right to enjoy your work. If that means changing jobs, so be it!

Judy was a pioneer—trying every career avenue that nursing had to offer: emergency room, psychiatric, visiting nurses, school nursing, and managed care. Along the way she was concerned that she was changing jobs too frequently, but then the job market changed. New careers were opening up; companies expected up-to-date skills—and Judy was ready to jump into new and challenging areas. She was also a traveler, she worked in different countries and in the mid-'80s she even moved from California to

Massachusetts, leaving a great salary and retirement to start again. In three years, she brought her salary back to what she was making in California by applying her skills to new career areas in her profession and by taking the risk to move to more lucrative positions in the area.

Judy is a person who needs new challenges and will never be happy settling for doing the same thing for all her life. It's no longer a job market that requires life-long loyalty to one company. Today organizations are looking for people who are up-to-date in their areas of expertise, are open to continual learning, and contribute to bottom-line results. Employees are looking for companies that will enable them to master and add new skills and provide increasing challenges and opportunities. When there is a *mutual benefit* to employer and employee, then everyone wins. When there is not, they part ways. Judy was a pioneer to the way life is being lived today.

Career Lingo

Mutual benefit between employee and employer has replaced loyalty. It used to be that employees would pretty much work for one company for their whole working lives. In exchange for their loyalty, they received the security of employment and often retirement benefits. In today's work world, the exchange is different. Employees are looking for opportunities to learn, to keep their skills up, and to remain employable. Employers are looking for employees who have the skills they need right now. As long as the employee and employer are meeting one another's needs, you have mutual benefit. When you don't, there is a parting of the ways.

Myth #5: Lack of Motivation and Knowledge

"I don't have the energy or motivation right now, and I don't know how to go about it anyway"—coming from a person who has just lost their job and has no knowledge of career planning.

This is such a tough position to be in. While it may be little comfort, there are thousands of people facing this situation every day. Let's begin by addressing how to bring your motivation up. While it's a very difficult time, the best way to move through it successfully is to begin by addressing your loss. When you lose your job for any reason—downsizing, rightsizing, layoffs, firing—you receive a blow to your self-worth. You often go through a period of grieving for the loss of your job, your co-workers and friends, and your status or role association. It's important to acknowledge these feelings in order to put them in perspective and eventually let them go. Find a friend, another co-worker, a coach, or a counselor—someone to actively listen to you. This is not a weakness—it is being proactive and taking charge of your own life!

The good news is that this book will provide knowledge on career planning. You will be able to walk yourself through this book and plan your career strategy. You will also learn to lead yourself through this process. It's important to think about your career planning as your new job. You are hiring yourself to find your perfect career. You are your own boss with goals and expectations, a sense of purpose and mission, defined tasks to hold yourself accountable, time lines and deadlines to meet, and plenty of support and recognition for milestones along the way.

Career Lingo

A **milestone** is an important event. In career terms it indicates that you have reached a certain plateau in your journey to identifying your perfect career. Setting milestones is a way to break down your long-range goals into manageable pieces. A milestone is when you have accomplished a big chunk of your goal. It indicates specific results achieved along the road to goal accomplishment. Milestones need to be acknowledged and celebrated. Sometimes goals are so big that we get discouraged along the way. Milestones help us to recognize that we are truly making progress and motivate us to continue the journey.

Dan was laid off from his job of 10 years. He never thought about being laid off. The university was laying off more than 300 staff members due to budget cuts, but somehow he never thought he would be one of them. He loved his work in the alumni office of a state university. He liked the event planning and travel involved in meeting with alumni groups across the country.

Dan decided to ask a career coach to work with a small group of people that had each been laid off. The group was able to talk about their feelings over the loss of their jobs and to go through a structured career planning and job search process. Over a six-week period, Dan and his small group created a *Career Profile Map* that provided the paths to new career options. Dan decided to apply his love of event planning, travel, and his outgoing personality to the sports entertainment industry. He now works for a sports arena where he books talent, plans events, and travels.

Career Lingo _____

Your **Career Profile Map** is in Appendix A—take a look—it might be blank for now, but as you follow along in this book, you will fill it up quickly. This is your career profile—what is really important and of interest to you in a career. It ranges from values that are important to you to skills you want to use or learn in the work you do. It will be your guide in making sure you choose a career direction that matches who you are and what you want.

Obstacles and Drivers

If you didn't see yourself in any of these myth-busting stories, take the time to write your own right now. Use the following examples of obstacles and drivers to get started:

- **Success obstacles:** What do you say to yourself about your career/life situation that can stop you from finding your perfect career?

- **Success drivers:** What is motivating you to do this career exploration now? Be specific about the drivers, dissatisfactions, unfulfilled dreams, unused talents, and desired lifestyle changes.

_____

_____

_____

The Least You Need to Know

- If you are dissatisfied with your career, you are not alone. More than half the population is with you!

- You can face the myths and fears about finding your perfect career and be successful.

- Ask yourself what is driving you right now to find your perfect career. Keep this motivation right in front of you at all times!

2

What Is Your Calling?

In This Chapter

- ◆ Know what you don't want in a career

- ◆ Start to dream big

- ◆ Learn how to figure out your career must haves

Most of us have some idea of what we are interested in doing and the life we want to lead. Unfortunately, it is easy to get distracted and muddled in our thinking. The societies we live in, the families and communities we grow up in, the schools we attend all send messages to us as individuals about who we should be and what type of career is best for us. Sometimes these messages drown out our own feelings. We dismiss or ignore what is really important to us.

So let's get started by focusing on you, and what you want from your career and your life. This chapter is all about you thinking about what's important to you and writing your thoughts down. Right now, let's begin by focusing on what you know you don't want to do!

Career Lingo

Lifestyle is an important aspect of career decision-making. It takes into account all those individual preferences that we have in life. Things like the amount of time we spend relaxing versus working or traveling versus home and community. Lifestyle encompasses parts of us that need to be taken into consideration in our career choices.

What Is Your Job from Hell?

Let's have a little fun by coming up with work situations that you know you would hate! Why start here? Because it helps us to ground ourselves in the certain knowledge we have about what we don't like. Although we may struggle with what we do like, we usually know what we want to stay away from.

Remember in Chapter 1 when Scott hated the idea of wearing a business suit, working from 8 to 7 for someone else? He knew what he really didn't like (even though he thought he had to do it). We are going to begin by looking at some of the work environment and *lifestyle* issues that we love or hate.

Place a **checkmark** next to the descriptors that definitely *would not* describe your perfect work situation:

- ❑ Up and out the door early
- ❑ Make your own schedule
- ❑ Drive to the city
- ❑ Live in the city
- ❑ Walk to work
- ❑ Bike to work
- ❑ Live in the country
- ❑ Work from home
- ❑ Suit up for work
- ❑ Wear relaxed attire every day
- ❑ Work with a team
- ❑ Work alone
- ❑ Relaxed/stress-free environment
- ❑ High expectations
- ❑ Energy-filled environment

- ❑ Deadlines to meet
- ❑ A boss who mentors me
- ❑ Being my own boss
- ❑ Freedom to be creative
- ❑ Clear guidelines and assignments
- ❑ Business lunches
- ❑ Inviting the work gang over
- ❑ Time for socializing and friends
- ❑ Advancing rapidly
- ❑ Learning new skills
- ❑ Variety
- ❑ Routine
- ❑ Challenging work
- ❑ Good people to work with

Coach Wisdom

Have you ever noticed when you ask people about their bosses, their jobs, or their lives that most people feel much more comfortable telling you the negatives. They start with what is going wrong. The down side of situations is what is taking up space in our thoughts and bogging down our feelings. This is a very good reason to get this out first—then we can turn to the positives. We can identify what we really enjoy, prefer, and want to experience.

The Jobs You *Never* Want to Do

Let's clear some space in our brains by throwing out jobs that you know you would never want to do. One person's palace is another's prison, so there are no right or wrong answers here. It's about whether or not a particular job appeals to you.

Let's take a walk in the park to look at the different categories of jobs that are available for us to do. As we do this, **circle** those jobs that you know you would hate to do:

On the right is the gazebo, flower gardens, and restrooms. People are engaged in careers that require working with their hands. They are building, landscaping, and repairing. Jobs involved in this category are carpenters, landscapers, plumbers, electricians. (Producing Orientation)

Then there are the police who are directing traffic around the soccer game being played in the center of the park. People who like adventure and risk-taking are involved in these careers. (Adventuring Orientation)

On the left is a building that houses the first-aid station, environmental studies, and the computer lab. People are enjoying careers that engage them in analyzing what is going on, investigating, and researching. They are performing jobs in the field of science such as a biologist, chemist, physician, medical technician, and *environmental scientist*. Others are involved in careers in computers and math. Still others are more interested in sociology and psychology or being a veterinarian. (Analyzing Orientations)

Career Lingo

Environmental scientists use their knowledge of the physical makeup and history of Earth to protect the environment. They locate water, mineral, and energy resources; predict future geologic hazards; and offer advice on construction and land-use projects. Environmental scientists make $29,000 to $50,000 per year.

As we move down the path, we see people in careers where they are being creative. They are engaged as artists, dancers, architects, musicians, photographers, interior decorators, and curriculum specialists—any career that engages them in using their imaginations! (Creative Orientation)

Next we come across the camp counselors and teachers. People who like to help people, teach them how to do things, and provide comfort and care to others are in this group. Jobs in this area range from nurses, to ministers, to counselors, to teachers in school systems and communities. (Helping Orientation)

> **Career Lingo**
>
> **Curriculum specialists** are also known as instructional coordinators, staff development specialists, or directors of instructional material. They play a large role in improving the quality of education in the classroom. They develop instructional materials, train teachers, and assess educational programs. Income ranges from $35,000 to $72,000 per year.

At the far end of the park, we see the booths set up to sell us all kinds of ser-vices and products. People in these jobs like to sell, influence, and use their skills of persuasion. We see chefs, travel agents, hair stylists, florists, life insurance agents, realtors, and many other people who love to make their business or part of it run. (Influencing Orientation)

Last but not least, we go behind the scenes of the career garden to see the people who hold jobs that support what we see out front. We see accountants, bookkeepers, administrative assistants, and others who process data, maintain records, and keep everything organized. (Organizing Orientation)

In our walk through the garden, you have been introduced to the world of work according to the Seven Interest Orientation model of David Campbell. This gives you your first look at how various jobs fall within particular interest areas. The good news for you is that you will be able to assess your interests in Chapter 9 and then look at all the jobs that match your interests in Chapter 16. There is a wide world of work out there, and you can find work that captures your interests.

Your Career *Don't* List

What else don't you want in your career? You have started to think about some of the work environment and lifestyle areas you don't want, some of the jobs you absolutely don't want, so what else do you have for your list?

Make a list of all the jobs you have held so far in your life:

_____   _____

_____   _____

_____   _____

_____   _____

_____   _____

If you haven't had very many jobs, think about jobs that you have seen other people do. Think about your week and all the places you go. What jobs are people doing? What do you read about people doing in books, newspapers, and on TV?

In the blank table provided on this page, list all of the things you can think of that you dislike and like about your own experiences on jobs as well as what you see other people experiencing in their jobs.

Dislikes	Likes

Here is an example from Mia:

Dislikes	Likes
Boss telling me what to do	Working with friendly people
Standing on my feet all day	Boss treating me with respect
Boring work	Variety of things to do in a day
Nasty customers	Can take a walk during lunch break
Wearing a uniform	Clean and bright work environment
Last minute changes in schedule	Lots of things to do—day goes by fast
	Sending me for training

Now you have had a chance to think about what's important to you in your work environment. When we think about spending 8+ hours a day on a job, our work environment really matters. You now have a snapshot of what you want your work environment to look like and feel like. In Chapter 14 you will be even more specific about your ideal work environment.

Starting to Dream BIG

Now let's turn this picture around and capture those things that you think you would like to have in your perfect career. A little later in Chapter 5, you will look at your dreams in depth. Right now we just want you to start the process of thinking BIG—out of the box—anything you want!

> **Coach Wisdom**
>
> If you could be anything, anyone you wanted to be—what and who would it be? Who do you most admire and why? Dreams and wishes give us so much information about what we truly want, truly think, truly feel. This information will help us to be more creative in looking at our career options.

Read this paragraph and then sit back, put your feet up, and dream big. Think about all the jobs you've ever seen, known about, read about, or made up. Let your mind wander over the landscape of career options and see which ones pop out, put a smile on your face. Look at the whole picture of living this career—see your-self in this career. Then ask yourself what the elements are that make this career so appealing to you. Is it the environment you are working in? Is it the work you are doing? Is it the people you are working with? Is it who you are working with or learning from? Is it the power, the glory, the anonymity, the discovery, the contribution?

Write down the elements here:

_____   _____

_____   _____

_____   _____

Who Are You?

This question, "Who am I?" is a recurring one in our lives. When we are children, we don't worry about it. When we are in our 20s and 30s, we think we have it figured out. When we hit 40, then 50, then 60—oh my—here we go again. Each of us experiences different intensities and levels of discovering who we are and what is important to us at different times in our lives. The question needs to be asked and revisited often—it's part of the career check-up. You wouldn't let your health go for 10 years would you? Well, your career/life satisfaction and direction deserves attention, too. In fact, health and happiness are closely associated!

Insider Tips _____

Over the years we go through stages of growth and development. Each stage presents us with new areas to focus on—defining who we are as individuals, who we are as a partner and/or parent, career aspirations, career plateaus, and retirement. We are always discovering more about ourselves through experiences and life stages. It is normal and healthy to adjust our career paths and goals.

Particular aspects of ourselves make up our career check-up. Starting in Chapter 6, we are going to break each aspect of the check-up into discreet tests and assessments that will help you uncover and focus on yourself in that area.

For now, we want to introduce you to each of these aspects. Do a little brainstorming with yourself before you take any of the assessments—just to prime your pump. The process of defining what you really want takes concentration, focus, and revisiting to bring the true answers to the surface. So we begin by learning about each aspect and asking you to write down your initial thoughts—what comes to mind right away.

What Are My Values?

Values are attitudes and beliefs that we hold as most important in our lives. They are demonstrated through consistent behaviors in relation to these values. Values range from being security minded to seeking adventure and risk or from maintaining independence to facilitating interdependence. Values are our guideposts to selecting the work, the work environment, and the lifestyle that is most important and fulfilling for us. Every Career Profile Map needs an anchor, and values are just that—they keep you on course.

Stop-Look-Listen _____

Let's look at friendship as an example of a core value. What behavior might demonstrate friendship? Perhaps making time for friends, listening to their concerns, checking in with them, and so on.

What's important to you—what are your beliefs and attitudes that you choose to act upon? Quickly write down a list and circle the three you act on the most often.

1. _____
2. _____
3. _____
4. _____
5. _____
6. _____
7. _____

"Values are not reflected by what we think, or even by what we intend, they are a reflection of what we do."—Anonymous

What Do I Like To Do?

These are your interests, things you enjoy doing. What you are drawn to doing. Do you like to play sports? Do you love walking or jogging? What types of books do you like to read? Do you like to bird watch, parachute out of planes, or travel? Think back over the past three months and write down three things you spent time doing that you are really drawn to, three things that you can't wait to get to—or that you wish you had more time to do.

1. _____
2. _____
3. _____

What Do I Do Best?

If someone asked you what you think your special talent is, what would you say? Things that we do best are probably skills or talents that have come easily to us from a young age. Ellie has a talent for observing other's behavior. She uses this talent in her work with leaders when she observes their behaviors and gives them feedback. She can remember using this talent in elementary school! Take a few minutes to think about what comes easily to you. Do people ask you to figure out the tip for them at a restaurant—math skills? Do you find yourself being the office "counselor"—people see you as a good listener and problem solver? Are you good at analyzing complex situations? Write down two of your talents. Don't be shy about owning these—it's only between us for now.

1. _____

2. _____

Where Do I Want to Live?

For some people this can be the most important question to answer in their career/life decisions. We desire to live in certain places for many different reasons. Do you love to live in different cultures? Want to be close to family? Need a certain climate for your health? Figure your business will be more profitable in a certain location or climate? A few years ago I changed lawn-care companies and went with two young men just starting their business. I made them promise me a long-term business relationship. For three years they were great. Then, they moved to Florida. You can guess why—lawn care all year long. They don't have to worry about how much snow falls in the winter to sustain their business. Right now, today, where do you want to live and why?

_____

_____

_____

How Much Money Do I Want to Have?

You might be able to answer this question very quickly. You might be very clear that money is a main driver for you in choosing a career path. Or, you might be sure that doing something that makes a difference is most important, and money is secondary. A simple life, a comfortable life, a luxurious life—what will it be? We will go more in-depth about the complicated issue of money in our lives in Chapter 5. For now, take a temperature check on the amount of money you want to make each year. How much money do you want to have and why?

_____

_____

_____

The Least You Need to Know

◆ It's okay to eliminate jobs that you really don't like—it narrows the field.

◆ It takes time and focus to uncover what we really want in a career.

◆ Your values drive all your career decisions—pay attention to them.

◆ Your career choices will change over time with your life-work experiences.

3

Setting Up for Success

In This Chapter

- What gets in the way of progress
- How to keep focused on career planning
- Set SMART goals
- Start a support group

Let me say right from the start—discovering your perfect career is not a quick or easy task for most people. Staying the course to figure it out takes persistence. Here are a few things to keep in mind that can happen to you in this process:

- It's hard to retain a clear picture of what you are learning about yourself as you go through the exercises and tests in this book.

- It's easy to get distracted. Keeping the focus on you is tough. Other things become much more interesting.

- It's not easy to keep talking to your friends and family about your career exploration. Most of us don't get enough airtime to talk about what's important to us on a daily basis. Philosophical life and career conversations are definitely put on the back shelf compared to daily must do's.

◆ It's easy to start wondering whether you are getting a true picture of yourself. There is only so much insight we can provide for ourselves. We begin to ask ourselves whether we really do have talent in a certain area—or whether we are just kidding ourselves?

With these cautions in mind, you can keep your motivation up and your focus steady in several ways.

Going Solo

Some parts of this career exploration you must do on your own. And you might want to do this whole process on your own. Some of us prefer to work on our own; others will prefer to use a variety of approaches. The sections that follow will high-light things that are important for everyone to do.

Capture Your Thoughts

In order to be able to retain all the information we are learning about ourselves, the first thing we need to do is *capture our thoughts*. In Appendix A there is a Career Profile Map where you can write down all your assessment and test results as well as weigh the importance of each aspect of your career/life profile. There is also a place on this Career Profile Map to write down your insights and thoughts as you go along. These are indicated as Career Implications (notes to yourself). Writing all of this down is extremely important. This is going to aid in your ability to get a clear picture of what your preferences are for your career/life decisions. In the end, you're Career Profile Map will by your guide to making decisions about the types of jobs and careers that are right for you.

Get into a "This is Your Job" Mind-Set

Visualize this career exploration as your job. Discovering your perfect career is not a pastime, it is a mission. It is a job that you have hired yourself to do, and it comes with accountability and rewards. When you work for an organization, you have responsibilities and deadlines to produce. Think of your career mapping in the same way.

Set SMART Goals

People who set goals for themselves tell us that they achieve their goals faster for two reasons. First, goals help them to focus their energy and take actions on a daily basis. Second, goals help them to stay motivated. Being able to look at your goals every day provides guidance for your actions as well as motivates you to get results.

Here are some guidelines for writing goals. These are called SMART goals because they contain all the elements that are going to help you set goals that will stretch you without breaking you.

S—Be *specific* about what you want the end result of all this work to be for you. For example, "One year from today I will be in a job that matches my career and life preferences on my Career Profile Map."

M—Make your goal *measurable*. How else will you know when you have succeeded? In the previous "S" example, the measurements are one year from today (time) and match the preferences on my Career Profile Map (demonstrated quality). Measurements can involve cost, time, quantity, and quality.

Career Lingo

Measurables are a way of demonstrating the kinds of results your goal is achieving. You will know whether you have been successful. Results can be seen in the difference in cost, time, quantity, or quality.

A—Your goal has to be *attainable*. Goals are motivating when they stretch you. By stretching I mean moving out of your comfort zone into a learning zone. You don't, however, want to move into the danger zone. A danger zone is when you don't have much chance of success. Stay in the learning zone where you can succeed. Perhaps landing your perfect job in one year is unrealistic for your circumstances. Your goal may need to be broken down into multiple stages. For example, in one year you will devote one-third of your time to your new career interests or you will complete a training/education program. You want to be able to celebrate your milestones and successes along the way. You don't want to suffer under a heavy and unattainable goal. The idea is to free us and motivate us to grab our brass ring.

R—Each goal must be *realistic*. You need to set goals for yourself—not for other people. You need to consider who you are, what your strengths and weaknesses are, and what would add to your satisfaction. Setting goals for other people or just for "these circumstances" is not motivating or inspiring. We each have talents and gifts that make us very special. This is what will make us successful in life.

T—*Time-framed* goals are what get results. Always set a time frame for achieving your goals. You can break your goal down into steps that are attainable for you. For example, "My job this week is to read and complete exercises in Chapters 1 to 3 and to set a goal for the next week." If you are familiar with project maps, you can plan ahead for the next two months. Your day planner or PDI might have a project map that you can use.

Take the time now to write your goal. What do you want to accomplish? What is it that you are hoping to get as a result of going through the exercises in this book? What is your desired result? When you are finished writing your goal, post it on your refrigerator, put it in your planner, or anywhere you frequent on a daily basis. Make sure you see it so it can motivate and guide your actions!

SMART Goals

Goals	Description
S (specific)	
M (measurable)	
A (attainable)	
R (realistic)	
T (time-framed)	

Give Yourself Rewards That Work

Can you imagine a world where no one ever said thank you, slapped your back in appreciation, or bowed in reverence to your wisdom? Well, we don't always have to look to others to let us know we are doing a good job. As your own taskmaster, you can also reward yourself. Rewards can be short—10 minutes to check e-mails, 5 minutes for a personal phone call, or a hot fudge sundae. They can also be more lengthy—a walk in the park, a trip to Hawaii, or a day off! The important thing is to choose things that feel like a reward to you. What gift would you like to receive after

completing your first three chapters? After completing your Career Profile Map?
Think about it and write a few rewards down here:

_____

_____

_____

Support Options

Wouldn't it be nice to know that someone has set aside time to talk with you about
your career/life directions? You wouldn't have to try to fit it into the conversation;
it would be on the agenda. Although some of us can do this work on our own—and
actually prefer it that way—others like a sounding board. Talking out loud (to another
human being!) helps us to sort out our true thoughts and feelings. Having someone
else ask us questions—provide feedback about what they think we are saying—can
deepen our exploration. Another thing it does is hold us accountable. We are
expected to report in on what we have learned about ourselves this week—WOW—
a time for me. There are many ways to build in support, the sections that follow list
a few.

Buddy Up

Find someone else who is using this book to discover their perfect career. Perhaps it
is a family member, a colleague, a friend, or someone you met at the bookstore buying the book! All you need is one other person who wants to make a commitment to
themselves—and to you. Set up a meeting once a week by phone, in person, or a
combination of the two. Agree to a 1-hour meeting, 30 minutes each. Set a weekly
goal; focus your discussion on something you want to discuss more in depth. For
instance: I just did the Values Sort Assessment in Chapter 6, and I had trouble
deciding on my Top 5 Values—I have too many. My focus this week would be on
talking about the values I chose and why they are important to me. My buddy might
want to ask me how he sees me acting on my values—what they see as most important to me. Or you can make it simple—what I learned about myself this week and
what I recorded in my Career Profile Map. Conversation will follow from there.

Success Group

This is another version of buddying up, just with a few more people. Having four or five people that are committed to going through the same process can give you even more information, ideas, and insights.

To get the maximum benefit from working with a success group, try the following:

1. Think about what you want to get out of your discussion beforehand.

2. Establish that each person has a specific amount of discussion and support time.

3. Give a two-minute summary of your goal and what you have accomplished since setting the goal.

4. Identify where you are stuck and where you need help.

5. Ask the group to brainstorm ideas for getting you moving.

6. State your goal for next week.

When you get to the part about brainstorming career/job options, the more people focusing on what you can do, the better. Over time people get to know one another and can observe one another's special talents. This provides a source of verification, confidence, and motivation for group members.

Career Coach

If you know you can't do it yourself and you have the resources to work with a professional—do it. Check the telephone directory under Career and Vocational Counseling. Ask your local colleges for a referral. Call the college you graduated from to see whether they have a service for their alumna. If you don't have the monetary resources, see whether you can barter with someone or network to find free community services through colleges, employment offices, or career centers. Look in the paper for ads for free career services. Some people offer free introductory workshops. Always check on credentials by asking whether you can talk to people they have worked with or going to their websites for backgrounds.

> **CAUTION**
>
> **Stop-Look-Listen**
>
> If you need support, ask for it, negotiate for it, and give it in return. We only go around once (at least in this lifetime) so get over yourself. Be proactive in making your career exploration the best it can be. If that involves having support—work it out—be proactive!

Support Network Components

As we go through our lives, it is important to have a network of people who we can go to for different types of support. Often we look to only one or two people we can talk to about everything. This proves to sometime ask too much of too few. In the area of career/life conversations and decisions, here are the support categories that can be useful:

◆ *Challenging People* who will challenge you. These are people who will nudge you out of your comfort zone. They are able to see your potential. They en-courage possibilities, risk taking, and growth. These people might come in the form of a mentor or a boss.

◆ *Trustworthy People* in your life that you trust. People who can give you honest feedback and who will listen. These people can provide insight and observations on your strengths and weaknesses.

◆ *Are Like Me People* who are like you. In thinking about your career/life experiences and goals, it is helpful to talk with people who are the same as you. This similarity in culture, age, gender, sexual orientation, race, or nationality can be helpful in understanding and sorting through common experiences. It also allows an honest sorting out of thoughts and decisions.

◆ *Praise Me People* who just like you. We need people in our lives who will tell us how wonderful we are. People who encourage us, celebrate our successes, and always remember the best about us.

◆ *Hard Timers People* you can go to in hard times. Throughout the process of making career/life decisions, we sometimes come across setbacks and hard times. We need people we can talk to who don't need any sugar coating. People who don't need us to be totally "to-gether." People who can listen and encourage our feelings.

Coach Wisdom

Most of us spend our time putting out fires and responding to crises or wasting our time on TV and surfing the Internet. The place we need to focus on is those areas that are important in our lives—like our careers, our important relationships, coming up with solutions to recurring problems. It isn't a matter of time—it's a matter of focus!

Write the names of people in your current support network who fulfill your needs in each of these five categories:

Challengers	Honest Feedback	Are Like Me	Praise Me	Hard Timers

Check to see whether you have the same person down in several categories. You might be overloading these people. If you don't have at least three names down for people in each category, start thinking about who else in your network you could call on more frequently in these categories. Think about the people whom you like, admire, spend time with, and have connections to already.

If you don't have people in your network right now, then start to do more networking. Get to know people better through volunteer work, committee work, starting your own support group, as well as joining associations locally and nationally.

The Least You Need to Know

♦ There will be obstacles to staying the course in finding your perfect career, but you can overcome these obstacles.

♦ Choosing methods to keep you focused on your career planning is crucial to your success.

♦ Support comes in many forms, and we need different people for different types of support.

Part 2

Assess Yourself: Uncovering the Real You

In this section, you will be creating your Career Profile Map, which will guide you in making decisions about the perfect career for you. This section begins with an overview of what assessments are and how you can use them. Before you begin to take your assessments, you will have a chance to think about what you wanted to do when you were growing up and how satisfied you feel about the life you are living right now. Then you will assess your values, temperament and personality, motivation, interests, skills, and lifestyle. At the end of this section, you will sum it all up in your Career Profile Map and be ready to match careers to your profile.

Dig a Little Deeper

In This Chapter

♦ Discover self-assessment

♦ Learn how to self-assess using tests

♦ Uncover what self-assessment tests can tell you

♦ Tests you will take and some to consider

♦ Find out how you'll use your results to discover your dream career

Discovering your dream career, the career that will make you happiest, involves more than just figuring out what you want to do. Also important is discovering what you'll be good at—determining what kind of work will best fit with your values, your temperament, and your interests. To accurately uncover who you are and what you want, self-assessment tests are invaluable.

Don't worry, these tests aren't like the ones you took in school. You won't get a grade, and no matter what, you can't fail! Best of all, these tests are easy and fun; let me explain.

What Are Self-Assessments?

First, what does *self-assessment* really mean? If you pick up *The Collins English Dictionary*, you'll find self-assessment defined as "an evaluation of one's own abilities and failings." But that definition doesn't really fit self-assessment for our purposes. Instead, let's give self-assessment the more accurate definition psychologists use: an appraisal of one's own personal qualities and traits. This type of self-assessment focuses on recognizing your strengths, not your weaknesses. It's this self-assessment that can help you best uncover your dream career.

Career Lingo

Self-assessments are appraisals of your own personal qualities and traits that help you identify your strengths.

How Self-Assessments Help

Self-assessments can provide you with all kinds of information about your hidden talents, personality characteristics, and interests. I would be willing to bet you'll learn at least one thing about yourself that you didn't know. Truth be told, you'll probably learn dozens of things from taking the self-assessments in this book.

But don't misunderstand, these assessments (or any assessment for that matter) will not lay out quick and easy answers about what you should or shouldn't do with your life. However, by taking the information you'll learn about yourself as a whole, and by using the guidance you'll get in this book, you can more quickly and easily discover the path to your dream career.

The key thing to remember: Don't put all of your eggs in one basket. This translates to: don't rely solely on one self-assessment test. That's why this book is filled with information and direction to numerous self-assessments and exercises, so you'll get as complete a picture as possible of who you are. Then you can determine what area of work will bring you the most overall satisfaction.

The following sections will highlight and provide an overview of the assessment tests contained in this book. They will also give you references to online assessments and books.

Dreams Assessments

Dreams are sources of information. In this book, we want to tap into the dreams you had when you were young, the dreams that are hanging around still. These dreams can be keys to unlocking elements of what you want in your perfect career. Along with checking out your dreams, we also want to take a look at the different aspects of your life and see how satisfied you are right now.

Looking at how satisfied you are currently with the amount of money you make, the work you do, family and friendships, health and fitness, body/mind/spirit, work and living environments, and fun and recreation, is going to give us even more clues to what you may want instead! This is the next step in moving our dreams foreword in time, so we will ask you to create a vision statement for five years down the road. In summary, we take your dreams (past and future), compare them with your current state, and you are able to see the gap or distance between your ideal state and your present reality. This is called a GAP Analysis:

> Future State
>
> GAP
>
> Present Reality

Here are some assessments for uncovering your dreams and looking at your life satisfactions:

- **Early Career Dreams Assessment**—Chapter 5 contains three exercises that capture your favorite things to do, your early dreams, and dreams that are still with you today;

- **The Wheel of Life Assessment**—In Chapter 5, you will also find this assessment on your level of current satisfaction with the following: money, career/work, family and friends, health and fitness, spirit/mind/emotions, significant other, environments, fun and recreation;

- **Five Years From Now Exercise**—This is a visioning exercise to help you think about where you want to be five years from now. This vision can be a motivator and guide for you in your career exploration process.

Values Assessments

Values are attitudes and beliefs you hold dear and will act upon—what's most important to you in life. Despite what many people believe, it *is* possible to find a career that aligns work with your values. When you can do this, your work is much more rewarding because it fulfills your personal needs as well as your financial needs. You feel satisfied through and through.

> **Stop-Look-Listen**
>
> Remember how much you railed at your parents' values—well now you get to decide what's really important to you. Take the time to decide for yourself!

The interesting thing about values, however, is that the values you have when you are 25 might not be the same values you have when you're 35, 40, or even 50. This is just one of the reasons people grow disillusioned with their chosen careers and they start searching for a different line of work. Examining your values is something you should do regularly each year to see what's changed and how you can adapt your work and lifestyle to match what's important to you. The assessments in this book can help you do this.

Here are some values assessments you can check out:

- ◆ **Values Sort Assessment.** Helps you to identify and prioritize values that are currently important to you in your life. You can take this assessment in Chapter 6.

- ◆ **Super's Work Values Inventory.** Identifies the work characteristics that are important to you in selecting an occupation. Can be found at www.Kuder.com for cost of $11.00, which also includes two other assessments. Super's Work Values is a part of the whole Kuder Career Planning System. It is one of the three assessments within the system, Kuder Career Search (interest), Kuder Skills Assessment, and Super's.

- ◆ **Work Preference Inventory.** Helps you understand your work style based on your values. Free at www.CareerPerfect.com.

Temperament and Personality Assessments

An important part of self-assessment is pinpointing characteristics of your personality. Your personality is more than just how you define yourself. It's the sum total of all of your qualities and traits. It's a complex pattern that includes emotional characteristics, mental traits, and behaviors that make you uniquely you.

Some of your most important characteristics, the ones that can help direct you to your dream career, may not be the ones of which you're aware. In fact, the human personality is so complex, hundreds of years of research have been devoted to understanding the way a person thinks, feels, and relates to others. Self-assessment testing can help you uncover your hidden behaviors and who you really are.

Here are some examples of personality assessments:

- **The Shorter Personality Sorter™.** Based on David Keirsey's work in the areas of *temperament* and personality. There are four distinct temperaments, each of which has a predisposition to particular attitudes or behaviors. Our temperaments influence our values; communication style; interests; self-image; and how we approach our past, present, and future. This assessment, found in Chapter 7, identifies 16 personality types that are based on our temperament as well as our character.

  The last page of this book contains a discount coupon code to take the "Bundle—the Kiersey Temperament Sorter and the Campbell Interest and Skill Survey." Go to www. KeirseyCampbell.com and follow the instructions for inputting your code to receive your discount. David Keirsey's latest book is *Please Understand Me II: Temperament, Character, Intelligence* (Prometheus Nemesis Book Co. Inc., 1998).

> **Career Lingo**
>
> **Temperament** is your disposition. It represents tendencies you were born with to have certain attitudes and to behave in certain ways. It is known as the core or driving force of your personality.

- **The Myers Briggs Type Indicator (MBTI).** Identifies 16 personality types based on different ways you take in information and how you make decisions based on this information. In order to take the MBTI, you must work with someone who is certified to administer this test (career counselor, human resource staff, guidance counselor). For more help with referral sources for test administrators, visit www.cpp.com.

Stop-Look-Listen

Watch how much stock you put in the results of any test. Check it out with your friends and family—is this really what I'm like? Do you see me behaving in these ways?

◆ **The Enneagram Type Indicator.** Looks at nine basic personality types to help you recognize and understand an overall pattern in your behavior. The Enneagram can help to orient you to your higher spiritual and psychological qualities that each type has in abundance. The Enneagram Type Indicator Sampler can be found at www.enneagraminstitute.com.

Motivation Assessments

Do you know what motivates you? What makes you start your day with enthusiasm? Some motivations are based on needs that might change over time such as money, relationships, being recognized and respected, contributing to society, or spirituality. Other motivations may run deep, such as what we really value in our careers.

◆ **The Four Boxes of Life Assessment.** Makes you think about and prioritize what you want from four basic areas of motivation: security, relationships, recognition, and contribution. You will find this assessment in Chapter 8.

◆ *Career Anchors, Discovering Your Real Values* (Pfeiffer, 1985). Edgar Schein's book contains a self-assessment and gives terrific examples of career motivators, for example:

1. Being seen as an expert

2. Wanting to lead and manage others

3. Working independently

4. Having ongoing security

5. Being an entrepreneur

6. Giving service

7. Experiencing challenges

8. Enjoying a specific lifestyle

Interest Inventories

Your interests are another part of self-assessment that people often forget about. For decades, people chose careers without regard to their interests and hobbies. And because of that, many professionals never experienced sincere job satisfaction.

Yes, work is work. But you can also get paid for doing something you love. This area of self-assessment will help you determine what you really enjoy doing. What your favorite hobbies are or could be. It might come as a surprise to you to know that many leisure activities can be converted into profitable careers.

- ◆ **Orientation Scales Assessment.** This was developed using David Campbell's theoretical model of seven specific orientations that match our interests to occupations. Chapter 9 will start you on your journey to identifying interests that you have in each of the seven interest orientations. Later, in Chapter 16 you will match your interests to actual jobs. The Campbell Interest and Skills Survey (CISS) is available at a discount if you use the bundle coupon on the last page of this book. To use the discount coupon go to www.KeirseyCampbell.com. Otherwise, you can take the CISS at www.AdvisorTeam.com for $17.95.

- ◆ **Strong Interest Inventory.** Matches your interests to occupations where people have similar interests. It must be administered by a certified person. Look to your guidance counselor, human resources department, career counselor, or check out www.cpp.com for a referral.

- ◆ **The Career Key.** Matches your interests, needs, values, abilities, and skills to occupations. You can find this assessment at www.CareerKey.com, and it costs around $4.95.

- ◆ **Talent Identification.** In Chapter 8, which focuses on your many different types of skills, we ask you to pick out those skills that you have always had, use regularly, feel very comfortable using, and essentially are your talents.

Skill Assessments

Self-assessments can also accurately gauge your skills. These skills include what you've learned from past work and life experiences. These skill sets are often placed in three categories:

- ◆ Transferable or functional skills: These are skills that can be transferred from one job to another, for example, typing or knowledge of computer software.

◆ Self-management or adaptive skills: These are behavioral skills that you have learned from your work and life experiences. For example, maybe you excel under pressure or you're a good communicator.

◆ Technical or work content skills: These are the skills you have learned from specific training, for example, a degree in teaching or in accounting.

Some examples of skills assessment tests include the following:

◆ **Skills Inventory Assessment.** This is a self-assessment to identify skills you have, skills you want, or skills you never want to use in the areas of working with data, things, and people. You will also identify your transferable skills based on this assessment. These assessments can be found in Chapter 10.

◆ **Self-Management Grid.** This is an assessment to help you identify your self-management skills (also in Chapter 10).

◆ **Skills Profiler.** This tool has you list your skills, identify occupations that require your skills, and look at the gaps in your skills and/or education for each occupation. It is highly recommended that you check this out at www.CareerOneStop.com.

◆ **SkillScan.** This assessment takes you through a process of identifying your transferable skills, your knowledge-based skills, and your personal traits and attitudes. The cost is $14.95, and it takes approximately one hour to complete. It can be found at www.skillscan.com.

Lifestyle Assessments

Getting a clear picture of your preferred lifestyle includes understanding how much money you want to make along with the type of balance you want to maintain between career and home life. How do you see yourself spending time after work or on weekends? What's important to you in your life—relationships, leisure time, and fun, community involvement? This area of assessment is critical in directing your career choice. It takes into consideration all the other important aspects of your life.

Do we stay the same throughout our lives—absolutely not. For example, in your 30s, your career may take up more of your focus and time, but in your 60s and 70s you may want to have more leisure time and involvement in the community. It's important to check in with yourself periodically to see whether your lifestyle preferences have changed and what implications that has on your career path.

◆ **Lifestyle Preference Assessment.** Helps you to determine which lifestyle aspects are most important to you right now and how this might influence your career choices. You will take this self-assessment in Chapter 11.

Ideal Work Environment Assessments

What kind of work environment do you like? For example, do you like to work alone? Do you like to work with other people? Do you hate the idea of being confined to an office? How you'll answer questions like these will help you uncover your preferred work environment and help you determine in which career areas you'll be most comfortable and happiest. It also helps you to narrow down your search of organizations that fit your criteria for a good place to work.

◆ **The Ideal Work Environment Assessment.** Focuses on three work environment components: location, work environment, and work style. This assessment helps you to narrow down those work environment areas that are most important to you. We will cover this assessment in Chapter 14.

◆ **Preferred Work Style Inventory.** This describes the way you learn and operate in new work situations. Neil Yeager is the author of this inventory. You can order this inventory from Charter Oak Consulting Group, Inc. Go to their website at www.COCG.com to contact them about purchasing inventories.

How to Use Self-Assessments

All of the assessments included in this book have been designed specifically to be clear and easy to use. Each of the tests is unique and is structured differently. For some, you'll answer two dozen questions; in others you'll pick and choose interests and skills with which you identify. And still in others, you'll take a survey asking your preferences for people, things, job, and lifestyle content. No test has more than 100 questions. And no test should take you longer than 30 minutes to complete. Where applicable, you will be instructed to include your test results in the Career Profile Map in

Insider Tips

When taking self-assessment tests, you should respond with your first instinct. Don't agonize over questions. When you do, you just allow your preconceived beliefs about who you are and what you want to shape your answer, which might not necessarily be the true you.

Appendix A. This will allow you to keep all your results together for your reference and reflection.

With the varied range of assessments, you will have a clear profile of who you are and what a good career/job match is for you. We will also give you many other resources online that are available for free and for purchase.

Most important, when you start taking the self-assessment tests in this book, and the ones you'll be directed to online, it's important to keep all of your results in perspective. For example:

♦ Never depend on self-assessments to determine what you want to do with your life. Self-assessments are helpful in making you think about who you are, what's important to you, and what *might* be some possibilities to research further.

♦ Always step back and think about the results of each assessment. There may be new information for you to consider. Or, the information might not match who you know yourself to be. So, make up your own mind about the value of each assessment to you.

♦ One of the reasons we give you so-o-o many assessments is because we want you to look for consistent themes in your results. We want you to be able to look at yourself from a number of angles and to really check what your preferences and passions are for the work you want to do. Your assessment results can be influenced by many things that can cover up your true self, for example:

I'm having a bad day—don't like anything;

Other people tell me that I'm good at using a particular skill, so I might not pay attention to skills I really want to use;

My current job pulls on me using particular skills and approaches to my work, and this can cover up the styles and skills I prefer to use.

CAUTION

Stop-Look-Listen

Don't rely on a single test for direction. It's important that you take all the tests included in this book to obtain the clearest view of who you are.

♦ Assessments help you to look at yourself from different angles. Take advantage of this. Keep track of what you are finding out by recording your results in your Career Profile Map in Appendix A. It won't be a new you, but it might be a more informed you.

♦ Don't throw out the baby with the bath water. Take the gems—the good information—and let them help you to guide your thinking about your career and lifestyle choices.

We've tried to make it easy for you to get the right perspective on your self-assessment test results and to make taking a "misstep" like misinterpreting your results next to impossible.

We've organized the second half of this book into sections to help you specifically understand and put to use the culmination of your test results. You'll learn how to take your assessment profiles and match them to different career areas, how to narrow those areas down into job preferences, and how to discover what you need to know about each one. The result is that you can make an informed decision and choose a career path that is *most* right for you!

Your Career Profile Map

Each time you take an assessment, you will be asked to write your results in your Career Profile Map located in Appendix A. This is your own personal career map to guide your decisions about jobs, occupations, and careers that match up with what you really want. It also helps to keep all these assessment results straight!

> **Coach Wisdom**
>
> Don't be overwhelmed by the information in this chapter! Take three deep breaths. You will take these assessments one at a time. You can take a break between chapters and reflect. In the end, you will have a picture of who you are. Then, you will be ready to match your authentic self to the right career areas.

The Least You Need to Know

◆ Self-assessments can help you to discover more about your values, your interests, your personality, your skills, your preferred lifestyle, your motivations, and the kind of work environment you want to be in.

◆ Self-assessments cannot teach you all you need to know about yourself, but they can give you a good start in reflecting on who you are and what is most important to you in your life.

◆ Keep track of your results on all your assessment tests in your Career Profile Map in Appendix A. This will be your guide to selecting a career that matches your personal requirements.

5

Your Dream Career

In this Chapter

- ◆ Get in touch with your early dreams
- ◆ Assess your current satisfaction with your life and work
- ◆ Look five years down the road

How often have you heard people joke about still not knowing what they want to be when they grow up? Let's reverse that and say maybe we knew what we wanted to be when we were children and growing up got in the way! There are actually so many clues from our youth that go undetected. So we are going to take a retrospective look at what our early dreams were.

Think about this as solving a mystery. You are in search of clues from your early life. Clues that will give you information about your true character and preferences. The mystery tour will continue when you jump to the present and assess how you feel about the life you are living today. You will look at how satisfied you actually are with the choices you have made so far. And last but not least, you will create a five-year vision to see what the future may look like for you.

There is so much information stored in our minds and our imaginations. Visioning can help us to release this knowledge. When we are finished looking back, looking at the present, and looking ahead, we will have our dream board started. Your dream board can take the form of drawings, pictures, or writing. It can be in a notebook or journal or pasted on your wall. It is a tangible representation of you and your dreams. And, it can be a motivation and guide for the pursuit of these dreams. It can also change and develop over time.

We actually know quite a bit about ourselves and what we really want. It's more a matter of making the space and having a way to get at that information. This chapter will give you both!

Early Career Dreams

What did you want to be when you grew up? Yesterdays are often forgotten in the bright glare of today's realities. But in those early years of our childhood we all had dreams about what we would be when we grew up. Part of those dreams was based on liking the red fire trucks and the great noise they made on the way to a fire. Not so fast—how about the adventure and excitement and risk involved in being a fireman (or woman)!

There is usually information in our early dreams that can remind us of hopes and aspirations and parts of our character that we might have lost over the years. For example, my son used to spend hours with his small plastic armies, moving them around, sending them to battle. I hated the battle part, but he loved the strategy, and that's what he uses in his business today.

My Favorite Things to Do

Remember, you are on a mystery tour to find out what really interested you and excited you when you were young. What were your favorite playtime activities? What were you drawn to doing when you were alone? What did you like to do with other children? Start from the earliest age you can remember (some of us are better at this than others). Did you like to build things, make things, watch people or things, talk, sing, dance, help to do things around the house, plant flowers, do risky things (without permission), or read books?

Write down all the fun and interesting things you did during these different time periods. If you are having trouble remembering, ask those who were around you (parents, siblings, cousins, friends, and extended family). They often have wonderful and insightful stories to tell about what you spent your time doing! List the activities and write down why you liked them. What about them interested you, excited you, drew you to them?

Activities from ages 1–5	**Why did you like this activity?**
_____	_____
_____	_____

Activities from ages 6–11	**Why did you like this activity?**
_____	_____
_____	_____

Activities from ages 12–16	**Why did you like this activity?**
_____	_____
_____	_____

Too often we skip over information that has important clues to what we really enjoy doing in our lives. Solving a mystery can be very gratifying. And, you have to pay attention to all the subtleties that lead you to the right answer. Looking back over your life and uncovering those early interests and dreams will help you to solve the mystery of finding your perfect career.

Capturing Early Dreams

This is where you capture your early career/job dreams. What did you want to be when you grew up, and why do you think that was so interesting to you? From a very early age, my child wanted to be in business for himself. At around age 10, he wanted to own a Toy Store—well, this made sense for age 10. The part that remained true was being a business owner. The content of the business changed over time.

Write down your early dreams. Did you want to be a dancer, a clown, an actor, a police person, a cook, an architect, a teacher, a doctor, a farmer? What appealed to you and why? Figure out what about these jobs/careers drew you to them. Again, ask other people in your life what you talked about being when you grew up.

My Early Dreams:

_____

_____

_____

Dreams That Linger Still

It's never too late to pick up themes that were present in your youth. You may not want to pursue being a doctor today, but what was it about that career that interested you? Was it the helping people, or analyzing and problem-solving, or interest in how the body works? These themes can still be used to create career choices that bring to life your early loves. It's never too late to uncover information about yourself that you can use today in your career search.

> **Career Lingo**
>
> **Elements** means parts of a whole. Career elements are parts of you that are important, such as talents or skills you like to use, environments you like to be in, amount of adventure you want in your life, pieces of your personality you enjoy using in work, etc.

Of the jobs, careers, and activities that you loved to do when you were a child, what still remains true for you? What do you still like about them today?

Look at the reasons you liked the activities you engaged in and careers/jobs you wanted to do when you grew up. Now, make a list of those career _elements_ that are still true for you today. Do you still like to be outdoors? Do you have a flair for being on stage? Do you love finances?

My Career Elements:

_____

_____

_____

The Wheel of Life Assessment

Now we have jumped to the here and now of your life. This is what is happening today. You will be asked to rate your level of satisfaction, on a scale of 1 to 10, with many aspects of the life you are living today. Career satisfaction is often influenced by many of these other aspects of our life. The amount of time and energy we want to spend with family and friends can affect our choice of career. Our desire for a lifestyle that allows for living in $400,000 homes and traveling around the world will affect our career choices. This means we need to take all of these areas into account. You will be presented with eight aspects of your life:

- Money
- Career/Work
- Family and Friends
- Health and Fitness

- Spirit, Mind, Emotions
- Significant Other
- Environments
- Fun and Recreation

These aspects make up your wheel of life. The eight sections on the Wheel of Life represent balance. Seeing the center of the wheel as 0 and the outer edges as 10, rank your level of satisfaction with each life area by drawing a straight or curved line to create a new outer edge. The new perimeter represents the wheel of your life. If this was a real wheel, how bumpy would your ride be?

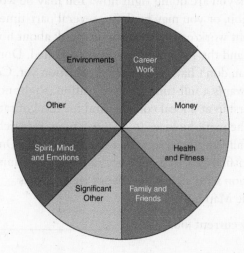

The Wheel of Life.

Money

How satisfied are you today with the amount of money you are making? Does it allow you to live the lifestyle you want to live right now? Are you able to support yourself, uphold family obligations, or support those you want or need to support?

On a scale of 1 to 10 (1 being not at all satisfied and 10 being very satisfied), choose the number that represents your level of satisfaction with your money right now and consider the reasons for this level of satisfaction. Record this number in your Career Profile Map in Appendix A.

Reasons: _____

_____

Career Goal: _____

_____

How much money would you like to make three years from now? _____

_____

Career/Work

Think about the work you are doing right now. You may be working for yourself, or you have a full-time job, or you may be doing several part-time jobs at one time. Whatever your current work/career situation is, think about how satisfied you are with doing the work and the reasons why you are satisfied. Don't automatically say you are unhappy if you don't have your perfect situation yet. Consider Jim who has his Ph.D. and really wants a full-time faculty position. Right now he is has a temporary visiting professorship at a local college. And his level of satisfaction is a 7, because he is doing the work he loves to do—teaching, research, and advising. It isn't a 10 because it isn't full-time, secure, with a good pay scale. On a scale of 1 to 10 (1 being not at all satisfied and 10 being very satisfied), the number that represents your level of satisfaction with your career/work right now is ___. Record this number in your Career Profile Map in Appendix A.

What I like about my current job: _____

_____

What I dislike about my current job: _____

_____

Family and Friends

How satisfied are you with your relationships with your family and friends, the time you spend with them, the distance or closeness? At different times and stages of our lives, our relationships shift and change with family and friends. Tap into where you are right now, and don't worry about past or future. On a scale of 1 to 10 (1 being not at all satisfied and 10 being very satisfied), the number that represents your level of satisfaction with your family and friends right now is ___. Record this number in your Career Profile Map in Appendix A.

What am I currently doing that is satisfying? _____

_____

What could I be doing to increase my level of satisfaction? _____

_____

In our teens and twenties we often feel more attached to friends than to family. We are forming our own identities. We want to be independent. Having fun is centered on things we do with friends. In our thirties we start getting the urge to move closer to home. We may want support for our new families. We appreciate the history and family connections. Friends are moving around for jobs and their own families. We want to support and enjoy our aging parents.

Health and Fitness

What is the state of your health? Are you taking care of any problems that are recurrent or beginning to happen? Do you feel in shape, satisfied with your physical ability? Do you go for regular checkups for your health? Do you have a routine to keep you physically fit? This is the vessel—our body—that makes everything else in our lives possible. And, it is often forgotten or pushed to the background as we juggle everything else in our lives. It's easy to forget that paying attention to the health and fitness of our body often gives us the energy and stamina for all our other activities. So, how satisfied are you with your health and fitness? On a scale of 1 to 10 (1 being not at all satisfied and 10 being very satisfied), the number that represents your level of satisfaction with your health and fitness right now is ___. Record this number in your Career Profile Map in Appendix A.

What am I currently doing that is satisfying? _____

_____

What could I be doing to increase my level of satisfaction? _____

_____

Make sure you consider the types of exercise that really works for you. Things you would actually do!

Spirit, Mind, and Emotions

These three life forces complement and support our physical health and fitness. The ability to feed our *spirit*, stimulate our mind, and understand and communicate our emotions can have a profound effect on our overall effectiveness in life. Let's look at each one of these separately:

> **Career Lingo** _____
>
> **Spirit** is another dimension of knowledge beyond the cognitive, the tangible, the concrete. It gives us access to inspiration, peace, and insight into ourselves. Ways to be in touch with spirit can come through meditation, yoga, walking, spiritual practices, contemplating spiritual writings, and more.

Spirit: Do you feel satisfied with the amount of time and attention you give to your spiritual needs? For most people, spirituality is a form of inspiration. If you are seeking worldly success, inner peace, or enlightenment, spiritual knowledge provides another dimension beyond cognitive knowledge. Spiritual satisfaction can bring work, wisdom, love, peacefulness, and service to our lives. This can take the form of practicing a religion, meditation, yoga, or spiritual readings and practices. How satisfied are you with the time, attention, and practice you give to spirituality in your life? On a scale of 1 to 10 (1 being not at all satisfied and 10 being very satisfied), the number that represents your level of satisfaction with your spirit right now is ___. Record this number in your Career Profile Map in Appendix A.

What am I currently doing that is satisfying? _____

_____

What could I be doing to increase my level of satisfaction? _____

_____

Mind: In today's world it's important to be a continual learner. You want to keep up with changes in your career/work area so that the business you are in remains viable. And there is a world of new learning all around us to keep us stimulated and energized. Reading, learning a new leisure-time activity, crossword puzzles, strategy games, house projects, and repairs. All of these require thought, exploration, and learning. Where are you in terms of being satisfied with the amount of learning you are doing right now? On a scale of 1 to 10 (1 being not at all satisfied and 10 being very satisfied), the number that represents your level of satisfaction with your mind right now is ___. Record this number in your Career Profile Map in Appendix A.

What am I currently doing that is satisfying? _____

_____

What could I be doing to increase my level of satisfaction? _____

_____

Emotions: Understanding our own emotions and being able to appropriately express them gives us a wealth of information for our career/life decision making. When we are able to identify what makes us happy, interested, stimulated, productive—then we have solid information about ourselves. When we ignore our feelings, tough it out, rationalize why we have to do work we don't like—we are doing a disservice to ourselves. The important role of emotions has had some good press lately. Research has shown that the stronger our emotional intelligence (EQ) is, the more effective we are in conducting our lives and relationships with others.

Leaders who have a high EQ know their own emotions, can communicate them effectively, and understand the emotions of others. The more we pay attention to our feelings, the more information is available to help us make good choices in our lives. Where are you with your current satisfaction with being able to access your emotions? On a scale of 1 to 10 (1 being not at all satisfied and 10 being very satisfied), the number that represents your level of satisfaction with your emotions right now is ___. Record this number in your Career Profile Map in Appendix A.

What am I currently doing that is satisfying? _____

_____

What could I be doing to increase my level of satisfaction? _____

_____

Significant Other

What is your level of satisfaction with your partner or significant other in your life? Or what is your level of satisfaction with not having a significant other in your life right now? In the realm of relationships, satisfaction can fluctuate due to circumstances or to lack of attention.

Whatever the situation, your level of satisfaction with this primary relationship can have many impacts on your career/life choices and levels of happiness. Often we consider this relationship our base of operations. If everything is running smoothly here, we have more energy and enthusiasm for the rest of our lives. What is your level of satisfaction with your primary other right now? On a scale of 1 to 10 (1 being not at all satisfied and 10 being very satisfied), the number that represents your level of satisfaction with your significant other right now is ___. Record this number in your Career Profile Map in Appendix A.

What am I currently doing that is satisfying? _____

_____

What could I be doing to increase my level of satisfaction? _____

_____

Environments

At home and work what do your environments feel like to you? Do you feel good when you are in these environments? Do they energize you, calm you, or comfort you? Again we are all different in what types of environments might do this for us. Some of us would prefer to look out on lawns and gardens and forests in the distance. Others prefer the sound of traffic and people coming and going at a fast pace. Knowing what types of environments we like to be in can give us great clues to the type of work and lifestyle we want. How satisfied are you with your work and home environments? On a scale of 1 to 10 (1 being not at all satisfied and 10 being very satisfied), the number that represents your level of satisfaction with your environment right now is ___. Record this number in your Career Profile Map in Appendix A.

What am I currently doing that is satisfying? _____

_____

What could I be doing to increase my level of satisfaction? _____

_____

Fun and Recreation

Last but not least, are you having any fun lately? Do you have time for other things in life besides work, school, or self-study? What comes to mind when you think of the word "fun?" Laughter, play, freedom, relaxed, connections, joy, creativity, letting go—yes! Fun and recreation do not have to be separate from work, although it often is. Studies show that having a good laugh keeps us healthy—releases those good endorphins—and it definitely makes us more creative. How satisfied are you with the fun and recreation you are currently having in your life? On a scale of 1 to 10 (1 being not at all satisfied and 10 being very satisfied), the number that represents your level of satisfaction with your fun and recreation right now is ___. Record this number in your Career Profile Map in Appendix A.

What am I currently doing that is satisfying? _____

_____

What could I be doing to increase my level of satisfaction? _____

_____

Five Years from Now Exercise

Vision means giving yourself a picture of the future that inspires you and motivates you to take action. It moves you closer to the reality you see for yourself. Now that you have given some thought to your early dreams of career and your current level of satisfaction with your life, you are ready to move to your future. So rev up your engine and change your mindset to five years from now.

If you wonder why we want you to visualize five years from now, it is because it helps you let go of things dragging you down in the present. Instead you can take those things from the present that you want to continue to have and imagine work/life in the future that gives you the *most satisfaction*.

You are going to imagine what you are doing for a week, five years from now. After you have read these over, find a quiet place to imagine your future. It helps to close your eyes so that your mind can bring forth pictures to accompany your thoughts. Afterward you can write down your vision in the space provided.

Career Lingo

Our **vision** describes what we aspire to become, to achieve, and to create. The first component of a vision is the stretch goal. This has a specific time frame— 5 years from now. It states our future dream, hope, or aspiration. The second component of a vision provides a vivid description or visual image of the stretch goal. You want the words you use to be descriptive and upbeat and exciting. This vision will be carried around in your head and keep you focused on where you want to go. An example of a Vision Summary might be, "In 2009, I am sitting on the deck of my newly renovated house looking into my beautiful office space. My consulting and coaching business is flourishing; I have been writing a follow-up book to *The Complete Idiot's Guide to Discovering Your Perfect Career*, and the pace of my life is just right for enjoying family, friends, and the work I love to do."

Here is a way to move through your week and focus on various aspects of your work/life:

- Five years from now you are getting up on Monday morning. Notice the time on the clock next to your bed. For those of you who are night owls (by choice or profession) your Monday morning may be late afternoon! Please adjust all the other times accordingly as you go through your day. Look around at your surroundings. Where are you? What do you see? What is the temperature? Look outside and see where you are. What does the landscape look like? What noises do you hear?

- Determine your relationship to others in this environment. Who do you see around you? Are you with your partner, family, friends, yourself, children.? How do you interact with them?

- Now you are ready to move on with your day. How are you dressed? Are you walking or traveling by car, train, bus, or limousine? Are you going to a space in your home environment? Some of you may be going to work, other's are engaged in their volunteer work, or, perhaps your days are filled with travel and leisure activities. Adapt your vision to fit your reality, please!

- You have now arrived where you will spend your day. How do you feel? What do you see? What is in this environment that interests you? Who else is in the environment?

◆ Go through the day now and pay attention to the types of skills you are enjoying using. What are you doing? What strengths and talents are you using? With whom do you interact?

◆ Look ahead to other days during the week and visualize what you are doing. Do you have a daily routine, or is every day different? What goes on during lunch and other break times during the day? Where are you?

◆ Now imagine your evening. Where do you go? What do you do? Who are you with? Are you at home, at the opera, at a baseball game, out star gazing, exercising, walking, having dinner with family or friends, dancing, or going to school?

◆ Make plans for the weekend. What do you like to do on weekends? Gardening, hiking, biking, sports, movies, hanging out, museums, or studying?

◆ Thinking back over your week, what do you like about yourself five years from now? What do the days look like and feel like for you?

Now write down anything that came to mind as you walked through your week five years from now.

Vision Summary:

_____

_____

_____

Record your Vision Summary in the Career Profile Map in Appendix A.

The Least You Need to Know

◆ There are clues to who you are and what you want to be in your early childhood play and dreams.

◆ Assessing your level of satisfaction with your life today will help you plan for your future.

◆ Visioning your future inspires you to action and reminds you of your potential in life.

Your Values

In This Chapter

♦ Understand the role of values in your career choice

♦ Take the Values Sort Assessment

♦ Make the link between your values and work/life preferences

As you build your profile of what is really important to you in choosing a career path, values will sit at the very foundation of your decision making. Values are key in helping us determine our career/life direction.

While value decisions are always part of our lives, sometimes we think about our values only when situations arise that force us to consider them. Think about a recent time in your life when you were faced with a critical decision. What were the value choices involved? A common example most of us face in our lives is having a friend or co-worker ask us to lie for them—or "bend the truth." In this chapter, you will have the opportunity to reflect on your values and choose those values you want to guide your career and life decisions.

Defining Values

Have you ever stayed up with friends for half the night debating the rights and wrongs of a situation? Think about the controversial topics over the centuries. The death penalty, civil rights, going to war, abortion rights—all of these ongoing debates involve principles of right or wrong. Values are driving our positions and beliefs. Values of equality, national security, salvation, freedom, a world of peace are just some that might underlie these issues. Values are the basic notion that each individual holds about what is right and wrong. They are highly regarded beliefs and attitudes, in which we have an emotional investment. And we are willing to act upon them. Our values are reflected in our behavior.

In a speech given at a recent leadership conference, a senior executive stood before 250 people and said that values were the key to his company's success. His company focused on identifying company values and having each employee practice these values on a day-to-day basis. Companies see a clear connection between having a well-defined value system that guides actions and gets results and achieving company goals. In the same way that companies use values as guides to decision making and behaviors, individuals can do the same in making their career and work environment choices. Our ability to identify our *core values*—those most important to us—is a basis for making clear decisions about what will make us happy in our career/life choices. Our values shape our character and define who we really are.

Career Lingo

Core values are the big ones—your most important values. These are the ones that really make a difference in how you behave and directions you choose. We all have many values that are important to us, but we are looking for those that are at the core of defining who we are.

There are several influences on how we choose our values. These include parents, extended family, friends, environments we grow up in, and our national and ethnic cultures. The greatest influence is just who we are, the outlook and personality that we bring into the world. Values are complicated. They have a tendency to be pretty stable, although some can change as we grow and develop. We rarely throw out the baby with the bath water. But selected values may come and go. There are times when we might want to throw out values that were important in our family. Then when we turn about 35, we start to reclaim some of them. Family behaviors can also be a source of helping us define values that are opposite from ones we observed growing up. Then there are times we embrace change and adopt values that make us better people. If we have bent the truth, we decide that honesty is a value we want to have. This becomes a guide for our behavior going forward.

There are two basic types of values that operate in our lives, and the following categories are adopted from the values studies published by Milton Rokeach in his book, *The Nature of Human Values*, (Free Press, 1973). Let's take a look at these two types of values: the life you want to live and the day-to-day actions you take.

> **Stop-Look-Listen**
>
> It's never too late to rethink your values. Don't box yourself into a definition of yourself that is based on old beliefs or attitudes. You are constantly changing and having new experiences and insights. Take advantage of this, and choose new values that will guide your behavior.

The Life I Want to Live

These are values that we hope to achieve in our lives. They represent the way we want to be living our lives and/or the type of life to which we aspire. They represent states of being such as having a comfortable life, being happy, and having mature love. Being clear about how we envision our lives and what states of being would be most satisfying is a basis from which we can make good career/life decisions. After all, who wouldn't want to line up their values with the work they do and the life they lead?

Day-To-Day Actions

These are the values that guide our behaviors on a daily basis. They also can be directly connected to helping us achieve the life we want to live. Day-to-day values include being loving, courageous, capable, and self-controlled.

As an example, Sam's highest value in life was attaining a state of happiness on an ongoing basis. In order to do this, she practiced the values of cheerfulness, being loving, honest, and forgiving. She chose these values because that is how she attains happiness in her life.

Values Sort Assessment

This assessment will help you to determine your top five values for "The Life I Want to Live" and for your "Day to Day Actions." In total, you will end up with 10 values that represent your long range goals for your life as well as day-to-day actions that will help you to achieve your long-term goals. Your final list of values will provide guidance for the career and life decisions you will be making. They are the foundation for who you are right now and the way you want to live your life.

Part 1: The Life I Want to Live

Circle those values that most reflect the life you want to live. Put a check in front of the five values that are most important to you.

❏ Fairness

❏ An exciting life

❏ Self-respect

❏ Happiness

❏ Beauty/aesthetics

❏ Community

❏ Wisdom

❏ Inner harmony and peace

❏ A comfortable life

❏ Wealth and prosperity

❏ Health and wellness

❏ Accomplishment/Achievement

❏ Faith/spirituality

❏ Friendship

❏ Love

❏ Family

❏ Financial security

❏ Peaceful world

❏ Power and influence

❏ Fun

❏ Loyalty

❏ Equality/Equity

Part 2: Day-to-Day Actions

Circle those values that most reflect your day-to-day actions. Put a check in front of the five values that are most important to you.

❏ Collaborative

❏ Ambitious

❏ Honest

❏ Kind

❏ Make a difference

❏ Loving

❏ Respectful

❏ Operate with integrity

❏ Open minded   ❏ Capable

❏ Fight for a cause   ❏ Forgiving

❏ Responsible   ❏ Take risks

❏ Intellectual   ❏ Help others

❏ Imaginative/creative   ❏ Self-controlled

❏ Trustworthy   ❏ Independent/self-reliant

❏ Being an expert   ❏ Logical

Now that you have identified those values that are most important to you in guiding your behavior and decisions, it's time to dig a little deeper. Each of us has a slightly different twist on why we chose a value. Say you chose an exciting life as a primary value. It might mean travel and adventure in different cultures to you. For someone else, it might mean living in the Big Apple, dressing to the nine's, and going to clubs every night. So now I want you to take each of your ranked values from both lists and be very specific about the reasons you chose each value. Then identify any career implications that come to mind right now based on these chosen values.

Insider Tips

Take the time to delve into what the values assessment results really mean for you. Ask yourself some questions. For example: Why am I drawn to these values? What do each of these values really mean to me? When you can answer questions based on your results, then you can begin to identify possible career implications.

Part I: The Life I Want to Live

Ranked Values	Reasons for Choosing	Career Implications
1. _____	_____	_____
2. _____	_____	_____
3. _____	_____	_____
4. _____	_____	_____
5. _____	_____	_____

Part 2: Day-To-Day Actions

Ranked Values	Reasons for Choosing	Career Implications
1. _____	_____	_____
2. _____	_____	_____
3. _____	_____	_____
4. _____	_____	_____
5. _____	_____	_____

Now that you have ranked these values in order, record The Life I Want to Live and Day-To-Day Actions in your Career Profile Map in Appendix A.

The Least You Need to Know

◆ Values are key in helping us determine our career/life direction. They are highly regarded beliefs and attitudes, in which we have an emotional investment that forms our decisions and behaviors.

◆ "The Life I Want to Live" values represent the type of life we envision for ourselves. If we looked back at the end of our lives we could say that we lived these values. Examples are an exciting life, one of self-respect, having recognition, and happiness.

◆ "Day to Day Actions" are a second category of values. They complement and support "The Life I Want to Live" values, and they guide our day-to-day behaviors. Examples are being creative, open minded, respectful of self and others, and being truthful.

◆ Sorting out our values helps us to lay the foundation for making career decisions that will make us happy and productive in our lives.

Chapter 7

Your Temperament and Personality

In This Chapter

◆ Learn about temperament

◆ Find out what your personality type is

◆ Connect your temperament to careers

This chapter is adapted from the theory and writings of David Keirsey, who is the renown author of the best seller, *Please Understand Me II: Temperament, Character, Intelligence*. Professor Keirsey has been studying personality differences for over 20 years and his theory of temperament is well suited to helping you understand yourself and others better. When you get to Chapter 15, you will look at careers that best match your temperament. All references and adaptations of Dr. Keirsey's work come directly from the following three sources: *Please Understand Me II: Temperament, Character, Intelligence;* www.AdvisorTeam.com, and www.Keirsey. com.

Picture a world where everyone wears sun glasses that are either green, blue, brown, red, yellow, orange, purple, or black. Each of the shades provides a different way of seeing the world and a different approach to interacting and making decisions. One way of viewing the world is not better than another, just different.

People who wear the green shades tend to take time to think about what they are going to say before they speak. In contrast, people who wear the blue shades love to talk out their ideas with anyone who will listen. People wearing the brown shades prefer to pay attention to the specific, observable facts in a situation, while people wearing the red shades take in the big picture and collect information using their intuition. Then there are the people wearing the yellow glasses that make decisions based on logical conclusions vs. the people wearing orange classes who rely on their feelings to make decisions. Last but not least, are the people wearing purple glasses who live a very orderly life as compared with people wearing the black glasses who prefer to live a much more flexible life.

When people wearing each of the different shades come together to solve problems, they come up with win/win solutions because they can consider all the different perspectives.

This example helps us to begin to think about all the different behaviors that come together to make up our personality type and our temperament. This chapter will highlight David Keirsey's work in the areas of temperament and personality. And you will have an opportunity to assess yourself on these dimensions in the Shorter Personality Sorter. There is also an opportunity for you to use the bundle coupon on the last page of this book to take the Keirsey Temperament Sorter and the Campbell Interest and Skill Inventory at a $5.00 discount on www.KeirseyCampbell.com.

Defining Temperament and Personality

Temperament is a predisposition to particular attitudes and behaviors. It is how we are wired. It means that we have preferences for the way we think and behave that we automatically use in our daily lives and interactions. Our temperaments influence our values, the language we use in communicating, our interests, our self-image, how we approach our past, present, and future, and how we apply our intelligence. So, there is a wealth of information that can help us to understand ourselves and our orientation to the world. The four temperaments are Artisan, Guardian, Idealist, and Rational.

Each of the temperaments has four personalities associated with it, giving us 16 personality types in all. Our personality combines our temperament with our character. We develop the habits of character over our lifetime, while our temperament remains fixed. Thus, each temperament breaks down into four personality types that reflect the over-all behaviors of the temperament while distinguishing itself from the other personality types through the habits of character. An example of this would be the Artisan Temperament breaks down into the following four personality types: The Promoter, The Performer, The Crafter, The Composer.

Let's begin the journey of discovering your temperament and personality type by taking the shorter Personality Sorter. After you have taken this assessment, you can read about your temperament and your specific personality associated with your temperament. In Chapters 15, 16, and 17, we will look at some of the careers and jobs that could be a fit with your personality type.

Shorter Personality Sorter

Circle either a or b for each of the thirty-six questions that follow. Make your choice based on the response that best represents your preferences. You want to focus on who you are today—your real self, not your ideal self (smile)! Try not to spend too much time thinking—your first choice is usually the most accurate.

1. I prefer to have …
   a. lots of friends
   b. a few friends

2. Which is more your style …
   a. trial and error
   b. a well thought out plan

3. Which appeals to you more …
   a. peaceful relationships
   b. consistent thinking

4. If you agree to meet friends at a specific time, but they are late, do you …
   a. get annoyed
   b. shrug it off

5. Waiting in line, do you often …
   a. chat with others
   b. keep to yourself

6. Is it worse to …
   a. be a daydreamer
   b. always repeat things

7. Would you say that your feelings get hurt …
   a. more often than others
   b. less often than others

8. Do you …
   a. plan ahead
   b. just jump into things

9. At large social gatherings, do you …
   a. talk to many people, even strangers
   b. talk with just a few friends

10. Are you more ...
    a. sensible   b. inventive

11. Is it better to ...
    a. show pity   b. be fair

12. Are you more satisfied having ...
    a. a finished product   b. several ongoing projects

13. Does interacting with strangers ...
    a. energize you   b. make you tired

14. Do you tend to be more ...
    a. practical   b. imaginative

15. Are you more often ...
    a. kind and friendly to all   b. logical and even-tempered

16. At school, do you want your activities ...
    a. scheduled and planned   b. unscheduled and open

17. When a new person invites you to do something ...
    a. you readily accept   b. wait until you get to know them better

18. Are you better at ...
    a. imitating others   b. imagining wild possibilities

19. You are more likely to forgive someone if ...
    a. they express sorrow   b. they have a logical explanation
       and remorse

20. Do you more often prefer ...
    a. endings   b. beginnings

21. Do you think of yourself as ...
    a. an outgoing person   b. a private person

22. Are you better at ...
    a. doing a good job   b. coming up with unusual ideas

23. If a troublemaker is harshly punished, do you feel ...
    a. a little bit sorry for them   b. that they probably deserved it

24. Do you more often ...
    a. calculate   b. estimate

25. Are you the kind of person who ...
    a. is really talkative
    b. is quiet and watchful

26. Which is more your motto ...
    a. united we stand
    b. express yourself

27. Do you more often relate to others in ...
    a. a personal manner
    b. an objective manner

28. Are you inclined to be more ...
    a. driven
    b. relaxed

29. The thought of making new friends ...
    a. makes you excited
    b. makes you nervous

30. Which do you prefer ...
    a. describing an experience
    b. solving a problem in your head

31. It is easier for you to ...
    a. identify with others
    b. analyze others

32. Is it preferable to ...
    a. make sure things are arranged
    b. just let things happen naturally

33. Are you better at ...
    a. talking to your friends
    b. listening to your friends

34. In stories, do you prefer ...
    a. action and adventure
    b. fantasy and heroism

35. Do you see yourself as a ...
    a. sensitive person
    b. logical person

36. Is your room at home ...
    a. neat
    b. messy

CAUTION

Stop-Look-Listen _____

Please keep in mind that this is a shorter and less accurate version of the Keirsey Temperament Sorter. You are invited to use your discount coupon on the last page of the book for the "bundle" to take the original Temperament Sorter along with the Campbell Interest and Skill Survey at www. KeirseyCampbell.com.

Here are the instructions for how to determine your personality type:

1. Using the answer sheet that follows, enter a check for each answer in the column for **a** or **b**.

Answer Sheet

	a	b		a	b		a	b		a	b
1	__	__	2	__	__	3	__	__	4	__	__
5	__	__	6	__	__	7	__	__	8	__	__
9	__	__	10	__	__	11	__	__	12	__	__
13	__	__	14	__	__	15	__	__	16	__	__
17	__	__	18	__	__	19	__	__	20	__	__
21	__	__	22	__	__	23	__	__	24	__	__
25	__	__	26	__	__	27	__	__	28	__	__
29	__	__	30	__	__	31	__	__	32	__	__
33	__	__	34	__	__	35	__	__	36	__	__
	↓	↓		↓	↓		↓	↓		↓	↓
	E	I		S	N		F	T		J	P

2. Add down the **a** and **b** columns and write the total number of checkmarks at the bottom of each column.

3. For each of the four letter pairs, circle the letter with the higher number. If you have a tie between any of the four pairings, read the descriptions for each (in the sections that follow) and decide which one most accurately represents your behavior.

4. Write the four letters that you circled—these represent your personality type.

My Personality Type is _____.

Record your Personality Type in the Career Profile Map in Appendix A.

Please keep in mind that this is a shorter and less accurate version of the Keirsey Temperament Sorter III. The Shorter Personality Sorter is for educational purposes only. The results from this instrument may not be correct.

Please verify your results for yourself by reading through the descriptions of temperament and personality that follow in this chapter.

16 Personality Types

There are 16 personality types in all. Each type has four letters—one from each of the following pairs of behaviors:

E for Extroversion/I for Introversion

S for Sensation/N for Intuition

T for Thinking/F for Feeling

J for Judgment/P for Perception

Coach Wisdom

Each of us has a preference for one of each of the pairings being described (E or I, S or N, T or F, J or P). Our preference is seen as a strength because we use it in most situations. However, we can develop our ability to use the opposite of our preference and often do. Work, life experiences, and relationships all present us with opportunities to use all parts of our temperament and character.

As we take a look at what the differences are between each of these four pairs, circle those words or phrases that describe your preferences in the tables that follow.

Extroversion and Introversion refer to your social style—how you interact and whether you access your energy from external interactions or internal reflections.

Your Social Style

Extroversion (E)	Introversion (I)
Gregarious	Private
Expressive	Reserved
Socialize with groups	Solitary activities
Outgoing	Contemplative
Large circle of friends	Few, long-term friends
Get energy from others	Get energy from internal reflection

Sensation and Intuition differentiate between two distinct worlds of human interest or focus. Sensing focuses on the outside world of concrete things, and Intuition focuses on the abstract internal world of ideas.

What You Focus on to Gather Data

Sensation (S)	Intuition (N)
Concrete	Abstract
Physical and material world	Conceptual and theoretical world
See details	See big picture
Practical	Possibilities
Focused on here and now	Focused on future
Common sense	Speculation
Focus on facts	Focus on symbols

Thinking and Feeling shows us how people govern themselves and make decisions. The distinction here is between making decisions with one's head or with one's heart.

How You Make Decisions

Feeling (F)	Thinking (T)
Heart	Head
Personal	Impersonal
Subjective	Objective
Feelings	Hard data
Concerned	Critical
Sympathetic	Tough-minded
Gentle, kind	Straightforward

CAUTION

Stop-Look-Listen

Thinkers have powerful feelings, too. However, a strong show of emotion usually embarrasses them. They like to keep their feelings in check and retain self-control. Feelers may not have stronger or deeper feelings than Thinkers, but they let their feelings show more easily.

Judgment and Perception measure how people process information and arrange their lives. The difference comes out in either making one's mind up quickly and committing or keeping ones options open and remaining flexible.

How You Process Information and Arrange Your Life

Judgment (J)	Perception (P)
Quick decision maker	Keep options open
Commit to schedules	Flexible timetables
Closure	Possibilities
Orderly procedure	Fun
Deadlines	Open ended
Routine	Spontaneous and has a purpose
Neat	Cluttered

Descriptions of Temperament and Personality

Understanding your personality type starts with a description of each temperament. Remember, your temperament is the driver of your personality—what really makes you tick. Under each temperament will be listed the four Personality Types personality types associated with it.

Two of these letters refer to your temperament:

◆ The four Artisans have the following letter combinations: ESTP, ESFP, ISTP, and ISFP. *Note:* These four share the letters SP (Sensation and Perception).

◆ The four Guardians have the following letter combinations: ESTJ, ESFJ, ISTJ, and ISFJ. *Note:* These four share the letters SJ (Sensation and Judgment).

◆ The four Rationals have the following letter combinations: ENTP, ENTJ, INTP, and INTJ. *Note:* These four share the letters NT (Intuition and Thinking).

◆ The four Idealists have the following letter combinations: ENFP, ENFJ, INFP, and INFJ. *Note:* These four share the letters NF (Intuition and Feeling).

Each of these different personality types are described in the sections that follow.

Artisan Temperament

All Artisans (SPs) share the following core characteristics:

♦ They tend to be fun-loving, optimistic, realistic, and focused on the here and now.

♦ They pride themselves on being unconventional, bold, and spontaneous.

♦ They make playful mates, creative parents, and troubleshooting leaders.

♦ They are excitable, trust their impulses, want to make a splash, seek stimulation, prize freedom, and dream of mastering action skills.

Artisans are smart and crafty like a fox. Known for their ability to be tactical, they look for ways to improve their present position. Being able to see the nuances and details in front of them ensures the full use of all existing resources. They look for opportunities to advance the picture on their canvass, the fleet at sea, the novel being written, the character on stage, the country they are leading, the pitch they are throwing, and so on.

Famous Artisans include Barbara Streisand, Elvis Presley, Franklin Roosevelt, George W. Bush, Donald Trump, and Ernest Hemingway. Thirty-five to forty percent of the population are Artisans who are creating much of the beauty, grace, fun, and excitement the rest of us enjoy in life.

The four personality types of Artisans are: the Promoter (ESTP), the Performer (ESFP), the Crafter (ISTP), and the Composer (ISFP). Each is described in the sections that follow.

The Promoter (ESTP)

Ten percent of the population are Promoters—people of action. They make things happen with a theatrical flourish, demanding new activities and new challenges. They are bold and daring and take tremendous risks to get what they want. Charming, confident, and popular, Promoters delight their friends and investors with their endless supply of stories. However, they rarely let anyone get really close to them. They have a low tolerance for authority and commitment and are likely to leave situations in which they are expected to toe the mark or play second fiddle. They are always looking for the next deal or ways to negotiate a better one.

The Performer (ESFP)

Performers see "all the world as a stage," looking for ways to stimulate those around them to lighten up and enjoy life. They have a special ability to delight those around them with their warmth and good humor. They often have extraordinary skills in music, comedy, and drama.

More than 10 percent of the population are Performers. Performers aren't comfortable being alone and seek the company of others whenever possible. They haven't a mean or stingy bone in their body. What's theirs is yours, and they seem to have little idea of saving or conserving. They will avoid worries and troubles by ignoring them as long as possible. Performers are open to trying almost anything that promises them a good time, not always giving enough thought to the consequences.

The Crafter (ISTP)

Crafters are masterful at the operation of tools, equipment, machines, and instruments of all kinds. Most Artisans use tools in some capacity, but Crafters (as much as 10 percent of the population) are the true masters of tool work. They have an innate ability to command tools and to become expert at all the crafts requiring tool skills.

More than anything, Crafters want to be free to do their own thing. They are proud of their ability to do it with an artist's skill. They are impulsive, spontaneous, and playful. They thrive on excitement and are fearless in their play. Of all the types, Crafters are most likely to be risk takers, pitting themselves, or their technique, against chance or odds. They are hard to get to know, communicating primarily through their actions instead of with their words. However, they are generous to a fault, going out of their way to help people in their lives.

The Composer (ISFP)

More than the other Artisans, Composers are in tune with their senses. Although the other Artisans are skilled with people, tools, and entertainment, Composers have an exceptional ability to work with subtle differences in color, tone, texture, aroma, and flavor. They act in the here and now, with little or no planning or preparation. Composers are seized by the act of artistic composition, as if caught up in a whirl-wind. Composers paint or sculpt, they dance or skate, they write melodies or make recipes simply because they must.

On the social side, Composers show a kindness unmatched by all the other types. They are especially sensitive to the pain and suffering of others. Many Composers have an instinctive longing for the wild, and nature seems to welcome them. They are nonverbal communicators, expressing their character quite eloquently through their artistic expressions.

Guardian Temperament

All Guardians (SJs) share the following core characteristics:

- ♦ They pride themselves on being dependable, helpful, and hard-working.

- ♦ They make loyal mates, responsible parents, and stabilizing leaders.

- ♦ They tend to be dutiful, cautious, humble, and focused on credentials and traditions.

- ♦ They are concerned citizens who trust authority, join groups, seek security, prize gratitude, and dream of meting out justice.

Guardians are like fish out of water if they do not belong to a group or community. Belonging and contributing to the ongoing stability of their organizations is the driving force for Guardians. They take their duties and responsibilities quite seriously and take pride in being dependable and trustworthy. If there's a job to be done, they can be counted on to put their shoulder to the wheel. In fact, they usually end up doing all the indispensable but thankless jobs the rest of us take for granted.

Practical and down-to-earth, Guardians believe in following the rules and cooperating with others. From supervision to maintenance and supply, they use all their skills to keep things running smoothly in their families, communities, schools, churches, hospitals, and businesses. Guardians also believe in law and order and respect for authority. Guardians are meticulous about schedules and have a sharp eye for proper procedures. They are cautious about change—look before you leap. Making up from 40 to 45 percent of the population, famous Guardians include the first President George Bush Sr., Barbara Walters, Justice Sandra Day O-Connor, and J.C. Penney.

The four types of Guardians are: the Supervisor (ESTJ), the Provider (ESFJ), the Inspector (ISTJ), and the Protector (ISFJ). Each is described in the sections that follow.

The Supervisor (ESTJ)

Supervisors are highly social and community-minded, with many rising to positions of responsibility in their school, church, industry, or civic groups. They are generous with their time and energy. They often belong to a variety of service clubs, lodges, and associations, taking outspoken leadership roles. Supervisors like to take charge of groups and are comfortable issuing orders. They are cooperative with their own superiors, and they would like cooperation from the people working under them. They tend to judge how a person is doing in terms of his or her compliance with, and respect for, schedules and procedures.

Comprising at least 10 percent of the population, Supervisors enjoy and are good at making schedules, agendas, and inventories. They much prefer tried-and-true ways of doing things over speculation and experimentation. Supervisors are friendly and talk easily with others. Although they can seem a bit formal in their manners, Supervisors are pretty easy to get to know. At ease in polite company, they tend not to confuse people by sending double messages or putting on airs. They are what they seem to be.

The Provider (ESFJ)

Providers take it upon themselves to ensure the health and welfare of those in their care. They are also the most sociable of all the Guardians. They are the great nurturers of social institutions such as schools, churches, social clubs, and civic groups. Providers make up more than 10 percent of the population. Wherever they go, Providers happily give their time and energy to make sure that the needs of others are met and that social functions are a success.

Highly cooperative themselves, Providers are skilled in maintaining teamwork among their helpers. They are also tireless in their attention to the details of furnishing goods and services. They make excellent chairpersons in charge of dances, banquets, class reunions, and charity fund-raisers. They are without peer as masters of ceremonies, able to speak publicly with ease and confidence. Providers are extremely sensitive to the feelings of others, which makes them perhaps the most sympathetic of all the types. They are happiest when given ample appreciation both for themselves personally and for the tireless service they give to others.

The Inspector (ISTJ)

The one word that best describes Inspectors is extremely dependable. They see to it that rules are followed, laws are respected, and standards are upheld. Inspectors (as much as 10 percent of the general population) are the true guardians of institutions. Whether at home or at work, Inspectors are extraordinarily persevering and dutiful.

Inspectors will see to it that goods are examined and schedules are kept. Resources will be up to standards and delivered when and where they are supposed to be. And they would prefer that everyone be this dependable. Inspectors can be hard-nosed about the need for following the rules in the workplace and do not hesitate to report irregularities to the proper authorities. Because of this they are often misjudged as being hard-hearted, or as having ice in their veins. However, people fail to see their good intentions and their vulnerability to criticism. Although not as talkative as Supervisor, Inspectors are still highly sociable. Their words tend to be plain and down-to-earth, not showy or high-flown.

The Protector (ISFJ)

Making up as much as 10 percent the population, their primary interest is in the safety and security of those they care about. This includes their family, their circle of friends, their students, their patients, their boss, their co-workers, or their employees. Protectors have an extraordinary sense of loyalty and responsibility in their makeup and seem fulfilled in the degree they can shield others from the dangers of the world. They prefer to make do with time-honored and time-tested products and procedures rather than change to new.

At work, Protectors are seldom happy in situations in which the rules are constantly changing. Protectors are willing to work long, hard hours quietly doing all the thankless jobs that others manage to avoid. Protectors are also quite happy working alone. When Protectors undertake a task, they will complete it if humanly possible. They also know better than any other type the value of a dollar. They abhor the squandering or misuse of money. To save, to put something aside against an unpredictable future, to prepare for emergencies—these are actions near and dear to the Protector's heart.

Idealist Temperament

All Idealists (NFs) share the following core characteristics:

- They are enthusiastic, trust their intuition, yearn for romance, seek their true self, prize meaningful relationships, and dream of attaining wisdom.

- They pride themselves on being loving, kindhearted, and authentic.

- They tend to be giving, trusting, and spiritual, and they are focused on personal journeys and human potentials.

- They make intense mates, nurturing parents, and inspirational leaders.

Idealists (NFs) can be described as enthusiastic, creative, insightful, idealistic, trusting, and subjective. They are wired to pursue their own and other's personal growth, being authentic in their behaviors and operating with integrity.

Diplomacy is at the heart of their interest and their behavior. From a very early age, Idealists are diplomats—helping others to resolve conflicts and encouraging win-win solutions. They are known for wanting to uncover meaning and significance in the world. And they have a sixth sense about people that comes out in their hunches and ability to listen to their feelings. Being tuned into body language, tone of voice, and facial expressions adds to the Idealists' ability to help others to develop their human potential and awareness.

Idealists are generally drawn to working with people in some capacity—counseling, spirituality, or personnel work. Abraham Maslow, Eleanor Roosevelt, Mohandas Gandhi, and Emily Dickinson are examples of Idealists. Idealists care about the morale of those around them and bring their enthusiasm and ability to lift others' spirits with them. Idealists are known for being self-less, trusting, open to mystical explanations, being future oriented, and always being on a journey to a higher stage of personal development. Making up about 8 to 10 percent of the population, Idealists want to be known as being empathic toward others, authentic in their actions, and always having goodwill toward others.

The four types of Idealists are: the Teacher (ENFJ), the Champion (ENFP), the Counselor (INFJ), and the Healer (INFP). Each is described in the sections that follow.

The Teacher (ENFJ)

Even more than the other Idealists, Teachers have a natural talent for engaging students or trainees in learning. Teachers (around 2 percent of the population) are able, effortlessly, to dream up fascinating learning activities for their students. In some Teachers, this ability to fire the imagination can amount to a kind of genius that other types find hard to emulate. Teachers look for the best in their students and communicate clearly that each one has untold potential. This confidence can inspire their students to grow and develop more than they ever thought possible.

In whatever field they choose, Teachers consider people their highest priority, and they instinctively communicate personal concern and a willingness to become involved. Warmly outgoing, and perhaps the most expressive of all the types, Teachers are remarkably good with language, especially when communicating in speech, face to face. And they do not hesitate to speak out and let their feelings be known. They are absolutely trustworthy in honoring their commitments.

Valuing as they do interpersonal cooperation and harmonious relations, Teachers are extraordinarily tolerant of others, are easy to get along with, and are usually popular wherever they are. Their insight into themselves and others is unparalleled, and they can read other people with uncanny accuracy. Teachers show a sincere interest in the joys and problems of their employees, colleagues, students, clients, and loved ones.

The Champion (ENFP)

Like the other Idealists, Champions are rather rare, say 2 or 3 percent of the population. But, even more than the others, they consider intense emotional experiences as being vital to a full life. Champions have a wide range and variety of emotions and a great passion for novelty. They see life as an exciting drama, full of possibilities, and they want to experience all the meaningful events and fascinating people in the world.

The most outgoing of the Idealists, Champions can be tireless in talking with others in the hope of revealing some truth about human experience, or of motivating others with their powerful convictions. They are the most vivacious and inspiring of all the types. Champions have outstanding intuitive powers and can tell what is going on inside of others, reading hidden emotions and giving special significance to words or actions. Champions are keen and probing observers of the people around them and are capable of intense concentration on another individual. They are likeable and at ease with colleagues and handle their employees or students with great skill. They are good in public and on the telephone and are so spontaneous and dramatic that others love to be in their company.

The Counselor (INFJ)

Counselors have an exceptionally strong desire to contribute to the welfare of others and find great personal fulfillment interacting with people. They nurture others' development, guiding them to realize their human potential. They are happy working at jobs (such as writing) that require solitude and close attention. However, Counselors do quite well with individuals or groups of people provided that the personal interactions are not superficial. They also require some quiet, private time every now and then to recharge their batteries. Counselors are both kind and positive in their handling of others; they are great listeners and seem naturally interested in helping people with their personal problems. Not usually visible leaders, Counselors prefer to work intensely with those close to them, especially on a one-to-one basis, quietly exerting their influence behind the scenes.

Counselors are scarce, little more than 1 percent of the population, and can be hard to get to know, because they tend not to share their innermost thoughts or their powerful emotional reactions except with their loved ones. Counselors tend to work effectively in organizations. They value staff harmony and make every effort to help an organization run smoothly and pleasantly. They understand and use human systems creatively and are good at consulting and cooperating with others.

Counselors have vivid imaginations and are highly intuitive. They can recognize another's emotions or intentions even before that person is aware of them.

The Healer (INFP)

Healers present a calm and serene face to the world and can seem shy, even distant around others. But inside they're anything but serene, having a capacity for personal caring rarely found in the other types. Healers care deeply about the inner life of a few special persons or about a favorite cause in the world at large. And their great passion is to heal the conflicts that trouble individuals, or that divide groups, and thus to bring wholeness, or health, to themselves, their loved ones, and their communities.

Healers are idealists with a deep commitment to pursuing what is positive and good. Their scarcity (1 percent of the population) and their pure idealism often lead to feelings of isolation. Healers™ are adaptable, welcome new ideas, and are patient with complicated situations. Healers are keenly aware of people and their feelings and relate well with most others. Because of their deep-seated reserve, however, they can work quite happily alone. They have a natural interest in scholarly activities and demonstrate, like the other Idealists, a remarkable facility with language.

Rational Temperament

All Rationals (NTs) share the following core characteristics:

◆ They tend to be pragmatic, skeptical, self-contained, and focused on problem-solving and systems analysis.

◆ They pride themselves on being ingenious, independent, and strong willed.

◆ They make reasonable mates, individualizing parents, and strategic leaders.

◆ They are even-tempered, trust logic, yearn for achievement, seek knowledge, prize technology, and dream of understanding how the world works.

Rationals (NTs) are the problem-solving temperament, particularly if the problem has to do with the many complex systems that make up the world around us. Rationals bring a keen insight, ability to grasp ideas, and a sharp intellect to abstract situations. The driving force for the Rationals is their ability to be competent and use their intelligence. They are interested in increasing the efficiency of any system of which they are part. This can include families and companies, plants and animals, and computers to automobiles.

Rationals are known as visionaries who are able to design new systems and efficiencies and strategize how to build them. They are interested in the sciences, technology, and systems. Rationals are known for seeking workable solutions. Often seen as skeptical about proposed ideas and views for the future, they weigh the importance of information based on the situation at hand. Their frame of reference and attention is on the particular situation in front of them. They evaluate their own self worth based on their ability to use their ingenuity, to retain their autonomy, and to keep their resolve in accomplishing what they set out to do.

Rationals value being calm, using their intellect and reason, being able to achieve what they set out to do, seeking knowledge, and being asked to discuss their rationale for work they have done. Rationals comprise as little as 5 to 7 percent of the population, but because of their drive to unlock the secrets of nature and to develop new technologies, they have done much to shape our world. They aspire to being seen as a wizard—to produce magic! Albert Einstein, Dwight Eisenhower, and Thomas Edison were all Rationals.

The four types of Rationals are: the Field Marshal (ENTJ), the Inventor (ENTP), the Mastermind (INTJ), and the Architect (INTP). Each is described in the sections that follow.

The Field Marshal (ENTJ)

Superb administrators in any field—medicine, law, business, education, government, the military, and so on—ENTJs organize their units into smooth-functioning systems, planning in advance, keeping both short-term and long-range objectives well in mind. Field marshals have a strong natural urge to give structure and direction wherever they are—to harness people in the field and to direct them to achieve distant goals. They are most interested in policy and goals versus regulations and procedures. They are likely to be good at systematizing, ordering priorities, generalizing, summarizing, marshaling evidence, and demonstrating their ideas.

They tend not to build organizations or push to implement their goals. When in charge of an organization, whether in the military, business, education, or government, Field marshals, more than any other type, desire to visualize where the organization is going, and they seem able to communicate that vision to others. They prefer decisions to be based on impersonal data, want to work from well thought-out plans, like to use engineered operations—and they expect others to follow suit. They are ever intent on reducing bureaucratic red tape, task redundancy, and aimless confusion in the workplace, and they are willing to dismiss employees who cannot get with the program and increase their efficiency.

The Inventor (ENTP)

Inventors begin building gadgets and mechanisms as young children and never really stop. As adults they turn their inventiveness to many kinds of organizations, social as well as mechanical. There aren't many Inventors, say about 2 percent of the population, but they have great impact on our everyday lives. With their innovative, entrepreneurial spirit, Inventors are always on the lookout for a better way, always eyeing new projects, new enterprises, new processes. Always aiming to "build a better mousetrap." "It can't be done" is a challenge to an Inventor and elicits a reaction of "I can do it."

Inventors are keenly pragmatic and often become expert at devising the most effective means to accomplish their ends. They often bring fresh, new approaches to their work and play. They are intensely curious and continuously probe for possibilities, especially when trying to solve complex problems. Inventors are filled with ideas, but value ideas only when they make possible actions and objects. Thus, they see product design not as an end in itself, but as a means to an end. The prototype that works can then be brought to market!

Inventors are confident in their pragmatism. A rough idea is all they need to feel ready to proceed into action. Inventors are usually easy-going and seldom critical. Inventors easily express their ideas and have well-developed debate skills. Inventors are usually nonconformists in the workplace and can succeed in many areas as long as the job does not involve too much humdrum routine. They make good leaders on pilot projects that test their ingenuity. And they are skilled at engineering human relationships and human systems, quickly grasping the politics of institutions and always wanting to understand the people within the system rather than tell them what to do.

The Mastermind (INTJ)

All Rationals are good at planning operations, but Masterminds are head and shoulders above all the rest in contingency planning. Complex operations involve many steps or stages, one following another in a necessary progression, and Masterminds are naturally able to grasp how each one leads to the next and to prepare alternatives for difficulties that are likely to arise on any step of the way.

Masterminds are rare, comprising no more than 1 percent of the population. They are rarely encountered outside their office, factory, school, or laboratory. Although they are highly capable leaders, Masterminds are not at all eager to take command, preferring to stay in the background. After they take charge, however, they are thoroughgoing pragmatists. They are certain that efficiency is indispensable. If they encounter any waste of human and material resources, they are quick to realign operations and reassign personnel.

Problem-solving is highly stimulating to Masterminds, who love responding to tangled systems that require careful sorting out. Ordinarily, they verbalize the positive and avoid comments of a negative nature. They are more interested in moving an organization forward than dwelling on mistakes of the past. Masterminds are highly theoretical, but they insist on looking at all available data before they embrace an idea, and they are suspicious of any statement that is based on shoddy research, or that is not checked against reality. They are confident and easily make decisions.

The Architect (INTP)

Architects are the master designers of all kinds of theoretical systems, including school curricula, corporate strategies, and new technologies. For Architects, the world exists primarily to be analyzed, understood, explained—and redesigned. External reality in itself is unimportant, little more than raw material to be organized into structural models. What is important for Architects is that they grasp fundamental principles and natural laws and that their designs are elegant—that is, efficient and coherent.

Architects show the greatest precision in thought and speech of all the types and are about 1 percent of the population. They tend to see distinctions and inconsistencies instantaneously and can detect contradictions no matter when or where they were made. It is difficult for an Architect to listen to nonsense, even in a casual conversation, without pointing out the speaker's error. And in any serious discussion or debate Architects are devastating—their skill in framing arguments giving them an enormous advantage. Architects regard all discussions as a search for understanding and believe their function is to eliminate inconsistencies, which can make communication with them an uncomfortable experience for many.

Ruthless pragmatists about ideas, and insatiably curious, Architects are driven to find the most efficient means to their ends. They will listen to amateurs if their ideas are useful and will ignore the experts if their ideas are not. Able to concentrate better than any other type, they prefer to work quietly at their computers or drafting tables, and often alone. Architects also become obsessed with analysis, and this can seem to shut others out. When caught up in a thought process, Architects close off and persevere until they comprehend the issue in all its complexity. Architects prize intelligence, and with their grand desire to grasp the structure of the universe, they can seem arrogant and may show impatience with others who have less ability, or who are less driven.

Using Your Results

You have already been given some important information about the relationship between your temperament and personality and your career and lifestyle preferences. Isn't this exciting? The more assessments you take, the more you will begin to see a consistency in your preferences, your values, your outlook on life, and your occupational preferences.

My Temperament is _____.

Right now, you are still building your profile, so remember to put your Temperament in your Career Map Profile in Appendix A. If you have any doubts about whether or not your temperament and personality type are correct, use the following tips:

1. Read over the descriptions of the four behaviors that combine to make up your personality: Extrovert and Introvert, Sensation and Intuition, Thinking and Feeling, and Judgment and Perception.

2. Give your friends a blank copy of the descriptions of the four behaviors and ask them to pick out the one they think describes you best.

3. Pay attention to your behavior over the next week. Where do you go to regain energy? How do you take in information? What do you rely on to make your decisions? Do you live your life in an orderly, planned fashion, or are you spontaneous and flexible?

By this time, you have a pretty good picture of which temperament best describes you and which of the four personality types under this temperament best reflects your type. Hopefully you have learned and confirmed more about who you are, what's important to you in terms of values, how you see yourself in the world, and some primary areas of interest. All of this will serve you well in figuring out which careers can be good matches for your temperament and personality—more on this in Chapter 15.

The Least You Need to Know

- Temperament is a predisposition to particular attitudes and behaviors that we use every day.

- Our temperament affects our values, the way we communicate, our interests, our self image, our own particular form of intelligence, and how we approach our past, present, and future.

- Personality is made up of our temperament and character. Character is influenced by our temperament and is developed over a lifetime.

Chapter 8

Your Motivation

In This Chapter

- ◆ Understand the role of motivation in making career choices
- ◆ Introduction to the four primary sources of motivation
- ◆ Assess your primary sources of motivation

Motivation is what can make you jump out of bed with gusto in the morning. It's what can make you look forward to the day. It's what can keep your behavior directed on accomplishing your goals. According to Kleinginna and Kleinginna, "motivation is an internal need or want that activates and energizes your behavior and gives it direction." (Kleinginna, P., Jr., & A. Kleinginna. [1981a]. A categorized list of motivation definitions with suggestions for a consensual definition. *Motivation and Emotion*, 5, 263–291.)

If you are having trouble sustaining your performance and/or your enthusiasm for the work you do, then it's probably time to identify your wants and needs—what really will motivate you.

So many of us do not stop to consider what really motivates and keeps us excited and productive. In this chapter, you will have the chance to take the Four Boxes of Life Assessment and start your journey to discovering what truly motivates you.

Understanding My Motivation

Understanding our own needs and wants helps us in three ways. First, we can more accurately choose jobs and careers that are suited to meeting our needs. Second, we can choose organizational settings that have the best chance of *motivating* us based on our needs. Third, we can acknowledge that work alone does not fulfill all our needs. This means looking at all aspects of our life/work and making sure that we are purposeful in making choices that will create the right balance for us.

Career Lingo _____

Motivation is an internal need or want that activates and energizes our behavior and gives it direction. Motivation can come from our need for security, for relationships, for recognition, or for making a contribution. Motivation sustains our performance and helps us to reach our goals.

Stop-Look-Listen _____

Never underestimate the importance of matching your needs and expectations to that of the organization you are thinking about joining. Organizations have needs just like people do. Often if these expectations don't match, you will find yourself demotivated to do your job. Understand your own needs and wants and ask what the organization can do for you!

Determining exactly what motivates people has been a challenge over the years. There are many theories of motivation and only limited agreement on the central areas of motivation. One area that most researches agree with is that some of our motivation comes from inside of us—again based on our own wants and needs. And that if we know our wants and needs we can use this information to energize and direct our behavior. The other side of the coin has to do with how our external environment plays a role in motivating us. Let's look at Erika's situation. Erika works in a counseling center at a large university. She is extremely motivated by her work in counseling and advising undergraduate students. Her main source of gratification is through her work with others, her ability to help others and to be appreciated for what she does. However, the counseling center where she works is a downer for Erika. Everyone on the staff is independent. They never work as a team; weekly meetings are full of conflict; and everyone remains in their private offices for the entire day with no interaction. Her need for affiliation, support, and acceptance from her peers is totally lacking. So Erika has chosen a career that meets her needs, but now needs to find an organization environment that will meet more of her affiliation needs with her peers.

For years, organizations have been trying to understand what motivates people. If they could only break the code, then productivity would be a snap. And to their credit many organizations do put programs and practices into place that do motivate many. Some of these include individual and team recognition and reward programs, teaching managers how to give positive feedback on a regular basis, providing ongoing training and development.

But the best way to know what motivates the individuals working for you is to ASK them. Some people need a friendly and supportive working relationship with peers and boss; others are driven by recognition for their achievements. Still others want to be able to continually learn and explore. Let's look at the Four Boxes of Life categories next.

Four Sources of Motivation

Although there is no universal agreement on theories and models of motivation, the Four Boxes of Life (see the table that follows) reflects a modified version of Abraham Maslow's Hierarchy of Needs. (Abraham Maslow, *Motivation and Personality*, 2nd ed., Harper & Row, 1970.)

The Four Boxes of Life

Security	Relationships	Recognition	Contribution
Money	Affiliation with others	Achievement	Self-Fulfillment
Physical Surroundings and Comforts	Acceptance	Approval and Recognition	Other's Fulfillment
Emotional Well Being	Belonging	Competence	Spirituality
Physical Well Being	Love	Knowledge	Exploration

In Maslow's theory, there is a hierarchy of needs, beginning with life needs and continuing to fulfillment needs. Maslow believed that after you satisfy a lower level need, you move on to the next level and that becomes your motivation. The Four Boxes of Life borrows from Maslow's categories but does not reflect his hierarchical theory.

The Four Boxes of Life is designed to help you to identify those wants and needs that give you the most motivation in doing your work and living your life. You may have several motivators or needs operating at one time. You may find yourself thinking, "Of course, I'm motivated by security and having enough income." We all need a certain amount of money and shelter to live. But, for some people money and status and grand living is a primary motivator. For others, having a comfortable and modest life supports their greater need for making a contribution to society. So you will be asked to make distinctions—to look for those wants and needs that consistently give you energy and enthusiasm for the work you do.

The Four Boxes of Life Assessment

Place a check in the box next to those motivators that represent what really motivates you. Which ones give you the most energy, help you enjoy your work and your life, keep your behavior directed toward accomplishing work and life goals?

❑ 1. Work with others on projects

❑ 2. The feelings of accomplishment from the work I do

❑ 3. Receiving recognition for my work

❑ 4. Knowing I belong—have a place in this group or organization

❑ 5. Exploring new territory or researching new areas

❑ 6. Financial security

❑ 7. Making a difference, contributing

❑ 8. Being accepted by others

❑ 9. Helping others to grow and develop

❑ 10. Having friends at work

❑ 11. Obtaining new knowledge, breaking new ground

❑ 12. Socializing with others

❑ 13. Having comfortable surroundings

❑ 14. Having a safe and secure life

❑ 15. Being able to pursue the full range of my talents and abilities

❑ 16. Continual development of my personal qualities (character)

❑ 17. Developing my spiritual awareness and practice

❑ 18. Emotional well being

❑ 19. Physical well being

❑ 20. Using my best and favorite skills

Let's take a look at how you came out on these motivators. Each of the Four Boxes of Life has five of the motivators associated with it (for example, questions 6, 13, 14, 18, and 19 refer to your need for security). Add up the number of check marks for each of the Four Boxes of Life and write down the total checked off. Here is the breakdown:

Security: #6, #13, #14, #18, #19 Total Checked Off _____

Relationships: #1, #4, #8, #10, #12 Total Checked Off _____

Recognition: #2, #3, #5, #11, #20 Total Checked Off _____

Contribution: #7, #9, #15, #16, #17 Total Checked Off _____

Rank order your motivators from highest number of check-offs to lowest number of check-offs and record the Total Checked Off and Rank in your Career Profile Map in Appendix A.

Using Your Results

You may have found yourself primarily in one motivation category or spread out in many categories. There are no simple answers to what motivates us. The important thing is to begin to recognize the consistency of some motivators over time. This assessment is a beginning. Continue to pay attention to which needs and wants give you the most motivation in your work and life. The following general comments about each of the Four Boxes of Life may give you some clarification or insight into which of the four is a primary motivator for you.

Security Motivators

If you found yourself primarily motivated by Security, then you may find yourself being more driven in your behavior to secure work that provides a certain income range and allows you to take care of your emotional and physical well being. You may also find yourself here temporarily if you have financial worries due to any number of circumstances. Everyone needs the basics in life, so they are always there in the background.

The questions for you are: Do these motivators drive my energy and behavior? Is it because I want to attain a certain income and live a certain lifestyle that motivates me to achieve my goals?

Relationship Motivators

Being primarily motivated in the Relationship category can mean that you are attracted to work and a life in which you can work collaboratively and comfortably with others. You like to belong to a group or organization and be accepted by others. You are happiest and work best when these things are in place for you in your work and life.

Most of us like to be with people and do things with people; the question for you is: Is working with others to accomplish goals and having a sense of acceptance and belonging a major driver in my happiness and ability to achieve goals? If the answer is YES, then it's important to find work environments and careers that will give you this motivation on a daily basis.

 Insider Tips _____

Organizations who have these things going are relationship oriented: rewards and recognition for teamwork; periodic social gatherings to celebrate reaching milestones or accomplishing goals; supervisors and managers who take the time to ask you how you are and take an interest in you as a person; teambuilding activities where people get to know one another, have fun, and build a feeling of belonging.

Recognition Motivators

Recognition motivators call out to you to do the work, achieve the goals, receive recognition and praise for your competence. Again, most of us can see ourselves in

these motivators—we all want to be competent and recognized for our good work,
don't we?

However, the questions for you are: Am I truly
driven, energized, happy when I can put my
competencies to work, see the results of my
achievements, and get recognition? Do I get up
in the morning to do the work and learn some
more—is that what does it? For those of us who
are *achievement oriented*, then we need to identify those competencies we want to use to
achieve those goals, find work environments
that reward achievement—are results oriented
and appreciate our work.

Career Lingo

Achievement oriented
means that you want to get
things done. You want to accomplish your goals, see the results
of your efforts. People who are
achievement oriented are doers.
They value being competent at
what they do and able to meet
and exceed expectations.

Contribution Motivators

Contribution motivators are all about being able to explore your full potential and
help others to live up to theirs. Do you want to explore all the gifts and potential you
were given? Do you want to help others to explore their gifts and talents fully? Is it
important to contribute to society and to others' development? Some people are
driven to leave a legacy of some kind—a contribution that will live on. This also may
have a spiritual component where one transcends the sense of self to the larger concept of spirit. Awareness and practice can be an important component of one's life.
Again, many of us want to explore our full potential.

The questions for you are: Do I find myself being most inspired and energized when
I am able to keep exploring my talents and interests? Do I enjoy making a contribution to the growth of others? Do I look for ways to make a difference in my own and
others' lives? Do I have a quest for self discovery? Those of us who see this as our
main motivator in life want the freedom to do this exploration. We want to work in
organizational environments that give us the freedom and opportunity to explore new
ways to develop ourselves and others. We want to do work that makes a difference to
our own lives and to the lives of others.

Work/Life Applications

Now that you know something about what motivates you, use this information to help guide your career and life decisions. Look for work environments that reward your motivations. Choose careers that lend themselves to fulfilling your needs. And, think about how what motivates you spills over into your choice of lifestyle. As you continue to take the other assessments in this book, you will begin to see patterns and themes among them. These will continue to affirm who you are, and the kinds of environments, work, and life you desire—and will fit you the best!

The Least You Need to Know

- ◆ If you want to understand your motivation, identify needs that energize you and move you to action.

- ◆ There are four major sources of motivation—security, relationships, recognition, and contribution.

- ◆ Understanding what motivates you can lead to choosing the right career for you, the right organization for you, and the right lifestyle for you.

Chapter 9

Your Interests

In this Chapter

♦ Understand the seven interest orientations

♦ Assess your own interests

♦ Prioritize your interests and map them to the seven interest areas

How do you gain a full understanding of your interests? Well you may have already begun by identifying interests you had in your youth. Or you may have developed more of your interests through extracurricular activities such as clubs, sports, or community groups. Perhaps you liked certain subjects in school more than others. Or you might have pursued relationships with people who were doing things you wanted to do. If you were lucky, you had a *mentor* to teach you and guide you in your interest. Other sources of determining our interests have to do with the books we read, the movies or shows we like, or what we do in our free time.

Seven Orientation Scales

The Seven Orientation Scales represent different clusters of interests that are found in major subsets of the world of work. Wouldn't it be nice to know how your interests line up with the world of work?

David Campbell, author of the *Campbell Interest and Skill Survey (CISS)*, lays out a way for us to understand just that. The CISS is a survey of self-reported interests and skills. Taking the CISS will help you to identify occupations in which people have interests similar to your own. It will also help you to determine the level of skill you have to meet job requirements. This survey is available onwww.KeirseyCampbell.com You may use the coupon on the last page in this book to take the Kiersey Temperament Sorter and the CISS for a reduced price.

We are using David Campbell's descriptions of the seven interest orientations to guide you in thinking about your own interests. Each of the Seven Orientation Scale categories (Influencing, Organizing, Helping, Creating, Analyzing, Producing, Adventuring) is described in the sections that follow. Afterward, you will take a self-assessment of your interests in each category. For now, see which of these descriptions fits you the best.

Influencing Orientation

People with an Influencing Orientation are drawn to leading and influencing others. They like to make things happen—to take charge and get results. Generally confident about being able to persuade others to their viewpoints, they love to debate.

Public speaking and visibility are comfortable for them. Typical careers for Influencers have to do with being in charge—manager, director, superintendent, or politician.

Organizing Orientation

People with Organizing Orientations bring order and planning to their work environments. They manage projects, plan procedures, and directly supervise the work of others. They see themselves as efficient and productive members of the work force. Organizers are good at details and enjoy solving day-to-day problems. They understand budgets and cash flow and are often good at investing. Typical occupations for people with Organizing Orientations are accountants, financial planners, and administrative assistants.

Helping Orientation

People with Helping Orientations like to help and develop other people. They are compassionate and deeply concerned about the well-being of others. Helpers enjoy having close personal contact with others. They like to help others live full and satisfying lives. Helpers understand the feelings of others and provide emotional support. Typical occupations for Helpers include counselors, teachers, human resource personnel, and spiritual or religious leaders.

CAUTION

Stop-Look-Listen

Pinpointing our interests and looking to them for guidance in selecting our work is a two-edged sword. On the one hand, our interests give us such great information and clues about the kind of work that will really motivate us every day. On the other hand, not all of our interests can be met through work. It's important to have a life beyond work. A life in which we can enjoy additional activities that give us joy and satisfaction. You can have it all—work you love and a life you really enjoy. The trick is not to put all your eggs in one basket—spread the wealth of your interests across your life.

Creating Orientation

People who have a Creating Orientation like to create new products, new visions, and new concepts in artistic areas. They see the world through innovative eyes and are frequently uncomfortable with traditional approaches. They are expressive and articulate. Typical occupations for Creators include artists, musicians, designers, and writers.

Analyzing Orientation

People who have an Analyzing Orientation are comfortable with data and numbers. They have a strong need to understand the world from a scientific viewpoint. They like working alone or in small groups in laboratories or academic settings. Analyzers need to be autonomous and like to work through problems by themselves. Typical occupations for Analyzers are scientists, medical researchers, statisticians, and doctors.

Producing Orientation

People who have a Producing Orientation like hands-on productive activities. They like to work with their hands and see the results of their labor. Working outdoors is often preferred by Producers. They are good with tools and new construction projects or repairing mechanical breakdowns. Typical occupations for Producers are mechanics, veterinarians, landscape architects, and carpenters.

Adventuring Orientation

People who have an Adventuring Orientation like to take risks, compete with others, and test their physical endurance. They enjoy physical activities and like competitive situations. They are confident in their physical skills and seek out excitement. Adventurers enjoy winning and bounce back when defeated. Typical occupations for Adventurers are sportsmen/women, military officers, police officers, and athletic coaches.

Orientation Scales Assessment

In column one (Orientation), place a check mark in front of those interests in column two (Interests) that represent activities you have been drawn to in your life experience. In column three (My Activities), list activities you have engaged in that are related to each of the interests listed in column two. In column four (Totals), count the number of activities you listed in column three for each interest.

Orientation Scales Assessment

Orientation	Interests	My Activities	Totals
Influencing			
___	Politics	_____	
___	Leadership	_____	
___	Positions in Organizations	_____	
___	Presenting/Speaking	_____	
___	Selling Products/Services	_____	
___	Debating	_____	
___	Motivating Teams/Players	_____	
___	Starting Businesses	_____	
___	Other	_____	
			Total ___
Organizing			
___	Keeping Records	_____	
___	Organizing Events	_____	
___	Secretary of Organizations	_____	
___	Reorganizing (rooms, files, closets)	_____	
___	Making things more efficient	_____	
___	Making investments	_____	
___	Keeping Detailed Records	_____	
___	Other	_____	
			Total ___
Helping			
___	Helping people to solve their problems	_____	
___	Supporting Others	_____	
___	Working with Children	_____	
___	Mentoring/Teaching Others	_____	
___	Spiritual/Religious Practice	_____	

continues

Orientation Scales Assessment (continued)

Orientation	Interests	My Activities	Totals
___	Interest in other cultures	_____	
___	Volunteer work	_____	
___	Other	_____	
			Total ___
Creating			
___	Writing	_____	
___	Art work	_____	
___	Approaching what you do with creativity	_____	
___	Playing music	_____	
Creating			
___	Acting	_____	
___	Designing workshops, clothing, and so on	_____	
___	Learning Languages	_____	
___	Other	_____	
			Total ___
Analyzing			
___	Doing Research	_____	
___	Keeping statistics	_____	
___	Solving puzzles/problems	_____	
___	Doing experiments	_____	
___	Computer Programming	_____	
___	Science Fiction	_____	
___	Novels	_____	
___	Studying Future Trends	_____	
___	Other	_____	
			Total ___
Producing			
___	Animal Care, Training	_____	
___	Building Things	_____	
___	Electronics	_____	

Orientation	Interests	My Activities	Totals
___	Fixing or Repairing	_____	
___	Nature	_____	
___	Gardening	_____	
___	Flower arranging	_____	
___	Other	_____	
			Total ___

Adventuring

Orientation	Interests	My Activities	Totals
___	Playing sports	_____	
___	Rafting/Canoeing	_____	
___	Outdoor Adventure	_____	
___	Trips	_____	
___	Fitness	_____	
___	ROTC, National Guard		
___	Military		
___	Testing physical ability	_____	
___	Other	_____	
			Total ___

Take your totals from column four for each of the orientations and list them here (also record each Total in your Career Profile Map in Appendix A):

Orientation Interest	Total	Orientation Interest	Total
Influencing	___	Analyzing	___
Organizing	___	Producing	___
Helping	___	Adventuring	___
Creating	___		

List in order of priority, your three highest totals:

1. _____

2. _____

3. _____

From the Interests listed in column two of the Orientation Scales Assessment table, write down the interests that would make it into your top five favorites.

1. _____
2. _____
3. _____
4. _____
5. _____

These are your Top 3 Priority Orientations and your Top 5 Interests, make sure that you record them in your Career Profile Map in Appendix A.

Using Your Results

Consider the interest orientations that you engage in most often along with your five favorite interests. What do these interest areas tell you about yourself and what you might be looking for in a career? Write your thoughts down. Be sure to capture any careers or jobs that come to mind based on this exercise.

_____

_____

_____

_____

The Least You Need to Know

◆ Your interests can be matched to major work areas where people are doing jobs with interests similar to yours.

◆ David Campbell's Seven Orientation Scales serve as a way to help you understand how your interests relate to these major work areas.

◆ The seven Orientations are: Influencing, Organizing, Helping, Creating, Analyzing, Producing, and Adventuring.

◆ Taking the time to identify your interests will prove pivotal in finding your perfect career.

Chapter **10**

Your Skills

In This Chapter

- ◆ Data, things, and people skills in the world of work
- ◆ Choose the skills you want to use in your career
- ◆ Skills that are transferable to other jobs and careers
- ◆ Identify your self-management skills
- ◆ Think about your natural abilities or talents

There are many sides to looking at your skills. Some of your skills seem like natural abilities or talents. These skills have been honed and developed over time and come easily to you. You also have self-management skills. Each of us has a different set of self-management skills that indicate how our attributes can contribute to getting results on the job as well as getting along with others. Then there are skills we use to work with data, things, and people. Most of us have a preference for one of the three. And most occupations are made up of one or more of these skill sets. Still other skills you have are ones that can transfer to other careers and occupations. Isn't that good news! This chapter will explore all these different aspects of your skills.

Three Types of Skills

Imagine that directly in front of you are three boxes, each of which contain a path to your future. You are supposed to choose one. One of these boxes is the right box for you and will bring you all the happiness in the world. The other boxes are filled with boredom and a life of discontent.

The first box represents using skills of the heart where you work with people most of the time. The second box is full of skills that keep your mind active as you work with data and ideas. The third box is filled to the brim with skills that use your physical ability to work with all kinds of things. Each box is beautifully wrapped and has colors and patterns that appeal to you. You are drawn to aspects of each, so how do you decide which one holds true happiness?

The boxes represent three categories of skills that are found in the world of work. All occupations are made up of some combination of the three basic skills. And, most occupations have one of these skills areas as their main requirement. The three basic types of skills are:

♦ People skills (box number one)

♦ Data skills (box number two)

♦ Things skills (box number three)

People Skills

All of us are involved in using people skills in our work place. These are the skills we use to influence others and to be of help to others. Leaders and salespeople are primary examples of occupations that directly relate to influencing skills. On the other hand, counselors, human resource personnel, teachers, and customer service people use primarily helping skills.

Data Skills

There are three ways of approaching working with data. One is through analyzing data. People who enjoy using their minds to figure out how to use data, how to organize it, and how to make it useful use analyzing skills. Accountants, air traffic controllers, and office assistants use analyzing skills.

Insider Tips

There are two sides to people skills. On one side is showing consideration for others. Being a good listener and understanding others' points of view are critical to your success. It doesn't matter what your job is or what your position is in the organization, you need to be able to get along with others. Getting along doesn't mean going along. The other side of people skills is being confident in expressing your own thoughts, ideas, and opinions clearly. Being a contributor is also critical to your success.

A second area of data skills is in the realm of ideas. Here you are often working with data to present it to others in the form of ideas. Speech writers and advertisers put data together to articulate ideas that their audience will be able to comprehend.

The third way to look at data skills is through a creative approach to the data. If you prefer to work with data to create something from scratch, then you fall in the "creative" skills area. Artists and people who invent or create new things out of data are found in the creative category of data.

Things Skills

Things skills are found in a couple of areas. People who like to work with concrete things such as materials, metals, tools, and plants are in the area of producing skills. You are using materials to produce an end product—a garden, a house, a bridge.

The second area is focused on using physical ability as the basis of your skill. Athletes, fitness trainers, and military personnel fall into the category of adventure skills.

One Box or Many?

Many people find that the skills they love to use or learn are primarily in one of the three boxes of skills. Brad is a good example of this. He is a sculptor, and he loves working with metal to create art. His total focus is on creating his work. His skill preferences are definitely in the things skills area. So for Brad, choosing the things box would bring him the most happiness. Often people in the arts need others to promote and sell their work because this is not where their skills lie. They need people with people skills!

How about the rest of us who don't find ourselves so neatly in one box? And that would be most of us! How about Jean who loves to work with people? She is a leadership consultant and takes great pride in helping people in positions of leadership to develop. So although she is solidly in the people skills area, she also loves to create watercolor paintings. These skills fall within the data skills box because she has to pay more attention to her use of materials, visualizing shapes and colors and working with the details involved in creating a work of art. She also incorporates her art in her work as a consultant, designing concrete models of growth and change that are artistically presented to her clients. So we can find ourselves combining the skills we really love into one career or occupational area.

The next section will help you to begin to think about your skills in each of the three work activity skill categories of data, things, and people. You may begin to see a relationship between your interests that you identified in Chapter 9 and the skills you like to use here.

Skills Inventory Assessment

Consider each skill listed under the three work skills categories: data, things, and people. Now perform the following steps:

1. Put a check mark in the "I Have This Skill" column if you have some expertise in using the skill.

2. Put a check mark in the "I Want to Use This Skill in My Work" column if you really love this skill and want to find an occupation where you can use this skill.

3. Put a check mark in the "I Need to Get or Develop This Skill" column if you want to learn this skill or improve your expertise in using this skill. Remember today's organizations require that you keep your skills up to date and be willing to learn new skills as the skill requirements for your job change.

4. Use the blank spaces (Other) at the end of each work skill list to write any skills you have that were not listed. This list is meant to stimulate your ability to identify your own skills in each of the work skills categories.

Skills Inventory

Work Activity Skills	I Have This Skill	I Want to Use This Skill in My Work	I Need to Get or Develop This Skill
People Skills			
Public Speaking	❑	❑	❑
Promoting	❑	❑	❑
Selling	❑	❑	❑
Persuading	❑	❑	❑
Giving Feedback	❑	❑	❑
Motivating	❑	❑	❑
Managing	❑	❑	❑
Supervising	❑	❑	❑
Results-Oriented	❑	❑	❑
Setting Goals	❑	❑	❑
Negotiation	❑	❑	❑
Risk Taking	❑	❑	❑
Change Agent	❑	❑	❑
Running Meetings	❑	❑	❑
Facilitating Groups	❑	❑	❑
Decision Maker	❑	❑	❑
Developing Trus	❑	❑	❑t
Helping Others Solve Their Problems	❑	❑	❑
Caring	❑	❑	❑
Comforting	❑	❑	❑
Active Listener	❑	❑	❑
Counseling	❑	❑	❑
Coaching	❑	❑	❑
Consulting	❑	❑	❑
Mentoring	❑	❑	❑
Good Communicator	❑	❑	❑

continues

Skills Inventory (continued)

Work Activity Skills	I Have This Skill	I Want to Use This Skill in My Work	I Need to Get or Develop This Skill
Encouraging	❏	❏	❏
Building Others' Self-Esteem	❏	❏	❏
Showing Empathy	❏	❏	❏
Advising	❏	❏	❏
Managing Conflict	❏	❏	❏
Developing Rapport	❏	❏	❏
Interviewing	❏	❏	❏
Inquiry	❏	❏	❏
Insight	❏	❏	❏
Instructing/Teaching/ Training	❏	❏	❏
Understanding the Backgrounds and Needs of Others	❏	❏	❏
Networking	❏	❏	❏
Expressing Feelings	❏	❏	❏
Collaborative	❏	❏	❏
Other 1:	❏	❏	❏
Other 2:	❏	❏	❏
Other 3:	❏	❏	❏
Other 4:	❏	❏	❏
Other 5:	❏	❏	❏
Data: Analyzing Skills			
Putting Things in Order/Structuring	❏	❏	❏
Analyzing Data	❏	❏	❏
Compiling Data	❏	❏	❏
Budgeting	❏	❏	❏

Work Activity Skills	I Have This Skill	I Want to Use This Skill in My Work	I Need to Get or Develop This Skill
Calculating/Computing	❑	❑	❑
Taking Inventory	❑	❑	❑
Using Technology to Analyze Data	❑	❑	❑
Managing Money	❑	❑	❑
Investing	❑	❑	❑
Filing	❑	❑	❑
Surveying	❑	❑	❑
Examining	❑	❑	❑
Following Instructions	❑	❑	❑
Making More Efficient	❑	❑	❑
Keeping Records	❑	❑	❑
Auditing	❑	❑	❑
Inspecting	❑	❑	❑
Synthesizing	❑	❑	❑
Keeping Statistics	❑	❑	❑
Organizing	❑	❑	❑
Checking for Accuracy	❑	❑	❑
Good at Repetitive Tasks	❑	❑	❑
Purchasing	❑	❑	❑
Testing/Evaluating	❑	❑	❑
Programming	❑	❑	❑
Forecasting	❑	❑	❑
Estimating Time, Costs	❑	❑	❑
Arranging	❑	❑	❑
Scheduling	❑	❑	❑
Researching/Investigating	❑	❑	❑
Solving Everyday Problems	❑	❑	❑
Other 1:	❑	❑	❑
Other 2:	❑	❑	❑

continues

Skills Inventory (continued)

Work Activity Skills	I Have This Skill	I Want to Use This Skill in My Work	I Need to Get or Develop This Skill
Other 3:	❑	❑	❑
Other 4:	❑	❑	❑
Other 5:	❑	❑	❑
Data: Idea Skills			
Editing	❑	❑	❑
Write Clearly	❑	❑	❑
Inventing	❑	❑	❑
Imaginative	❑	❑	❑
Quick Thinking	❑	❑	❑
Speech Writing	❑	❑	❑
Promotional Writing	❑	❑	❑
Advertising	❑	❑	❑
Publicity/Marketing	❑	❑	❑
Articulate	❑	❑	❑
Correspondence	❑	❑	❑
Reasoning	❑	❑	❑
Other 1:	❑	❑	❑
Other 2:	❑	❑	❑
Other 3:	❑	❑	❑
Other 4:	❑	❑	❑
Other 5:	❑	❑	❑
Data: Creative Skills			
Photography	❑	❑	❑
Painting	❑	❑	❑
Dance/Body Movement	❑	❑	❑
Performing	❑	❑	❑
Designing	❑	❑	❑
Mapping	❑	❑	❑
Mechanical Drawing	❑	❑	❑

Work Activity Skills	I Have This Skill	I Want to Use This Skill in My Work	I Need to Get or Develop This Skill
Visualizing	❑	❑	❑
Craft Making	❑	❑	❑
Illustrating	❑	❑	❑
Model Making	❑	❑	❑
Visualize Shapes	❑	❑	❑
Poetry	❑	❑	❑
Artistic Expression	❑	❑	❑
Other 1:	❑	❑	❑
Other 2:	❑	❑	❑
Other 3:	❑	❑	❑
Other 4:	❑	❑	❑
Other 5:	❑	❑	❑
Things: Producing Skills			
Fixing	❑	❑	❑
Repairing	❑	❑	❑
Driving	❑	❑	
Adjusting			
Operating Computer	❑	❑	❑
Operating Machines/Equipment	❑	❑	❑
Constructing/Building	❑	❑	❑
Operating Vehicles	❑	❑	❑
Using Tools	❑	❑	❑
Servicing Machines	❑	❑	❑
Gardening	❑	❑	❑
Harvesting	❑	❑	❑
Landscaping	❑	❑	❑
Working with Nature/Earth	❑	❑	❑

continues

Skills Inventory (continued)

Work Activity Skills	I Have This Skill	I Want to Use This Skill in My Work	I Need to Get or Develop This Skill
Lifting	❏	❏	❏
Moving Objects	❏	❏	❏
Shipping and Delivery	❏	❏	❏
Loading and Unloading	❏	❏	❏
Maintenance	❏	❏	❏
Assembling	❏	❏	❏
Keypunching	❏	❏	❏
Using Instruments	❏	❏	❏
Other 1:	❏	❏	❏
Other 2:	❏	❏	❏
Other 3:	❏	❏	❏
Other 4:	❏	❏	❏
Other 5:	❏	❏	❏
Things: Adventuring Skills			
Physical Fitness	❏	❏	❏
Sports	❏	❏	❏
Physical Strength	❏	❏	❏
Endurance	❏	❏	❏
Physical Coordination	❏	❏	❏
Competitive Game Skills	❏	❏	❏
Survival Skills	❏	❏	❏
Other 1:	❏	❏	❏
Other 2:	❏	❏	❏
Other 3:	❏	❏	❏
Other 4:	❏	❏	❏
Other 5:	❏	❏	❏

Why make a distinction between skills you have and skills you really want to use? Wouldn't you want to let an employer know all your skills? Well consider this example. Raul is great with numbers. His parents think he should be an accountant. He is happy to have this ability, but he doesn't see it as a driving force in his work. Raul loves sports—loves to persuade and influence people and sees himself right in the middle of the action. Maybe he'll be a recruiter or go into sports management. It's great to have many skills. And it's even greater to put the ones out front that we really love to use.

Rank Your Skills

Identifying the skills you want to use in your occupation helps you in several ways. You can be clear with everyone you speak to that these are the skills you want to use—no chance here of finding yourself in the wrong job! You can also use this combination of skills to locate occupations that use these skills—more on this in Chapter 17. Above all, this list will keep you focused on finding an occupation and a career that is going to allow you to use skills you love.

In the chart that follows, list the Data, Things, and People skills you checked off in the last two columns. Once you have listed the skills you want to use and develop, take a few minutes to rank order these skills, starting with the one you love the most. This rank order takes into consideration all the skills you listed in all three sections of Data, Things, and People. Think about the skills you really *must* be able to use in your perfect career. We realize this is tough to do, but it forces you to acknowledge to yourself the skills that will make you the happiest if you can use them every day on your job.

Now go to your Career Profile Map in Appendix A and record your skills chart in the Skills section. When we get to Chapter 17, look at the occupations that match the skills you have listed in this section of your Career Profile Map.

Skills Chart

Data Skills

I Want to Use This Skill in My Work	I Need to Get or Develop This Skill	Rank Order
_____	_____	_____
_____	_____	_____
_____	_____	_____
_____	_____	_____
_____	_____	_____
_____	_____	_____

Things Skills

I Want to Use This Skill in My Work	I Need to Get or Develop This Skill	Rank Order
_____	_____	_____
_____	_____	_____
_____	_____	_____
_____	_____	_____
_____	_____	_____
_____	_____	_____

People Skills		
I Want to Use This Skill in My Work	**I Need to Get or Develop This Skill**	**Rank Order**
_____	_____	_____
_____	_____	_____
_____	_____	_____
_____	_____	_____
_____	_____	_____
_____	_____	_____
_____	_____	_____

Skills to Go

We start to develop skills as soon as we arrive on Earth. And we continue to develop them through all kinds of life experiences—education, work, leisure activities and interests, and stepping up to challenges. It's important to understand the different ways in which we can identify and apply our skills. There are four unique ways we can look at our skills. Each of these is defined here:

♦ Skills you want to use on the job. The Skills Chart you just completed identifies the skills you want to use on your job.

♦ Skills that are "transferable." These skills that can move with you from job-to-job and don't have to be associated with only one occupation.

♦ "Self-Management" skills that employers look at very carefully. These are skills that set the tone for how you approach your work tasks and the people at work.

♦ Skills that you are naturally talented at using. These are skills that you have had from a very early age that you continue to perfect over time. They are generally skills that come easily and you have developed to an expert level.

These last three skill areas are great because you already have them! So wherever you go, they are packed and ready to go with you. The sections that follow will describe them in more detail.

Coach Wisdom
Do not, I repeat, do not underestimate your skills. Take the time to really look at skills you have been using in your life, work, home environment, community work, or volunteer work. Many times when people have been out of the workforce for a while, they think all their skills have atrophied. Guess what? You're using skills no matter what you are doing in life. So take out your microscope and really look at the skills you use in your everyday life.

Transferable Skills Assessment

Transferable skills are general skills that can be used in many different settings and activities. You can transfer these skills from one occupation to another and from one organization to another. Examples are communicating, supervising, analyzing, physical coordination, and operating. In fact, many of your work activity skills are transferable skills! Let's look at supervising as an example of a transferable skill.

You have been a supervisor in a high-tech company where you supervised five project managers. You decided to change fields and move into an educational testing firm where you will be expected to supervise three departments. You will have to learn another corporate language and some different organization culture behaviors. However, your knowledge about how to supervise people is a transferable skill that you can adapt to this new position. It makes you more attractive to a new employer because they don't have to train you in how to supervise. They also value having a person with experience in this skill area.

Identifying your transferable skills can help you to more easily move into new territory with confidence based on your experience.

Designing, supervising or managing people, instructing others, public speaking, sales, solving problems, project planning, running meetings, budgeting, and using computers are transferable skills. This list is meant to stimulate your thoughts about your own skills, so don't be limited by them. If you need to, go back to the Skills Inventory table in this chapter where you checked off the skills you have and want to use in your work.

Now, make a list of what you consider to be your top five transferable skills. These are key transferable skills that you see as strengths for you and ones you want to be able to use in your work.

Top Five Transferable Skills

1. _____

2. _____

3. _____

4. _____

5. _____

Record these skills in your Career Profile Map in Appendix A. Remember, you always want to put your best foot forward. In order to do this, you must know your strengths and which ones you really enjoy using.

Self-Management Skills

Self-management skills are our strengths in working with people and managing resources. Examples of these are being punctual, dependable, imaginative, and efficient.

Employers look to these skills to judge a candidate's character and ability to manage his own performance on any job. Employers want to know whether or not you can make a positive contribution to the work environment. They look for people who can provide the most value in terms of occupational skills and personal qualities.

Career Lingo _____

Self-management skills are personal qualities you use in your work. Your sense of humor, your tenacity, or your sense of responsibility can set you apart from others applying for a position. In addition, self-management skills are about assets you use to get along with others. These can be tone setters that contribute to a work environment such as being friendly and honest in your communication.

Take a look at the list of self-management skills on the Self-Management Grid that follows. Circle the skills that demonstrate the personal qualities you bring to your work. At the bottom of the grid, add any skills you have that are not already listed.

Self-Management Grid				
Honest	Adventuresome	Ambitious	Friendly	Dependable
Intuitive	Assertive	Conscientious	Helpful	Discreet
Flexible	Calm	Persistent	Patient	Punctual
Adaptable	Mature	Trustworthy	Sense of Humor	Positive
Motivated	Enthusiastic	Self-Motivated	Results oriented	Curious
Open-minded	Disciplined	Sociable	Hard-working	Cheerful
Good natured	Commitment to learning	Optimistic	Efficient	Independent
Reliable	Self-confident	Creative	Eager	Original
Sincere	Inquisitive	Expressive	Methodical	Versatile
Tactful	Authentic	Tenacious	Risk taker	Self-reliant
Empathic	Collaborative	Diplomatic	Emotionally stable	Easy going
Candid	Orderly	Playful	Poised	Loyal
Takes initiative	Quick Learner	Spontaneous	Energetic	Well-organized
Other_____	Other_____	Other_____	Other_____	Other_____

List the top five self-management skills that represent you the best.

Top Five Self-Management Skills

1. _____

2. _____

3. _____

4. _____

5. _____

Record these skills in your Career Profile Map in Appendix A.

Assess Your Talents

You have already assessed yourself on all the skill fronts, so now I want you to look at all the skills you have recorded in the skills section of your Career Profile Map in Appendix A. As you go down your list, highlight those skills you consider to be your special talents. Consider those skills that you can remember using from a very early age or that are easy and natural for you to do. Think about the ones that other people count on you to do. Talents can be in any category of working with data, people or things, self-management, or transferable skills. You may be really good at problem solving, or project management, or scientific experiments, or solving math problems, or helping people with their problems.

Many employers these days are looking for people who can identify their talents and use them easily in the workplace. Why? They can save a great deal of time and money spent in training people to do what some people are already very good at doing. It gives you an advantage when you can articulate what your talents are and how you have used them.

Once you have highlighted your talents, list them in your Career Profile Map in Appendix A.

Using Your Results

It's important to remember that *you* get to choose the skills you really want to use. The only way you get there—besides stumbling into a great career—is to identify what you want and plan to get it. You are on your way!

The Least You Need to Know

- There are three categories of skills in the world of work: working with data, working with things, and working with people.

- Identifying the skills you really like to use will help you to find occupations where you can use them.

- Everyone has skills that are transferable from one job to another or even to new career areas. Identifying these transferable skills makes it easier to transition into new areas.

- Employers want people with good self-management skills. These are skills that you use to work well with others as well as personal qualities that set you apart from others.

Chapter 11

Your Lifestyle

In This Chapter

- ◆ Understand what influences your choice of lifestyle
- ◆ Assess your lifestyle choices
- ◆ Place yourself on the stages of life continuum

Have you ever noticed how much focus our society puts on career and job? For instance, when we meet someone, one of the first questions we ask is, "What do you do?" Occasionally someone might ask, "How's your life?" and often we respond with, "What life?" In this chapter, we are going to focus on that aspect of life called "lifestyle." Lifestyle describes our living patterns. It is how, where, and what we spend our time doing. It means looking at the balance we need to sustain our work and our relationships and interests outside of work.

There is always a connection between our careers and our lifestyle. Our desire to maintain a certain type of lifestyle can influence our career or job choices quite dramatically. Becoming conscious of the lifestyle you want at this point in your life will influence your career choices in many ways. It impacts the amount of money you need to make, the time you want to spend with family and friends, and your ability to participate in activities outside of work that keep you motivated and inspired. Our lifestyle choices are very connected to our values, which make up what we feel is most important to us in life.

Lifestyle Influences

Many things influence our preferences for certain lifestyles over others. One of these influences is the generation into which we are born. The times we are born into impact our experiences and, thus, our choices. In the United States, we have designated the name "Baby Boomers" for those who were born between 1946 and 1964. Baby Boomers grew up in a time of social change. They demonstrated for peace and equality, and they experienced the sexual revolution. Jobs in the Peace Corps were preferable to jobs in corporate America. Experimentation and risk taking outweighed the desire for a secure life that their parents had experienced coming out of a Depression and two World Wars. As the economy boomed and Baby Boomers aged, many returned to traditional careers.

However, the Baby Boomers more than other generations, are unprepared for retirement. Living in the moment lingered for a long time!

Generation X and Generation Y who followed the Boomers find themselves in a world that has been heavily influenced by economic and technological changes. The high divorce rate and the latch key lifestyle with both parents working had a big impact on Generation X. They want more balance in their lives between work and leisure/family time. Generation Y experienced the technological boom of the Internet with its incredible access to information. They want organizations to give them skills and keep them competitive in the marketplace. They are known as multitaskers who like fun and work to go together.

Coach Wisdom

I bet you didn't know that most of the women born to the early Baby Boomer generation didn't even identify with the word "career." This was a totally new concept for women, which grew out of the Women's Movement. Men had always had careers. Women held jobs. Now women were expected to have a career and raise a family, too. Look what equality brought with it—additional expectations! Nothing taken off the plate, but we could add as much as we wanted—or thought we could handle.

Besides all the influences that come from our values, interests, and temperament, we are also influenced by our experiences. We grow up in particular cultures that include our race, ethnicity, economic class, and nationality. Our preferences for the type of life we want to live are often influenced either positively or negatively by our growing-up experiences.

Although we may value certain cultural, ethnic, or national practices and want to incorporate these in our lives, we might also want to change our economic status and live differently from what we experienced. Some cultures are very group oriented and want family, extended family, and friends to be the central focus of their lives. Other cultures are more individualistic and like their experience to be smaller and more private. Whatever the influences, it comes down to figuring out what is now important to us in our lives—and creating a lifestyle that reflects those preferences.

Lifestyle Preference Assessment

The Lifestyle Preference Assessment will help you to look at two aspects of your lifestyle:

♦ Part 1 addresses the issue of balance in your life. Where do you want to spend your time? And how much focus do you want to give to all the lifestyle categories?

♦ Part 2 will broaden your view of lifestyle by asking you to consider the specifics of how you want to live. You will be asked to make choices among various lifestyle descriptors.

Part 1: Finding a Balance Between Your Ideal and Actual Lifestyles

What is your ideal vision for your lifestyle and how you want to spend your time? Take 100 percentage points and divide them up among the following lifestyle categories:

My Ideal Lifestyle

___% Career/Job/Work

___% Personal Relationships (Family/Friends/Life Partner)

___% Fitness/Health

___% Spiritual Endeavors

___% Fun/Entertainment

___% Growth/Learning

___% Community

___% Other _____

100% Total

How do you actually spend your *time* right now in your life? Divide up 100 percent of your time among the following lifestyle categories:

My Actual Lifestyle

___% Career/Job/Work

___% Personal Relationships (Family/Friends/Life Partner)

___% Fitness/Health

___% Spiritual Endeavors

___% Fun/Entertainment

___% Growth/Learning

___% Community

___% Other _____

100% Total

Record the percentage points given for the specific categories of your Ideal Lifestyle and Actual Lifestyle in your Career Profile Map in Appendix A.

Now look at the similarities or differences between your Ideal and your Actual Lifestyle choices. If you are very close in your Ideal and Actual lifestyle preferences, than you are in good shape. If you have gaps, which most of us do, then consider the next set of questions.

What would you need to do in your life right now to close the gaps between these two lifestyles? Can you set a goal that will take a step in the right direction?

Goal: _____

_____

For example: Janet realized that her ideal lifestyle was one of spending more quality time with her children. Right now, she was spending all her time working or taking care of household chores and responsibilities. She was spending little or no time having any fun with her family or really tuning into their joys and sorrows. She could not afford to reduce her concentration on work right now. So, she set a goal for herself to *take each of her children out to breakfast one day a week; she would spend quality time focused only on that one child.*

Of course our lifestyle preferences can change over time. When people are going through the child-rearing years, they often find themselves more focused on wanting time for family activities vs. working until 8:00 every night. Implications during these years can take many forms, depending on economic and personal preferences. Some of these can be reduced hours, flexible work hours, long hours three days a week with three-day weekends, working from home a few days a week, learning to delegate work, etc.

When it comes to choosing a career based on the lifestyle we want to live, it's important to look at occupations that are going to support our lifestyle rather than work against it. For example, if you want to live in the country, but have culture and intellectual stimulation in your life, then working on a college campus might be the answer.

According to your lifestyle preferences, do you see any implications on the direction your career is taking, or the focus you place on your career? If so, write them down here.

Implications: _____

_____

Part 2: Specific Descriptions of Your Lifestyle

The second part of the Lifestyle Preference Assessment focuses on patterns and aspects of your life outside of work—the what, where, and how. For example, on the television show, *The Lifestyles of the Rich and Famous*, you get a glimpse of how rich and famous people live using such descriptors as the size and look of their homes, the locations in which they choose to live, and the formality or informality of their lifestyles.

Review the list of lifestyle descriptors that follow and circle the descriptors that represent the lifestyle you aspire to live.

Lifestyle Descriptors

A private life	A public life
Country living	City living
A place to throw my hat	A place to showcase my personality
Homes around the world	Regular attendance at plays, operas, cultural events
Out on the town regularly	Living the high life
A comfortable space to live in	A beautiful space to live in
An inspiring place to live in	High-energy living environment
A peaceful, calm place to live	A few close friends
Lavish entertaining	Small intimate dinners
Dedication to your communities	Active in social clubs and community events
Traveling all the time	Yearly vacation
Living near family	Living away from family
Family vacations	Exotic vacations
Loads of living space	Small, intimate living space
Time to myself	Camaraderie with friends or teammates
Living near the water	Living in the mountains
Living internationally	Exciting activities
Contemplation	Action going on all the time
Planned life	Open to the moment
Being in nature	Exercising regularly
Watching TV without interruption	Enjoying the simple things in life
Buy whatever I want	Go wherever I want
Build the biggest house	Own cars, boats, and flying machines
Dress to the nines	Live comfortably within my means
Save for the future	Being able to give freely to others
Live conservatively	Sharing what you have with others
Continuous education and learning	Helping my children with their homework

Lifestyle Descriptors	
Family dinners and rituals	Attending my children's plays, recitals, sports events
Family parties and get-togethers	Time alone with my partner
Invest in whatever I want	Always having time for my family and friends

Now, according to the lifestyle descriptors you circled, write down the top seven lifestyle descriptors that you feel are the most important to you.

Top Seven Lifestyle Descriptors:

1. _____
2. _____
3. _____
4. _____
5. _____
6. _____
7. _____

Record these in your Career Profile Map in Appendix A.

Life Stages

At different points in our lives we may be placing more emphasis on one or two aspects of our lifestyle preferences more than others. When we are just starting our careers, typically in our 20s, we might find ourselves in a steep learning curve where we need to spend a great deal of time focused on work. And we are still very focused on having a life of fun and engaging in doing things we like to do. We are young, full of energy, and can still go out and have a good time after work.

When we are in our 30s, our responsibilities usually begin to grow with the arrival of children, moving from one location to another, buying homes, keeping up with friends who may have moved far away. And these years continue to be prime work years when progressing in our careers through education, advancement, and achievement are critical. So the focus in the 30s is still on career, more on family, and less time for fun and entertainment or even fitness.

The 40s are seen as "the writing on the wall" time for our careers. We are right in the middle of whatever career direction we have chosen, and we are either advancing and succeeding, or we have leveled off and hit a plateau. This can be a critical time for many of us, because our identities and feelings of self-worth are tied up with "what we do." For some people, their lifestyle preferences come into focus in these years. We begin to reassess where our energy is going. Career may take a back seat to our family life at this point. Or, some people leave organizational careers behind and decide to do something less stressful or "what they really love" to do. It can be a major time of re-evaluation and change.

When we reach our 50s, we begin to think about the "R" word—retirement! Unfortunately, the economy and the government have both conspired to keep moving that retirement age right up to the 70s and beyond. So, what can one do? Most of us face our aging process head on. We have reached half a century, and the reality is that we probably can go another half century. So what do you want to do in that time span?

It's too early for most people to retire, and there's too little money to retire on. Some recommit to career goals at their current organizations by taking on new responsibilities and challenges. Others leave to pursue their own businesses. Some do retire—those that have planned well! Although most people go to an investment planner to start figuring out when they can retire—in earnest. It is another peak time for re-evaluating our lifestyle choices and seeing how we really want to live the next phase of our lives.

The 60s today are still a very active career time for many people. It is also the phase of life where we start to do some serious retirement planning. Our lifestyle focus becomes more on our future and what we want our lives to look like in semi-retirement or retirement.

Many other things influence our choice of lifestyle. Some of these include our values, interests, temperaments, and personality styles, and all kinds of life experiences that "happen"—some planned and some not. For example, taking care of our parents when we are in our 50s and 60s can be planned, but for most of us, this role reversal comes as a surprise.

Reminder!!! These stages and ages are not prescriptive—they won't necessarily happen to you. These are collective themes that do occur for many people at different ages and stages of life, but not all of us. For instance, one of your authors is over 60 and hasn't even started to think about retirement (except in terms of income!!!).

Your Age: _____

List the influences you are experiencing in your life right now that can impact your lifestyle choices:

_____

_____

_____

_____

Using Your Results

It's critical to take into consideration the balance we want in our lifestyle between all the life aspects that are important to us. You have taken the time to think about different aspects of your lifestyle and record them in your Career Profile Map. Now just sit back and think about what you have selected and what is currently influencing these selections. Are you embarking on your career and want to make sure you have an ideal in mind? Are you in a life transition that is changing your balance, and you want to be purposeful about your actions? Are you looking toward retirement years and deciding what that life looks and feels like to you? Consciously thinking about the lifestyle you desire can make it happen.

The Least You Need to Know

- ◆ Many things influence your choice of lifestyle. These include your values, the generation you grew up in, and economic and societal changes.

- ◆ Lifestyle includes making choices about how you divide up your time and focus among lifestyle categories: work, relationships, health and fitness, spiritual endeavors, community, growth and learning, and fun and entertainment.

- ◆ Lifestyle also includes lifestyle descriptors that look at your pattern of preferences for how you want to live your life. Descriptors involve choices about how you want to live: simple life to a grand life and all that implies.

◆ We all go through different stages in our lives that bring out different needs and experiences. These needs and experiences also influence our lifestyle choices. From early career through retirement, we see a shifting and changing of priorities in our lifestyle categories and where and how we want to live our lives.

Summing It All Up

In This Chapter

◆ Consider what all these tests mean to your career exploration

◆ First cut at generating your perfect career options list

◆ Revisit the "Five Years from Now" exercise

◆ Pull it all together into a statement of self

Now that you have taken all the assessments and filled out your Career Profile Map in Appendix A, it's time to put into focus what you have learned about yourself. Remember all of these assessments are meant to help you to understand what is truly important to you. After you identify what's important to you in all the profile areas of values, personality, interests, skills, and lifestyle preferences, you have a pretty good picture of yourself. You then can use this information in a couple of ways.

First, you have a wealth of information about possible career options to explore. In Chapters 15 through 17, you will be making a list of career ideas based on what you have discovered about yourself. Second, as you research career areas you think you might like, you can use your profile as your standard for whether or not a career option is a good fit for you. So always keep your profile handy in order to refer back to it as you explore career options.

This chapter is devoted to helping you pull together all the data from your assessments that you have compiled in your Career Profile Map. You will begin by generating ideas for careers and occupations that are a good fit with your Career Profile Map. Then we will address any lingering concerns that some of you may have about your assessment results so far, give you some additional resources, and encourage you to keep going! The remainder of this chapter will have you revisiting your "five year's from now" vision and updating it with any new thoughts or information you have received through the assessment process. And last but not least, write a statement of self that summarizes in a view short paragraphs your Career Profile Map.

What All These Tests Mean

Now it's time to take stock of the tests and assessments you have done. Here is a quick review of what all these tests and assessments can tell you about yourself. As you read through the descriptions and look at your own results, write down any career ideas that come to mind at the end of each profile section. At the end of this exercise, compile a Career Ideas List for inclusion in your Career Profile Map. Take out your Career Profile Map in Appendix A and follow along.

My Values Profile

Chapter 6 discusses your Values Profile which contains the beliefs and attitudes that you hold as most important in your life. You desire to live a life in which these values are consistently reflected in your behavior.

The type of work you choose to do, your organizational and work environment expectations, and the balance in your lives that this work affords you are all examples of how the match between your values and your work may impact your level of satisfaction.

There have been many articles in the past few years that highlight executive women deciding to leave corporations in order to start their own businesses. The question that arises, "Why would you leave a high paying, senior position?" Well, many of these women have responded that they want to live a different lifestyle, have more balance in their lives, and/or create a company with more collaborative values. Their values provide guidance for their career decisions.

It has also been documented over the years that as men reach their late 40s and 50s they find their values shifting to home and family and away from devoting all their time to work. Both of these examples point out that some values may shift over our lifetimes. Where for many years achievement was most important, family and balance may take on more importance due to entering new stages of life or changing life experiences.

Checking in periodically to consider the values that are most important to us right now is critical to helping us make good career choices. For some people, their values were always there, but they ignored them or didn't realize the importance they really held in their lives. They ended up in careers that didn't match their values and are finding that it is time to rethink career directions.

Write down any career/job ideas that come to mind based on your prioritized values.

_____

_____

My Temperament and Personality Profile

According to Chapter 7, your temperament tells you your predisposition to particular attitudes and behaviors. Your temperament influences your values, the language you use in communicating, your interests, your self-image, how you approach your past, present, and future, and how you use your intelligence. Your temperament is the most permanent and least changeable part of your personality. The other aspect of your personality is your character, which is made up of habits you develop over your lifetime that are consistent with your temperament.

Your temperament profile identifies whether you an Artisan (SP), Guardian (SJ), Idealist (NF), or a Rational (NT). Each of these temperaments then has four personality types associated with it that build off of the main temperament. Each one of the four has its own character traits that make each personality type a little different from the other three.

Read through your temperament and personality type and write down any ideas you have for careers/jobs that might be of interest to you based on your profile.

_____

_____

My Motivations Profile

As Chapter 8 states, your motivations are your internal needs or wants that activate and energize your behavior. Each one of us has different needs that we want met through our work. Knowing our motivations can help us to select the right work environments, tell our bosses what really works to motivate us, and help us to select the type of work that inherently satisfies our needs. Motivation comes in four categories of need: security, relationship, recognition, and contribution.

Look at the rank order list of motivators that you wrote down in your profile and write down any ideas that come to mind for careers based on this information. It's okay if you have repeat career ideas—try to continue generating new ones.

_____

_____

Coach Wisdom

Ray is a master mechanic, and his needs fall into two categories. He wants enough money to keep his family secure. This is a basic need that is ongoing and probably gets activated when lifestyle needs exceed salary. His most important need, however, is to be appreciated for his competence. This is what really motivates him on a daily basis. He speaks about the boss that gave him a gift certificate to take his wife out to dinner, or the thank you for a job well done he received from his manager. These are the things that really make his day!

My Interests Profile

Remember from back in Chapter 9 that your interests are those things in life that draw your attention. They are what you would like to spend your time doing. They include everything from games you like to play, to refinishing furniture, to learning something new all the time, to crafts and travel. Interests are whatever turns up the enjoyment factor for each of us.

Some people choose to incorporate their interests in their career choices. Scott loved sports so he went into the fitness business where he specializes in working with athletes who are training for their sport. Other people choose to pursue their real interests outside of work. Maybe they believe they can make money one way and enjoy life in another way. That's okay—whatever you choose is okay. I would encourage you to also consider how you can turn those interests into career ideas.

Write your ideas down based on the Orientation Scale categories that were of most interest to you.

_____

_____

Coach Wisdom
Amy is a school teacher who would like to go into business for herself. As Amy went down her list of interests with her career coach, she mentioned cooking. Amy didn't go into any detail about her interest in cooking, and the discussion went on to focus on a growing interest in real estate. Then Amy happened to mention the catering that she has been doing for small family and community functions. It turns out that Amy loves to cook and is great at catering. This would meet Amy's need to work part-time during her retirement while doing something she loves to do—cooking! So the moral to this story is, don't ignore or downplay your interests. They can uncover the core skills you really want to use and career paths to explore.

My Skills Profile

In Chapter 10 you selected seven skills to write in your profile that you want to use in your perfect career. Take a look at those again and remind yourself whether they fall mostly in the area of working with data, working with things, or working with people. You may have found yourself primarily in one of these areas, in two areas, or spread across three. No worry—we are all unique, and isn't that grand. We won't be tripping across each other for the same jobs!

In addition to looking at the top seven skills you want to use, also look at your self-management skills or attributes that you bring to a career/job. Based on both of these profiles, generate ideas about careers that would be perfect for your skills and attributes.

_____

_____

My Lifestyle Profile

Remember from back in Chapter 11 that your lifestyle choices help you to look at how you want to use your time on an ongoing basis. They help you think about the balance between work, relationships, health and fitness, spirituality, fun, growth and learning, and service to community. It also helps you to assess your "style" of living. Do you prefer the high life of big houses, boats, and cars? Or do you prefer a more laid back life of camping, community events, and spending time with family? Or perhaps something in between?

Look at your profile in terms of the percentage of time you want to spend on each category. Then look at the seven prioritized lifestyle choices. What ideas for careers come to mind as a result of looking at these?

_____

_____

Career Ideas List

Take all your career ideas and write them down in the Career Ideas List of your Career Profile Map in Appendix A. You will have many more opportunities to identify careers in later chapters, but this personal brainstorming session is a very important step in your creative process. When you have the time to focus on data about yourself, you often come up with ideas that really hit the mark.

What If You Don't Like Your Results?

The first thing to do is to ask yourself why you don't like your results. There are so many reasons to be discontent with information about ourselves. The sections that follow describe different scenarios that might fit your individual circumstances.

Family "Expectations"

I expected my tests to show that I am like my (father, sister, mother, brother) so I could easily fit in with everyone else.

Separating ourselves from family and expectations is often difficult. The question to ask yourself is: Do I want to live my life for someone else or really be successful at what I love to do? Okay, that's not fair … of course we want to do what we love. Sometimes we have to learn to speak our own truth and let those we love know what we are going to do. Often we are surprised by the response we get, perhaps they already knew and are happy for us—go figure! Other times, we have to be strong enough to march to the beat of our own drum.

Things Don't Seem to "Fit"

All my training and education is in a field that isn't fitting my personality or interests, and it's very unsettling to think I have wasted my time.

Try to remember that education and training is never a waste of time. Every experience you have adds to a depth of knowledge and wisdom that can be called on in many different situations. Whatever your training, there are always transferable skills that can be applied to new career areas. Often the field that we trained for has related career areas that are much more suited to who we are—so these can be explored. And as we have said so many times—it's never too late to follow your dreams.

"More" Education?

My assessment results are pointing to career areas that would require me to get more degrees, and I don't know if I really want to do that.

This can be a decision point for those of you who are faced with this type of scenario. It's important to find out more information about these career options—which you will be able to do in the remaining chapters of the book. There are also career areas related to fields that require degrees that may be of interest and would require less education. You are just at your first milestone for exploring career areas, so don't stop now!

Is This Really "Me"?

I'm just not sure that these assessments are giving me the whole picture of who I am and what I can do.

In order for us to fully understand ourselves, we need to get some information from those who know us and see us in operation. This is called feedback. All the self-discovery in the world will not give us the full picture of who we are; we need the view from outside of ourselves. Sometimes we miss things about ourselves. Others see the impact our behavior and skill has on people and achieving results. So you are going to have an opportunity to get this additional perspective—more to come in this chapter!

More "Proof"

I want to take some different versions of assessments and tests to see whether I get similar results from the ones I have taken. I would like more validation.

Always a legitimate desire, many tests you can take are available online that will provide a check for you. Just remember not to get too test happy. The real proof of the pudding is in whether or not you can validate the results you are getting. Do you think this is really a good picture of who you are?

If you would like to take more tests, here are some websites where you can take tests or view a list of test sites from which you can choose:

♦ www.KeirseyCampbell.com On this site you can take the Kiersey Temperament Sorter and the Campbell Interest and Skill Survey. You can use your Discount Coupon on the last page of this book for a reduced rate on taking these tests.

♦ www.careerkey.com This test matches your interests, needs, values, abilities, and skills toward certain occupations. The price is $4.95.

♦ www.QuintCareers.com This site has an online Career Assessments Tools Review with links to free as well as fee-based assessments.

None of the Above

No matter what your scenario for not liking your test results, it's okay. These are common reactions to really looking at ourselves and trying to come to terms with what is really important to us as individuals.

If your situation doesn't fit any of the scenarios already listed, write down your own here.

_____

_____

Taking the Next Step: Your Vision Statement

Okay you have reached a milestone—give yourself a pat on the back. You have completed your Career Profile Map, which was a terrific amount of work. You now have a map that tells you what is most important to you in your career and your life. Before moving on to looking at specific career information we want you to revisit your "Five Years from Now Exercise" from Chapter 5. It's important to update this now that you have spent time really thinking about who you are and what you want. This will provide a short version of your Career Profile Map—it is your *vision*.

A vision is something that you hold out in front of you in order to ...

♦ keep yourself focused on where you are headed

♦ help sort your actions and decisions that will get you there

♦ motivate you along the way

A vision describes what we aspire to become, to achieve, to create. The first component of a vision is the stretch goal. This has a specific time frame—five years from now. It states your future dream, hope, or aspiration. The second component of a vision provides a vivid description or visual image of the stretch goal. You want the words you use to be descriptive, upbeat, and exciting. This vision will be carried around in your head and will keep you focused on where you want to go.

An example of a vision statement might be, "In 2009, I am sitting on the deck of my newly renovated house looking into my beautiful office space. My consulting and coaching business is flourishing; I have been writing a follow-up book to *Finding Your Perfect Career*; and the pace of my life is just right for enjoying family, friends, and the work I love to do."

Although your Career Profile Map is great (and deserves to be placed on a wall in your home), your vision is short and can be pulled out anytime of the day or night. So let's do that vision exercise again and create your Five Years From Now Statement!

Five Years from Now Exercise—Again

You are going to imagine what you are doing for a week, five years from now. After you have read over the following guidelines for walking through your week, find a quite place to imagine your future. It helps to close your eyes so that your mind can bring forth pictures to accompany your thoughts. Afterward you can write down your vision in the space provided. Here is a way to move through your week and focus on various aspects of your work/life:

◆ Five years from now you are getting up on a Monday. Notice the time on the clock next to your bed. Look around at your surroundings. Where are you, what do you see? What is the temperature? Look outside and see where you are— what does the landscape look like? What noises do you hear?

◆ Who else is in this environment with you? Your partner, family, friends, children, … or are you by yourself? What is your relationship to others in this environment—who do you see around you, and how do you interact?

◆ Now you are ready to start your day. How are you dressed? Are you walking, traveling by car, train, bus, or limo? Or, are you going to a space in your home environment? Adjust this vision to prepare for the life you want to live— retirement, leisure living, career, small business, etc.

◆ You have now arrived at your place of work or leisure. How do you feel? What do you see? What is in this environment that interests you? Who else is in the environment?

◆ Go through the day now and pay attention to the types of skills you are enjoying using—what are you doing? What strengths and talents, transferable skills, self-management skills are you using? With whom do you interact?

◆ Do you have a daily routine, or is everyday different? Look ahead to other days during the week and visualize what you are doing. What do you do for lunch—where are you?

◆ Evenings after work—where do you go, what do you do, whom are you with? Home, opera, baseball game, star gazing, exercising, walking, dinner with family or friends, dancing, school ...?

◆ Making plans for the weekend. What do you like to do on weekends? Gardening, hiking, biking, sports, movies, hanging out, museums, studying ...?

◆ What do the days look like and feel like for you?

◆ Thinking back over your week, what do you like about yourself five years from now?

Step 1: Write down anything that came to mind as you walked through your week five years from now:

_____

_____

Step 2: Incorporate all the aspects of your life and work that you pictured in your vision exercise and wrote down in Step 1. Write a paragraph that starts with the following:

Five years from now I will _____

_____

_____

Record this Five Years From Now statement in your Career Profile Map in Appendix A.

What Is a Statement of Self?

So far, you have reviewed your Career Profile Map and generated a list of possible career options to explore, and you have a short Vision Statement from your Five Years From Now exercise to keep you focused and motivated going forward. Now it's time to prepare a more in-depth description of what you know about yourself. This "Statement of Self" will be a vehicle to share your knowledge and insights about yourself with people in your network. This is where you are going to get "the other view" of you.

You will benefit from sharing your statement of self with people who know you. They can give you their perceptions of your strongest skills and talents as well as verify those you have already identified. They may have some wonderful ideas about good career fits for you—even people who are in these careers for you to talk with. This statement of self also helps you to really take in what you have learned about yourself and summarize this information for yourself.

Stop-Look-Listen _____

If you are thinking to yourself, "I don't need to do this exercise; I just looked over my profile; and that's good enough—STOP! This is an opportunity to let all this information soak in. This is a time to own what you have learned (or confirmed) about yourself. We don't often take the time to focus on this knowledge in a written document. Sometimes we have difficulty articulating what we have learned to others so they can give us good feedback and input. This exercise helps you do both—focus through a summary statement and articulate to others in order to get more insight and input.

Once again, you will be relying on your Career Profile Map as a source of specific information for writing your Statement of Self. This statement should be no longer that one page. You want it to be a short summary that you can easily share in writing or verbally with others. Start with a simple opening, *"This is a summary of what I have learned (or affirmed) about myself so far in terms of what is important to me in my career and how I want to live my life."* Now you are on your way.

Once you have written your Statement of Self, put it in your Career Profile Map in Appendix A.

You may find it easier to follow your Career Profile Map categories in writing your statement (values, temperament and personality, motivations, interests, skills, and lifestyle). A simple way to do this is to use the outline that follows:

◆ In my life and career I want to be able to live these values.

_____

◆ I want to be able to use and value the strengths of my temperament and my personality in the work I do.

_____

◆ I acknowledge that these motivations are ones I want my work and/or work environment to address on an ongoing basis.

_____

◆ I want to be able to pursue these interests in my work or my life.

_____

◆ These are the skills I like to use the most and/or want to develop and use in the work I do.

_____

◆ This is the lifestyle that I want to live.

_____

Please feel free to be creative with this outline. You can throw it out and develop your own format and style. You can tweak the questions and make them more relevant to you. Or you can use them just as they are!

If you can, prepare this Statement of Self so that you can easily share it with others.

Getting Input from Others

Okay now you are ready for some input! Feedback is the breakfast of champions, and we don't get nearly enough of it. Would you like more feedback from your boss that would help you be more successful in your job? Most of us would like this as long as it is done in a supportive manner with an eye toward developing us versus punishing us. Let's think about who you might want to ask. Here is a list of criteria that might be helpful to you:

- People who have worked with me on a regular basis, know my work, and have been able to observe my competencies and skills (bosses, co-workers, clients, customers).

- People with whom I share my thoughts and feelings on a regular basis and know about my likes, dislikes, what excites me, what brings me down (friends, family members, close co-workers, support group members).

- People I have recently started to work with or get to know who can give me a fresh perspective. They may see things that others who have a history with me cannot.

- People I feel are trustworthy, will give me honest feedback, and will have my best interests at heart.

- People that will not threaten my current job status. In some organizations, talking about career exploration gets people thinking you are going to leave and can jeopardize your standing in the company. Be smart about whom you share information with.

Make a short list of four or five people you want to share your Statement of Self with and ask for input—these individuals make up your support network.

_____

_____

Next, you need to ask these individuals whether they would be willing to read over your Statement of Self and give you feedback and input. Here are some questions you can pose to them:

- Which aspects of my Statement of Self do you most agree with based on your experience of me?

- What can you tell me about myself that is not included in my Statement of Self that stands out for you (skills, behaviors, personality)?

- Based on my view of myself and your knowledge and experience of me, what careers/jobs do you think I should look into and why?

You can sit down and talk with them directly, give them your statement to read over and then meet with them for input, or ask them to write their responses down and send them to you (especially if they are far away). Please make sure you write down what they have said to you immediately after your discussion. Unfortunately, we have a tendency to readily forget feedback we get from others, making it even more important to capture right away.

Add this information to the Feedback (Statement of Self) portion of your Career Profile Map in Appendix A.

The Least You Need to Know

◆ Based on the information from the tests and assessments you have taken and documented in your Career Profile Map, you can begin to generate a good list of career ideas.

◆ Your vision for yourself five years from now needs to be updated to include what you have learned about yourself from your tests and assessments. This vision will provide the focus and motivation to continue your journey to your perfect career choice.

◆ Creating a Statement of Self that summarizes all you have learned about yourself from your tests and assessments helps you to internalize this information— this is who I am and what I want.

◆ Asking your support network for feedback and input on the Statement of Self can give you more information about your strengths and competencies as well as add ideas for career directions.

Part 3

Discovering Your Perfect Career Fit

Now you are ready to look at specific careers that might fit your profile. So begin with looking at the job market trends to give you an overview of what's hot, popular, stress free, and how much money you can make. Then you get to do your own assessment of your ideal work environment. Now you are ready to look at the types of jobs that fit your temperament, your interests, and your skills. You will have a pretty good idea of the careers that are good matches for you. If you decide that you need more education or training, we have a bunch of resources for you in this area.

Chapter

13

Job Market Trends

In This Chapter

- ◆ Learn what's hot and what's not in the job market
- ◆ Take a peak at the best and worst jobs
- ◆ Look at the least and most stressful jobs
- ◆ Tap into the most profitable jobs

In Parts 1 and 2 of this guide, you have tackled the first part of finding a good career fit. You now understand more about yourself and what your preferences are for careers, work environments, and lifestyle. Before you move on to looking at jobs that match your Career Profile Map, you can take a look at what's going on in the job market.

Having an understanding of why employment trends change over time helps you to tune into opportunities for yourself now and in the future. Of course, most of us want to know which jobs are hot right now, so we will take a look at those trends accordingly. If you are thinking about a couple of possibilities and one of them is in high demand, you can begin by looking into that one. High demand can also involve higher paying salaries.

Another angle on the job market is looking at those jobs that are considered to be the best jobs out there. These jobs usually involve lower stress, good working conditions, and decent salaries. Although some of us might love the high stress, others prefer much less of it. There is nothing wrong with choosing the type of work that is going to be most comfortable and enjoyable for you. That's what this whole process is about.

Last but certainly not least, salary is always of interest so we will look at the most profitable jobs right now as well as some not-so-profitable jobs. Sometimes we don't realize that the skills we have can be applied to more profitable jobs. Knowledge about what is going on in the job market is valuable in helping you to identify the career that matches all of your requirements.

Employment Trends

Employment trends can help us to figure out which jobs are going to be more in demand. In other words, we can figure out what and where the hot jobs are going to be now or in the near future. Employment trends change over time and are influenced by many different factors.

Let's consider the demand for goods and services that exist at any one time. The demand for goods and services depends on what people are buying. Consumers, government, and business form the major groups of buyers. Changes in buying patterns and habits can have a big impact on the jobs associated with the goods or services affected. For example, since mortgage rates have been low, people have been remodeling and building new homes. This has increased the demand and economic gain for workers in the construction trade (as well as the mortgage and refinance business).

When changes occur in the population, this also can increase or decrease the demand. Right now, the Baby Boomer generation is aging, and it is a very large population. This is causing an increase in the occupations that are related to the health of the boomers—elder care, nursing homes, and medical assistants. In addition, businesses are concerned about whether they will be able to fill the number of vacancies being left by the boomers. This may work to the advantage of boomers who will need to work beyond retirement age, providing full- to part-time jobs past age 65.

Any change in technology can also affect an increase or decrease in jobs. A good example of an increase is jobs that are being created for artists and designers in the website construction business. As the Internet becomes the business card and marketing arm for businesses of all sizes, websites need to be designed, built, and maintained. On the other hand, technology can also cause a decrease in jobs, which we have seen in the manufacturing sector where machines have replaced the number of workers required on a plant floor.

One of the most talked about changes in availability of jobs has been caused by employers deciding to outsource certain types of jobs to other countries. *Offshoring* has mostly affected low- to mid-level jobs such as customer service, manufacturing, and software development. Companies are able to attract more highly educated employees who will work for substantially lower wages in foreign countries. Although there is concern about higher-level positions being affected, this has not yet happened. Most experts agree that sales and marketing jobs will never be outsourced.

Career Lingo

Offshoring is a relocation of a product, production, or a service to a lower cost location, usually oversees. China is the preferred destination for production offshoring, and India is the major location for services offshoring.

Business practices can also be central to the increase or decrease in jobs. The shift from higher paying jobs such as nurses and librarians to nursing aids and library technicians takes place due to changing business practices. These practices can be brought on through a decline in people going into a profession or by the need to reduce costs.

Trends provide very useful information in helping us prepare for jobs that will be more abundant, new job areas opening up, and where to focus our education and training as we continue to make ourselves employable throughout our lives.

According to the Bureau of Labor Statistics, the 2002 to 2012 employment projections, published in the *News, United States Department of Labor* on February 11, 2004, include the following:

- Employment by Industry
- Employment by Occupation

Employment by Industry

In the service industry, the fastest growth will take place in education and health services and professional and business services. The goods producing industry has only one projected growth area: construction. The 10 industries with the fastest wage and salary employment growth are

1. Software publishers

2. Management, scientific, and technical consulting services

3. Community care facilities for the elderly and residential care facilities

4. Computer systems design and related services

5. Employment services

6. Individual, family, community, and vocational rehabilitation services

7. Ambulatory health care services except offices of health practitioners

8. Water, sewage, and other systems

9. Internet services, data processing, and other information services

10. Child day care services

Employment by Occupation

The two occupational categories expected to increase the fastest and add the most jobs are in the professional and related occupations category and the service occupations category of the *Dictionary of Occupational Titles*. The 10 fastest growing occupations come mainly from health or computer occupations:

1. Medical assistants

2. Network systems and data communications analysts

3. Physician assistants

4. Social and human service assistants

5. Home health aides

6. Medical records and health information technicians

7. Physical therapist aides

8. Computer software engineers, applications

9. Computer software engineers, systems software

10. Physical therapist assistants

As jobs that normally would not require postsecondary education become more in demand, we often see certification and associate degree programs crop up. This then ups the standards for candidates to have more specialized education. An example of this is a medical assistants who normally requires moderate on-the-job training and now is being asked to acquire certifications and more extensive training before seeking employment.

Best and Worst Jobs

The 2002 Jobs Rated Almanac, by Les Krantz (St. Martin's Griffin, 2002), develops a list of the 10 best and worst jobs based on 6 key criteria: work environment, income, employment outlook, physical demands, security and stress. The data comes from the U.S. Bureau of Labor Statistics and the U.S. Census Bureau as well as from trade and industry groups. Biologists ranked number one in 2002 based on low stress, high compensation, autonomy on the job, and the fact that they are in high demand. Coming in second was actuaries who work autonomously, with little stress in helping companies to assess risk. Six out of ten actuaries work for insurance companies. Financial planners are rated third in part do to the continuing demand from Baby Boomers to manage their money. The remaining best jobs are computer-systems analyst, accountant, software engineer, meteorologist, paralegal assistant, statistician, and astronomer.

The worst job list is headed by lumberjacks based on their work instability, poor pay, and danger inherent in the job. The rest of the worst 10 list are commercial fisherman, cowboy, ironworker, seaman, taxi driver, construction worker, farmer, roofer, and stevedore. It's important to remember that many of the jobs that made the worst list are also full of adventure. So for some people this lifestyle may be preferable. Different strokes for different folks.

The following are from *The 2001 Jobs Rated Almanac* list of the best jobs by industry:

 ◆ The Arts—motion picture editor, architectural drafter, symphony conductor

 ◆ Athletics—sports instructor, basketball coach, race car driver

 ◆ Business/Finance—accountant, paralegal assistant, financial planner

 ◆ Communications—technical writer, broadcast technician, publication editor

 ◆ Healthcare/medicine—hospital administrator, medical secretary, medical technologist

- Math/science—actuary, mathematician, math/science teacher

- Social sciences—historian, sociologist, political scientist

- Technical—website manager, computer systems analyst, software engineer

Most to Least Stressful

Most of the jobs listed on the best jobs list are there partly because they involve less stress than many other jobs. It's important to acknowledge that some of us thrive on stress while others prefer a job that is stress free. Let's talk a little about the role of stress on the job.

Learning and Growth

In today's job market, it is crucial that the workforce has up-to-date skills and competencies. This often means that no matter what job we have, we need to keep stretching and growing our skills. For many of us, this might mean stepping out of our comfort zone in order to learn a new aspect of our trade or profession. Or it may mean that we need to take our skills to the next level and become better at what we do. All of this can and usually does involve some stress. This stress is called "good" stress.

In order to grow and learn, we need to step out of our comfort zone into our learning zone. When we are in our learning zone, the stress we experience is moderate and manageable. It is providing the juice or energy to move us forward into our learning mode. An example of this is when Erika became a manager and was asked to give presentations to prospective clients. Erika was not a salesperson. In fact, she excels in one-on-one relationships as opposed to group settings. She was nervous and could feel her stress begin to build. In fact, she became quite anxious until she decided to look at this as a learning opportunity. As soon as she did this, she called her sister who was a public speaker to ask for some books to read and some coaching on preparing and delivering her presentations. So even though the stress was there for her, she turned it into "good" stress that motivated her to learn.

Erika also made her learning manageable by reaching out for instruction and coaching. Of course we know that next to the fear of snakes, public speaking comes in a close second. This could have been a situation that got out of hand and went into the "bad" stress zone. This is called the danger zone. What if Erika had not turned this into a learning opportunity? If she had just gone into giving these presentations without any instruction, she probably would have stretched herself way beyond her limits. The learning zone is where you can have success; the danger zone is where the odds are very limited for being successful.

Keeping our stress in the learning zone is what we need to do to keep ourselves current in our skills and lower our overall stress. All of us can use some "good" or healthy stress, and most of us want to stay away from the "bad" stress that can come with any job situation.

On-the-Job Stressors

Although everyone experiences stress, our reactions to stress vary depending on our temperament, our responses to change, and our outlook on different situations. For instance, some people love to be in the limelight and give speeches, others are very fearful. Some people love the pressure of deadlines—bring it on! Other people, however, would prefer a work environment in which expectations are consistent every day. Some people see changes at work as an opportunity, and others experience something being taken away from them.

Given today's economy and common practices in organizations, many of the common stressors involve the following:

1. Fear of losing your job (layoffs, rightsizing, downsizing)

2. Same amount of work (or more) with less people to do it

3. Accountability without being given the formal responsibility—lack of control

4. Dysfunctional work group

5. Supervisor or manager who doesn't care about your development

6. Not being recognized for the work you do—lack of rewards

The reality is that any job can be stressful. Even if you have one of the lowest stress jobs on the list! For instance, Stacy is a librarian in a private school setting. Librarians are always on the least stressful job list. In Stacy's situation, a co-worker's behavior over a two-year period was very abusive and nasty. Stacy's manager did not do anything about it for such a long time that finally Stacy took an early retirement package. She is still reeling from this experience and has lost her enthusiasm for her profession. She is seeking a low stress environment. How ironic is that?

Least to Most Stressful Jobs

Jobs can go on and off the stress list depending on the times. For instance, airline pilot was on the *1999 Wall Street Journal Almanac*, coming in at #22 on the list. Where do you think airline pilot would be today after 9/11? Some of the most stressful jobs include those in which you are a major decision maker for a large group of people—such as chief executive officer of a corporation, senator or statesman, president of a country. Other stress-related jobs relate to the amount of risk, danger, and unknown outcomes that are present in the work itself. Examples of these jobs are firefighter, race car driver, NFL football player, taxi driver in a major city, and photojournalist. Still other high-stress jobs involve being responsible for the lives of others. Some of these jobs include surgeon, emergency medical technician, air traffic controller, and police officer. Again it's important to remember that some of us are very attracted to high-stress jobs and are able to handle them very well. What is important here is figuring out whether these jobs are a good match for you.

If you know you are looking for a low-stress job, the number one low stressor is a *medical records technician*. And this is one of the fastest growing jobs in the country. Other technician jobs that are low stress include medical laboratory technician, electrical technician, and broadcast technician. Several low-stress jobs involve repair work, including musical instruments, appliances, vending machines, and piano tuner. Many of the low-stress jobs are ones where you have more autonomy on the job. Good examples of these are actuary, mathematician, dietitian, and repair workers. These jobs are also lower stress because of the unpressured environments that are associated with these jobs. Examples of this are florist, librarian, medical secretary, barber, dental hygienist and jeweler.

Career Lingo _____

Medical Records Technicians keep patient records that record observations, interventions, and treatment. They make sure that medical charts are complete and that forms are completed and signed. They assign a code to each diagnosis and procedure and record them on the computer. Contact with the public is very limited. An Associate degree and specific course work is required for this position, and there are several certificate programs that are available. Job outlook is very good with the highest growth in physician offices. The salary ranges from $21,320 to $26,160.

Best-Paying Jobs

The top 10 of the highest paying jobs list are still those that generally require extensive education and/or are high-risk/high-stress jobs. Doctors of all kinds, including anesthesiologists and psychiatrists are among the highest paid professions. Annual salaries range from $130,000 to $145,000+. Other professions that fall in the upper ranges of salary include pilots, flight engineers, and air traffic controllers; judges and lawyers; and dentists of all kinds. You will find mostly professional positions on the top 50 highest paid professions according to *America's Career InfoNet: Highest Paying Occupations* list.

As a note of interest, actuaries and mathematicians from the low-stress job category are also in the top 50. So there are many jobs that are not as high stress as you move from the top 10 down into the next 40 highest paying jobs.

According to the U.S. Department of Labor, Bureau of Labor Statistics, some of the highest paying jobs requiring two-year degrees include dental hygienists, registered nurses, paralegals, and radiologic technicians. Those jobs that are above average paying and do not require a college degree include automobile mechanic, carpenter, welder, electrician, firefighter, electronic technician, plumber, restaurant manager, and health technician.

For those of you who are interested in seeing the top 550 fastest growing occupations, go to America's Career InfoNet, www.acinet.org, where you can click on the *Fastest Growing Occupations* report or look up information on specific jobs to see what the outlook is over the next few years. This is a great list for just browsing career areas, seeing the growth in employment, finding out the salary range, and then having the opportunity to click on the job and read more information about each one. Terrific resource. America's CareerInfoNet is the prime site now for job projections and information. It even has videos giving overviews of occupational categories.

Coach Wisdom
It's important to remember that the reason we are able to do all the jobs that must be done to keep our societies running and provide the goods and services wanted and needed is because we have people who want to do these jobs. Thank goodness for our differences. If we all wanted low-stress jobs, who would clean the windows of our skyscrapers or put new roofs over our heads? If we all wanted to be brain surgeons, what would happen to the need for family physicians who care for our everyday needs? In other words—remember that the information in this chapter is meant to give you more information so you can make a good match between your wants and needs and the types of jobs out there in the marketplace. There are no rights or wrongs here—only what matters to you.

The Least You Need to Know

- The hottest jobs out in the market are usually ones that are in high demand with a low number of people to fill them or that are being fueled by a good economy.

- As the Baby Boomers grow older, elder care jobs become the hottest. When the economy is good, construction is going strong.

- Some of the best jobs are those that have good work environments, low stress, autonomy, and good pay. Examples of these are biologists, actuaries, and financial planners.

- Stress is in the eyes of the beholder. We all respond to stress differently. Some people look for high-stress occupations because they love the risk or danger or challenge.

- Generally, the highest paid occupations are professional jobs that require an advanced educational degree—such as doctors, lawyers, and computer scientists.

- People who do not have an advanced degree can make very good money, such as automotive mechanics, carpenters, and plumbers.

14

Your Preferred Work Environment

In This Chapter

- Look at work environment categories

- Assess your ideal work environment

- Know more about your own work style

- Understand job category lists

- Get an overview of how salary structures operate

Now that you have a handle on what is important to you in a career, it's time to start exploring your ideal work environment and getting prepared to look at jobs that match your temperament, your interests, and your skills. After all, what's the good of knowing all this great stuff about yourself if you don't have a specific job in mind? In this chapter, we will start with defining your ideal work environment and then set you up for looking at specific jobs in Chapters 15, 16, and 17.

My Ideal Work Environment—Think About It!

A large part of our satisfaction with work comes from being in the right work environment. This is the last piece of the puzzle on your Career Profile Map. It helps you to understand the work settings you prefer, the kinds of people you want to work with, the atmosphere in which you can thrive, and more.

For many people, this becomes the biggest clue to the kind of work they really want to do. Take Julio who was struggling with a decision between becoming a lawyer or pursuing his fantasy of running a small cottage farm. When we started to look at his ideal work environment, it became clear that he had to be in an outdoor environment. He loved nature, the earth, animals, and fresh air. He needed to use his hands to grow and build. The idea of becoming a lawyer had appeal from the viewpoint of helping others who could not afford legal council. Julio realized this need could be met in other ways and that his work environment would either sustain his motivation or drive him crazy. Being cooped up in an office or a courtroom paled in comparison to the open spaces and feel of the earth.

We are going to look at three aspects of your ideal work environment:

 ◆ Location

 ◆ Environment

 ◆ Work style

You will have a chance to put together your own ideal work environment using the Ideal Work Environment Assessment later in this chapter. For now, read over the descriptors of each category and start thinking about what's important to you right now.

Location

Location involves thinking about how important where you live is to you. People range in all aspects of this continuum from location is critical to "I'm open to experiencing anything." For some people, living near family is important in their lives. Perhaps a young couple is starting a family and would like to have support in caring for their children. Or family is a strong value for you, and no matter what your career, you want to be in proximity to them.

There are many reasons people choose a certain location. Some include being able to pursue interests and leisure activities in certain climates and locations, for example:

- liking the buzz of a city versus the quiet of the country

- wanting a social life versus a life of contemplation and solitude

- particular career opportunities only existing in certain locations

Although your preference for a certain location may change over a lifetime, try to focus on what is really important to you about location, right now. Your level of flexibility in being able to change locations is important in the type of organizations in which you choose to work. People who prefer to stay in one community for a number of years may find themselves less interested in working for a global company that moves their employees around every five years.

> **Insider Tips**
>
> An example of your location as related to career opportunities would be a ballet dancer or a professional actor. There are many more opportunities for work in major cities.

> **Coach Wisdom**
>
> If you are part of a two-income family, then thinking about geography for your needs alone is not sufficient. As partners in life, it's critical to consider the needs of both parties. So, life gets much more complicated, doesn't it? Actually going through the process of sitting down together and looking at your career goals and your lifestyle preferences can be a big help. Not only can you increase your understanding of one another, but you can engage in coming up with a life plan that satisfies the needs of both partners.

Environment

You may think that if you are doing the work you love to do, then your work environment may not be so important—WRONG! Your work environment is the stage or the backdrop for the work you do. If that stage is busy, messy, and ever-changing, and the way you do your best work requires soft lights, quiet, and order ... well, you get the picture.

Often the work we love to do and the work environment that generally supports that work are closely related. For instance, many stockbrokers love the thrill of working in a Wall Street environment in which the pace is fast; the stress is motivating; and the atmosphere is alive with phones, ticker tapes, and announcements about new trades. On the other hand, you can be a stockbroker and be working out of your own home office where your atmospheric stimulators are reduced, and you can talk to your clients while you take a walk through your kitchen.

There are always options for finding work environments that support your preferences for pace, stress, flexibility of work hours, working indoors or outdoors, hierarchy or flat structure organizations, complete autonomy—to teamwork—to being someone's right-hand person. It is important that you not settle for an environment that does not motivate or meet your needs when there are usually many other options out there.

Work Style

Your work style focuses on how you like to approach doing your work. Do you like to work alone or with others? Do you like to take action or sit back and observe first? Do you prefer to use a logical thought process in approaching your work, or are feelings more important to take into consideration? Understanding your own work style needs can help you to identify work environments that will support your styles.

You can also gain valuable information about what makes other people in your work environment tick. Everyone's not the same, and often your work environment brings you into contact with others who have a different work style. Valuing these differences and appreciating what everyone brings to the workplace decreases unnecessary stress and conflict.

The four basic work styles are described as follows:

◆ **Vision Focus.** This work style uses the powers of observation combined with being in touch with people's feelings to create a picture or a vision of the future. A person with this work style likes to approach their work creatively, support others in their work and development, and be able to discuss their insights and observations.

◆ **Team Focus.** This work style uses a combination of understanding people's feelings and their desire to take action. A person with this work style enjoys working with people and is very good at facilitating teams to come up with workable solutions to problems. They do well in an environment of change where they can motivate others to take risks, think outside of the box, and come to collaborative decisions.

◆ **Plan Focus.** This work style combines the ability to observe situations with logical thought processes. People with this work style prefer to work independently to produce plans that will be carried out in a very orderly and well thought out manner. They like to work with ideas that are developed over time and use a carefully planned approach to the work they do.

◆ **Results Focus.** This work style combines logical thought processes with a preference for taking action. People with this style enjoy solving concrete problems and testing out their solutions through trial and error. They focus on getting results in a very logical manner and not getting bogged down with having to work with others.

All four of these work styles are represented in organizations. Your department or group may be predominantly populated with people with your similar work style, because you all do the same type of work. However, you are bound to find other work styles that are dominant in other groups or offices. Think of a typical organization where there is a marketing department, a research department, an engineering department, a sales department, and so on. All of these have a slightly different work style preference in how they like to work with others, how they like to do their work, and how they focus on the type of work they like to do.

The beauty of our differences is that together our parts create a whole picture. For example:

◆ The Vision Focused style brings us a focus for the direction in which we are going.

◆ The Team Focused style brings us together to discuss our different points of view and helps us craft a way to move forward together.

◆ The Plan Focused style puts the Vision into a step-by-step plan.

◆ The Action Focused style moves us into taking action, trying out approaches, and getting results.

Although we are all different, we bring important perspectives and approaches to the table.

Ideal Work Environment Assessment

There are three sections to this assessment on your ideal work environment.

Location: Where do you want to locate yourself in the world?

Check off your must have's and fill in any blanks accordingly:

❑ Ocean   ❑ Lake

❑ Mountains   ❑ Plains

❑ Consistent Weather   ❑ Seasons

❑ Other _____   ❑ Other _____

❑ Country _____   ❑ State _____

❑ Province _____   ❑ City _____

❑ Town _____   ❑ Close to family

❑ Close to friends   ❑ Close to _____

❑ Wherever work takes me   ❑ Same place for ___ years

❑ Change as it comes   ❑ Change as much as possible

❑ Travel on regular basis   ❑ Staying in one place

Record your Top Five Must Have's for Location in your Career Profile Map in Appendix A.

Environment: What meets your needs for your ideal work environment?

Check off the must have's in your ideal work environment:

❑ Flexible work hours   ❑ 9 to 5 hours

❑ Low stress   ❑ Challenging

❑ Collaborative   ❑ Independent

❑ Structured   ❑ Unstructured

❑ Hierarchical   ❑ Collegial

❑ High tech   ❑ Low tech

❑ Modern architecture/furnishings   ❑ Rustic

❏ Friendly   ❏ Supportive

❏ Variety   ❏ Repetition

❏ Indoors   ❏ Outdoors

❏ Fast paced   ❏ Leisurely pace

❏ Consistency   ❏ Dynamic and changing

❏ Quiet   ❏ Activity

❏ Many people   ❏ A few people

❏ Large organization   ❏ Small organization

❏ Own business   ❏ Work from home

Record your Top Five Must Have's for Work Environment in your Career Profile Map in Appendix A.

Work Style: What best describes your approach to your work?

Put a check mark next to the one statement that best describes your behavior:

❏ A. Learn best when able to observe how others do something.

❏ B. Prefer to work with others to figure out how to do something.

❏ C. Like to thoroughly understand something before I try it out.

❏ D. Like to jump right in and try things out.

Put a check mark next to the one statement that best describes your behavior:

❏ E. Tune into other people's feelings as a source of information.

❏ F. Use my intellect to figure things out.

Put a check mark next to the one statement that best describes your behavior:

❏ G. I am very creative, love to use my imagination and intuition, can understand the big picture, care about others, like to support and help other people to develop.

❏ H. I am a people person who loves working with groups to come up with solutions we can all buy into. I like change and am able to mobilize others to take risks and go with the change.

❑ I. I am a planner who loves to put ideas into step-by-step plans that can be carried out. I have a rational and studied approach and am very organized. I prefer to work alone.

❑ J. I am a results-oriented person who likes to take action and talk about it later. I rely on facts to guide my actions, and I prefer to take control of situations independently.

Circle the specific letter you checked off next to each of the previous questions:

- ◆ Vision Focus   A   E   G
- ◆ Team Focus   B   E   H
- ◆ Plan Focus   C   F   I
- ◆ Results Focus   D   F   J

This is a quick assessment of your preference for a work style. The work style that has the most circled answers indicates your top preference. In the case of a tie, read the descriptions about each work style again and decide which one best describes you. Then, ask three people you work with to choose the work style that best describes your behavior.

My Work Style is: _____

Record your overall Work Style in your Career Profile Map in Appendix A.

Using Job Category Lists

The next three chapters will help you to begin to think about jobs that link to your temperament, interests, and skills. Specific jobs will be listed by job category. The job categories primarily follow the ten Bureau of Labor Statistics categories, such as:

- ◆ Construction Trades and Related Workers
- ◆ Farming, Fishing, and Forestry Occupations
- ◆ Installation, Maintenance, and Repair Occupations
- ◆ Management and Business and Financial Operations Occupations
- ◆ Office and Administrative Support Occupations
- ◆ Production Occupations

- Professional and Related Occupations

- Sales and Related Occupations

- Service Occupations

- Transportation and Material Moving Occupations

For each of the four temperaments (SP, SJ, NT, NF) described in Chapter 7, jobs will be listed in job categories that fit each of these temperaments.

For the seven interest orientations (Influencing, Organizing, Helping, Creating, Analyzing, Producing, Adventuring) described in Chapter 9, jobs will be listed in career categories that match each of these interest orientations.

For the three skill areas (Data, Things, People) described in Chapter 10, jobs will be listed by career categories that link to these skill areas.

What will you find as you go through Chapters 15, 16 and 17? Probably you will have quite a few of the same jobs listed under your temperament, interests, and skills. This overlap is natural because these three parts of us are usually interconnected and over-lapping. This overlap will confirm jobs that are most attractive to people with your temperament, interests, and skill sets.

You also might find that some of the same jobs are listed under more than one temperament and interest area. That is because one job can attract people for very different reasons. For example, an Artisan person who loves adventure and likes to live on the edge may want to be in the military as a pilot; however, a Guardian who wants to preserve law and order and maintain the traditions of our country can also be attracted to military service. An Idealist may also be attracted to a military career, but they will almost always want to work more in the human resource and organization development aspects of the military organization.

You are at the beginning of your selection process for looking up jobs that are at least in your areas of temperament, interest, and skill. You will be making a list of jobs that sound interesting to you. You will be looking these jobs up online to learn more about them. And eventually you will be narrowing your list to two or three jobs that fit your Career Profile Map criteria. These are the jobs on which you will be doing even more research. You can't afford to get sloppy at this point—you are heading to the finish line in finding your perfect career. So it's worth all the effort and research you will do to find out as much as possible about jobs that interest you!

Insider Tips

There are more than 12,000 different types of jobs out there, so the job lists presented in Chapters 15, 16, and 17 will not exhaust the possibilities! What it will do is point to some of the most popular jobs in each of the categories. You may want to then go to the *Occupational Outlook Handbook, 2004–05 Edition* published by the U.S. Department of Labor, Bureau of Labor Statistics to look at descriptions for most of these jobs as well as view more jobs in each job category that interests you. Just type www.bls.gov and click on Search A–Z in the right-hand corner, or type "occupational outlook handbook index". For a list of jobs put out by the United States Labor Department, see Appendix D.

Should you limit yourself to jobs that are *only* listed in categories that match your temperament, interests, or skills? The answer is a definitive, No! You can be anything you want to be—there are no restrictions. The true determinant of being able to do what you want to do is that you have the motivation to do it and the skill or ability to do it. So although these job lists are intended to point you in a direction that may be just right for you, it is not at all limiting. If you see a job that you really want to explore and it isn't in your area of temperament, interest, or skill—look it up anyway! Explore, have fun; you are the final judge and decision maker.

Salary Range Possibilities

Most of us are curious about what the salary range possibilities are for any occupation we are considering. Although this information is helpful in our decision-making process, it is also important to realize that no matter what occupational field you are in, there are wide ranges in salary based on several considerations. Here are some general guidelines:

Insider Tips

For more specific information on salaries, go to www.careerinfonet.com and click on "Labor Market Information" in the menu on the right and then click on "Occupational Report" in the box on the left. You can access salaries for any location in the United States.

- ◆ Higher education requirement
- ◆ Management positions
- ◆ Top tier professions
- ◆ Job location

Each is described in the sections that follow.

Higher Education Requirement

In any career category, the higher the education required, generally the more money you can earn doing the basic work involved. According to the U.S. Department of Labor, Bureau of Labor Statistics, occupations requiring a two year degree range in salaries from Radiologic Technician at $35,000 to Dental Hygienist at $46,000. Those occupations requiring a four year degree, range in salaries from Architect at $51,000 to Petroleum Engineer at $72,000. Occupations requiring a graduate degree range from $53,000 for Psychologist to $102,000 for Physicians. In education, a university professor or administrator is going to have a higher salary that most elementary through high school teachers. Again, more education is required for higher education positions.

Most occupational fields have a hierarchy of starting with those occupations within the field that are seen as more prestigious and demand higher salaries and position levels within the field. Also there are changing circumstances within fields that make some occupations more lucrative and in demand. This demand is often due to a variety of circumstances: technological advances, new products, services, trends, or a limited number of resources available to fill demand.

The explosion of biochemical research has placed a demand on educating more bio-chemists to prepare them for the breakthrough work that is being done in many small start-up and growing biotech companies. Some *colleges* are paying all tuition and fees for students to attend their masters and doctoral programs right now in chemistry because of the high demand.

Management Positions

Management positions in any organization generally pay more than other occupa-tional categories in that organization. And within the management ranks there are certain fields that pay higher salaries than others. For instance a CEO, and the com-puter and information systems manager pay about $300 more a week than the general operations manager and the marketing and sales managers.

Top Tier Professions

Some "elite" professions remain the most lucrative over time. Currently, the highest paying professions are doctors, chief executive officers, and dentists ranging from a $123,000 annual salary to more than $145,600. Those occupations that are in the next tier, from $90,000 to $100,000 are pilots, podiatrists, judges, air traffic controllers, engineering managers, and lawyers.

Again it's important to remember that these salaries are the potential within these occupations. Many doctors work for much less money at clinics and inner city locations that need their services and cannot pay competitive prices. The motivations that drive people to certain occupations can range from status, money and prestige, to service to community, and everything in between.

Job Location

Salaries can vary dramatically by location. Depending on where you are in the country (or the world), there will be differences in salaries. For instance, salaries in New York City are generally higher due to the cost of living in this area. You won't necessarily be taking home more money since you will have to pay higher living expenses. You can go to www.careeronestop.org to look up salaries for any occupation by location.

The Least You Need to Know

- ◆ The location of where you work may be an important factor for you. Identify where you want to be located in the world—in the country—in the city or town or country side—by the sea or in the forest.

- ◆ Understanding what you must have in your everyday work environment can help you find an organization that is a good match for you. Think about the work environment in terms of the kinds of relationships you want with co-workers, how much structure or flexibility you need in your schedule, and the size of organization that appeals to you.

- ◆ Your preferred work style will give you clues to how you work best with others and the type of environment that is going to be most pleasing to you. The four styles to consider are: Vision Focused, Team Focused, Plan Focused, or Results Focused.

- ◆ Salary ranges within all occupational fields have a wide range from the highest salaries being held by people with more education and in higher levels of responsibility in the organization.

Jobs for My Temperament

In This Chapter

- ◆ Take a look at job categories that match your temperament
- ◆ Understand some basic facts about job categories that can help you make good decisions
- ◆ Find out where to get more information on jobs that you want to research further

In this chapter, you are going to start looking at the jobs that match your temperament. The concept of temperament is based on David Keirsey's theory, which can be found in his latest book, *Please Understand Me II: Temperament, Character, Intelligence* (Prometheus Nemesis Book Co. Inc., 1998). And all references to temperament in this chapter are adapted from his book from the descriptions shared by the Advisor Team at www.AdvisorTeam.com., and from www.Keirsey.com.

An important aspect to remember is that within each temperament there are four role variants, which will be referred to as personality types. Although temperament is common to all four personalities, there are also some differences. These differences will be highlighted for each temperament so that you can keep them in mind as you review the job lists. You probably will find that you are attracted to some of the jobs listed for your temperament more than other ones due to your personality type.

You also may see some of the same jobs listed under more than one temperament. The clue here is what attracts each temperament to a career area. Although most career areas have some of each temperament represented in their career ranks, it is usually one or two temperaments that stand out as the ones that are most attracted to a career area. Remember: Don't be limited by the choices listed under your temperament. If you see something that interests you, check it off and look it up!

Artisan (SP) Jobs

The Artisan is unconventional, bold, and spontaneous. They tend to be fun-loving, optimistic, realistic, and focused on the here and now. Artisans like variety, are action-oriented and prefer having the freedom of expression. They like to have fun in whatever they do and are excellent troubleshooters. They are found primarily in career and job categories where there is an element of adventure and challenge and where they can apply their ability to see details, manipulate solid objects, and real-life events to get immediate results.

> **Coach Wisdom**
>
> The job categories and specific jobs related to each category will give you a good idea of the types of jobs that Artisans prefer. Please do not be limited by this selection. Each category can be explored more in-depth through the suggested professional and trade associations and the *Occupational Outlook Handbook* described in Chapter 14.

The Artisans (SP) are observant (S – sensation) and probing (P – perception). They gather information by paying close attention to the environment, its details and the nuances of a situation. They are practical and realistic about life, and are always looking for impact, so they are focused on living a spontaneous and flexible lifestyle. These two behaviors are primary drivers in the attraction to certain types of careers.

The four personalities represented in the Artisan Temperament are the ISFP, ISTP, ESFP, and ESTP. Although any of the jobs listed here can appeal to the Artisan temperament, there are specific job listings that may be more appealing if you are an Introvert (I) or an Extrovert (E).

The other distinguishing personality aspect of an Artisan is whether you are tough-minded (T – Thinking) or tender-hearted (F – Feeling). Those who tend to be tender-hearted may be drawn to careers where they are more involved with entertainment, service or helping others in an artful way, and those who are more tough-minded may prefer more freedom from authority, taking charge for a while, and directing others in a craft or technology they are skilled at.

Pay attention to the jobs that you are drawn to as you read over the list (organized by job category) and put a check mark in front of them.

Protective Service Occupations

❏ Correctional Officer

❏ Firefighter

❏ Police Officer

❏ Detective/Investigator

❏ Security Guard

❏ Military Service

Farming, Fishing, Forestry

❏ Farmer

❏ Marine Biologist

❏ Forester

❏ Park Naturalist

Management, Business, Finance

❏ Real Estate Broker

❏ Real Estate Investor

❏ Management Consultant

❏ Troubleshooter Manager

❏ Negotiator

❏ Sales

❏ Entrepreneur

❏ Insurance Broker

❏ Stockbroker

❏ Banker

Construction Trades Occupations

❏ Carpenter

❏ General Contractor

❏ Construction Worker

❏ Construction Inspector

❏ Electricians

Installation, Maintenance, Repair

❏ Computer Repair

❏ Electrical Installer

❏ Aircraft Mechanic

Transportation

❏ Pilot

❏ Air Traffic Controller

❏ Flight Attendant

❏ Travel Agent

Professional Occupations

Arts and Design

❏ Artists

❏ Interior Design

❏ Instructional Design

❏ Landscape Architect

Entertainers, Performers, Sports

❏ Actors

❏ Athletes

❏ Dancers

❏ Musician

❏ Entertainment Agent

❏ Special Effects Technician

❏ Sportscaster

❏ Photographer

❏ Fitness Trainer

❏ Wilderness Guide

Engineers

❏ Electrical

❏ Civil

❏ Industrial

Health

❏ Emergency Room Doctor

❏ Medical Technician

Computers

❏ Computer Programmers

❏ Software Engineer

❏ Systems Analyst

Guardian (SJ) Jobs

Guardians are the stewards of tradition in all their communities. They are dependable, helpful, and hard working. They like working in conventional structures where reporting relationships are clear and where their focus on credentials and practical experience is valued. They are always concerned citizens who trust authority, seek out membership in groups, and want security and gratitude for the contributions they make to their organizations.

Coach Wisdom

The job categories and specific jobs related to each category will give you a good idea of the types of jobs that Guardians prefer. Please do not be limited by this selection. Each category can be explored more in-depth through the suggested professional and trade associations and the *Occupational Outlook Handbook* described in Chapter 14.

Guardians usually seek out careers and jobs working for organizations with a history of stability, structure, and service. They are drawn to positions where they can keep things running smoothly and put their abilities at scheduling, following procedures, and attention to details to work. They are known for their talent at managing goods and services.

The four personalities represented by the Guardian Temperament are ISTJ, ISFJ, ESTJ, and ESFJ. The SJ is the DNA of the Guardian Temperament and makes all the following job lists possible. All Guardians are sensible (S – Sensation) and judicious (J – Judging). Although any of the jobs listed here can appeal to the Guardian temperament, there are specific job listings that may be more appealing if you are an Introvert (I) or an Extrovert (E).

However, Guardians are very social in general, making the temperament a strong factor in career choice. The following list of job categories and jobs is not exhaustive. Please remember to look up these job categories for more ideas about careers and jobs for the Guardian temperament. Put a check in front of those jobs that are most appealing to you.

Health and Service Occupations

❑ Dentist

❑ Dental Assistant

❑ Family Physician

❑ Medical Assistant

❑ Nurse

❑ Pharmacist

❑ Physical Therapist

❑ Medical Researcher

❑ Biologist

❑ Medical Equipment Sales

❑ Police Officer

❑ Military Service

❑ Underwriter

Professional Occupations

❑ Teacher

❑ School Principal

❑ Clergy

❑ Probation Officer

❑ Lawyer

❑ Librarian

❑ Social Worker

❑ Guidance Counselor

❑ Veterinarian

❑ Paralegal

❑ Legal Assistants

❑ Public Administrator

❑ Engineer (nuclear, environmental, mechanical—applied fields)

Office, Administrative Support

❏ Office Manager

❏ Administrative Assistant

❏ Financial Clerks

❏ Desktop publisher

❏ Customer Service Representative

❏ Information and Record Clerks

❏ Dispatcher

❏ Shipping, Receiving, Traffic Clerks

❏ Postal Service Worker

Management, Business, Financial Operations

Business, Financial Operations

❏ Accountant

❏ Auditor

❏ Budget Analyst

❏ Claims Adjuster

❏ Appraiser

❏ Banker

❏ Insurance Sales

Management

❏ Operations Manager

❏ Logistics and Purchasing Managers

❏ Project Manager

❏ Administrator

❏ Computer Network Manager

❏ Chief Financial Officer

❏ Maintenance Supervisor

❏ Lodging Managers

❏ Funeral Director

❏ Food Service Managers

❏ Farmer

❏ Administrative Services

❏ Public Relations

❏ Sales Manager

❏ Computer and Information Systems Manager

❏ Human Resource Manager

Rational (NT) Jobs

The Rational temperament is even-tempered, logical, and achievement oriented. Rationals seek knowledge, prize technology, and want to understand how the world works. They tend to be pragmatic, skeptical, and self-contained. They are known as the problem-solving temperament and are found tackling problems in organic systems such as plants and animals, in mechanical systems such as railroads and computers, or in social systems such as families, companies, and government. Rationals often seek out powerful positions where they find challenging environments and opportunities to employ their strategic minds and intellect. This temperament is what guides the selection of the job lists you will see here.

The four personality types associated with the Rational temperament are INTP, INTJ, ENTP, and ENTJ. Some jobs will look more attractive based on whether one is more gregarious and extroverted (E) or more reserved and introverted (I). In addition, Coordinating Rationals (NTJ) will be attracted to jobs that could manage projects or people whereas the Engineering Rationals (NTP) are attracted to problem-solving jobs that often do not require managing people. Look over the following list and put a check in front of those jobs that are most appealing to you.

> **Coach Wisdom**
>
> The job categories and specific jobs related to each category will give you a good idea of the types of jobs that Rationals prefer. Please do not be limited by this selection. Each category can be explored more in-depth through the suggested professional and trade associations and the *Occupational Outlook Handbook* described in Chapter 14.

Management, Business, Financial

❏ Consultant

❏ Inventor

❏ Sales Manager

❏ Marketing Manager

❏ Ombudsperson

❏ Human Resource Manager

❏ Investment Broker

❏ Real Estate Developer

❏ Business Analyst

Professional Occupations

Computer Occupations

❏ Network Integration Specialist

❏ Systems Analyst

❏ Computer Scientist

❏ Systems Administrator

❏ Data Base Administrator

❏ Software Engineer

❏ Webmaster

❏ Programmer

Professional Occupations

Engineering and Science

❏ Computer Hardware Engineer

❏ Design Engineer

❏ Biomedical Engineer

❏ Nuclear Engineer

❏ Civil Engineer

❏ Mining/Geological Engineer

❏ Environmental Engineer

❏ Aerospace Engineer

❏ Chemist

❏ Biochemist

Architecture

❏ Architect

❏ Landscape Architect

Education

❏ Curriculum, Instructional Design

❏ College Professor

❏ Administrator

❏ Dean

❏ Researcher

Law

❏ Judge

❏ Attorney

Health

❏ Surgeon

❏ Neurologist

❏ Psychologist

❏ Pathologist

❏ Coroner

❏ Researcher

Coach Wisdom

The jobs categories and specific jobs related to each category will give you a good idea of the types of jobs that Idealists prefer. Please do not be limited by this selection. Each category can be explored more in-depth through the suggested professional and trade associations and the *Occupational Outlook Handbook* described in Chapter 14.

Idealist (NF) Jobs

The Idealist temperament is focused on personal development and human potential. Idealists are enthusiastic, trust their intuition, seek self-knowledge, and want meaningful relationships. Idealists are loving, kindhearted, and authentic. They are naturally drawn to working with people in a variety of occupations—education, counseling, consulting, social ser-vices, personnel, journalism, and the ministry. They prefer environments where everyone's input is valued, people work collaboratively, and decisions are made democratically.

The Idealists are attracted to occupations where they can use their creativity and intuition in combination with their concern and attention for the well being and growth of people.

The four Personality Types associated with the Idealist Temperament are INFP, INFJ, ENFP and ENFJ. The preference for particular jobs in the following list can be affected whether or not you are an Introvert or an Extrovert. Moreover, a Mentoring Idealist (NFJ) can be more attracted to jobs that involve directing or guiding other people, whereas a Advocating Idealist (NFP) will be attracted to jobs that are more informative and involve gentle persuasion or inspiration. As you read through the following job lists, put a check in front of those to which you are most drawn.

Professional Occupations

Human Service and Counseling Occupations

❑ Career Counselor

❑ Educational Psychologist

❑ Personal Counselor

❑ Guidance Counselor

❑ Coach

❑ Dance Therapist

❑ Art Therapist

❑ Massage Therapist

❑ Minister/Clergy

❑ Outplacement Counselor

❑ Social Worker

❑ Public Health Educator

❑ Welfare Worker

❑ Elder Care Services Director

❑ Human Service Director

Education and Consulting

❑ University/College Professor of Humanities

❑ Student Affairs Staff and Administration

❑ Dean of Students

❑ Child Care Director

❑ Educational Program Director

❑ Program Designer

❑ Organization Consultant

❑ Trainer

❑ Employee Assistance Program Specialist

❑ Librarian

Artistic and Creative

❑ Writer

❑ Editor

❑ Newscaster

❑ Artist

Professional Occupations

Artistic and Creative

- ❏ Film Maker
- ❏ Wardrobe Designer
- ❏ Set Designer
- ❏ Exhibit Designer
- ❏ Producer
- ❏ News Analyst
- ❏ Actor
- ❏ Interior Designer
- ❏ Columnist
- ❏ Dancer
- ❏ Fashion Designer

Legal

- ❏ Family Lawyer

Health

- ❏ Physical Therapist
- ❏ Holistic Practitioner
- ❏ Occupational Therapist
- ❏ Managed Care Specialist
- ❏ Nutritionist
- ❏ Public Health Educator

Business

- ❏ Human Resource Specialist/Manager
- ❏ Employee Assistant Specialist
- ❏ Organizational Psychologist
- ❏ Trainer (diversity, teamwork, leadership)
- ❏ Recruiter
- ❏ Educational Software Developer
- ❏ Labor Relations Specialist

More About These Jobs

First of all, take all the jobs that you checked and add them to the Career Ideas List section of your Career Profile Map in Appendix A. As you proceed through the next two chapters, you can add selections. Right now, you are at the start of your identification and early research into jobs that you think might be of interest to you. It's important in this early stage to look up each of these jobs and read about them.

Your primary source of information is going to be the *Occupational Outlook Handbook*. The information is available online; you can get there using the following steps:

1. After connecting to the Internet, go to the Occupational Outlook Handbook web page at www.bls.gov/oco.

2. Click on the OOH Search/A-Z Index link in the upper-right corner of the web page. This will take you directly to the Search OOH page.

3. Type an occupation in the Search OOH text box (for example, one of the jobs you checked off in the previous set of job lists) and click the Search button.

4. Click on any of the listed occupations and review the significant points about the job. There are also a set of links you can click on for more information about the ...

   ♦ Nature of the Work

   ♦ Working Conditions

   ♦ Employment

   ♦ Training, Other Qualifications, and Advancement Opportunities

   ♦ Job Outlook

   ♦ Earnings

   ♦ Related Occupations

   ♦ Sources of Additional Information

If you do not like to use the Internet, any library will have a copy of the latest *Occupational Outlook Handbook.*

You can also go to www.KeirseyCampbell.com to access more information on your temperament. If you would like to use your discount coupon on the last page of this book to take the "Bundle," you can take the Keirsey Temperament Sorter along with the Campbell Interest and Skill Survey and get a full report on your temperament, personality, and jobs related to your interests.

Insider Tips

Although the OOH lists many jobs, there are specific job titles that you may not find. In that event, check out the information in Chapter 19 on utilizing additional Internet resources.

The Least You Need to Know

   ♦ The Artisan (SP) temperament is attracted to careers where they can live out their adventurous natures, take on new challenges, and apply their skill at seeing the details and nuances to manipulate solid objects and real-life events.

♦ The Guardian (SJ) temperament is attracted to careers where they can uphold the traditions in their organizations, keep things running smoothly and in an orderly manner, and maintain a social and civil working environment.

♦ The Rational temperament (NT) wants to use their problem-solving approach to tackle problems in systems—organic, mechanical, or social systems.

♦ The Idealist temperament (NF) wants to be able to focus on issues of personal development and human potential. They enjoy working in organizations that are more democratic and participative and in which the environment is collaborative.

16

Jobs for My Interests

In This Chapter

♦ Look at primary job categories that match your interests

♦ Identify occupations that match your interests or that seem interesting to you

♦ Find out where to get more information on jobs that you want to research further

We begin the focus on your interests by asking you to get out your Career Profile Map from Appendix A and look at the Orientation Scales Assessment section (originally presented in Chapter 9). These orientation scales are based on the theory developed by David Campbell for his Campbell Interest and Skill Survey, which can be accessed on www. KeirseyCampbell.com. All references to the seven interest orientations in this chapter were adapted from David Campbell's articles in his book (put reference here).

You already have identified one or more of these seven orientations as your primary areas of interest in Chapter 9. Using this as a guide, you will be able to look at job lists in this chapter that match your interest orientation. You will also continue to identify jobs that might be of interest to you to explore further. Remember, at this point you are not making final decisions. You are expanding your horizons and looking at all the options and possibilities there are that match up with who you are!

In looking at the jobs that match your interests, you will probably find some redundancy with what you discovered under your temperament. This is normal, because all the pieces of ourselves do fit together—like a challenging puzzle, it fits together in the end. And every one of us has slightly different shapes and sizes to our puzzle pieces, making us unique.

Although you can only have one temperament, your interests may fall in more than one category, throwing a wider net over the possible career areas. From this angle, we may pick up some new career possibilities. You will be asked to check off those jobs that are of most interest to you in each of the seven interest orientations and record your results in the Career Profile Map. You are building a good list of jobs that you can explore further.

In your decision-making process, you are in what is called the *divergent* stage of decision making where you remain open to generating possibilities. Later, you will get to the *convergent* stage where you narrow your choices down. Staying in the divergent mode right now is important. For those of you who favor the Judging behavior, you are going to have to fight your tendency to reach closer very quickly.

Career Lingo

Divergent means keeping your net thrown wide and generating possibilities. In this case, looking for your perfect career match requires seeing all the jobs out there that could be possible for you. **Convergent** means you narrow your focus and gather those nets in close. This is where you will bring your potential career choice down to two or three options and evaluate them based on criteria from your Career Profile Map in Appendix A.

Influencing Orientation Jobs

People with the Influencing orientation like to lead and influence others. They look for ways to make things happen and get results. You will find people with Influencing orientations in law and politics, sales, and management positions of all kinds. Influencers like using their people and data skills, and you will find this combination of skills is required in the jobs listed here. As you review the following job lists in each of the job categories associated with Influencing, put a check mark in front of those jobs that interest you the most.

Management, Business, Finance

❏ Marketing Manager

❏ Public Relations Manager

❏ Sales Manager

❏ Human Resource Manager

❏ Labor Relations Manager Executive

❏ Financial Planner

❏ Advertising and Promotions Manager Executive

❏ Organization Development Consultant

❏ Retail Store Manager

❏ Business Owner/Entrepreneur

❏ Financial Analyst

❏ Management Analyst

Professional

❏ Judge, Magistrate

❏ Lawyer

❏ Educational Administrator

Sales

❏ Real Estate Broker

❏ Insurance Sales Agent

❏ Stockbroker

Organizing Orientation Jobs

People with the Organizing orientation seek a career in which they can bring their efficiency and ability to plan and supervise others in the orderly accomplishment of tasks. They prefer structured and more traditional work environments in which their problem-solving skills can be used daily. Organizers love to work with data and are especially good at working in any environment that requires attention to ordering, planning, budgeting, and making things run smoothly. Put a check mark in front of those jobs that are of most interest to you for further exploration.

Management, Business, Finance

❑ Administrative Services

❑ Administrative Manager

❑ Financial Manager

❑ Food Service Manager

❑ Funeral Director

❑ Industrial Production Manager

❑ Lodging Manager

❑ Accountant

❑ Auditor

❑ Claims Adjuster

❑ Appraiser

❑ Investigator

❑ Cost Estimators

❑ Loan Officer

❑ Tax Examiner

❑ Bank Teller

Office, Administrative Support

❑ Financial Clerk

❑ Information and Record Clerk

❑ Material Recording, Scheduling Clerk

❑ Administrative Assistant

❑ Postal Service Worker

❑ Office Clerk

Professional/Health

❑ Dental Assistant

❑ Dietitian/Nutritionist

❑ Medical Records Technician

❑ Pharmacy Technician

❑ Veterinary Technologist

❑ Extended Care Administrator

Career Lingo

Veterinary Technologists usually love animals and are found performing medical tests and treating and diagnosing medical conditions and diseases in animals, under the supervision of a veterinarian. They work in either private clinics, animal hospitals, or research facilities where the median salary is $22,950 a year. The salary spread is from $16,170 to $33,750. Generally there is a requirement for completing a 2–4 year veterinary technology program and passing a state examination. The outlook for veterinary technologists is expected to grow faster than the average for all occupations.

Helping Orientation Jobs

People with a Helping orientation are committed to serving and developing others. They are compassionate and enjoy providing support and counsel in solving personal problems. Helpers like a harmonious work environment where they can apply their people skills to service occupations such as counseling, teaching, and spiritual guidance. Place a check mark in front of those jobs that are most appealing to you.

Management, Business, Financial

❏ Education Administration

❏ Human Resource Manager

❏ Corporate Trainer

Professional

❏ Clergy

❏ Counselor

❏ Guidance Counselor

❏ Art Therapist

❏ Dance Therapist

❏ Social Worker

❏ Life Coach

❏ Career Counselor

❏ Fitness Trainer

❏ Instructional Coordinator

❏ Teacher

❏ Student Affairs Staff

❏ College Professor

❏ Nurse

❏ Human Service Worker

❏ Psychologist

❏ Holistic Health Practitioner

Service

❏ Childcare Worker

❏ Personal and Home Care Aids

❏ Nurses Aid

Career Lingo

Student Affairs Staff are found in colleges and universities and includes people who are focused on providing services and programs for students on the campus. This category of jobs is highly populated by people with Helping orientation. There are several jobs that range from working with students to help them plan programs in the student activities or campus activities office to being a Head of Residence in a residence hall where you are in charge of the administration and programming aspects of residence living. Other jobs are in recruiting and admissions, financial aid services, health services and programming, and career and personal counseling. The environment of college campuses often draws people from the Helping Orientation to this setting.

Creating Orientation Jobs

People with a Creative orientation enjoy creating new products, new visions, and new concepts with an artistic focus. They are innovative and enjoy nontraditional work settings. Creators work with Idea skills in occupations such as commercial artist, musician, and interior design. Place a check mark in front of those jobs that peak your interest and that you would like to explore further.

Management, Business, Finance

❏ Public Relations Specialist

❏ Corporate Trainer

Professional

❏ Architect

❏ Landscape Architect

❏ Fashion Designer

❏ Fine Artist

❏ Art Teacher

❏ Musician

❏ Illustrator

❏ Instructional Designer

❏ Actor

❏ Director

❏ Dancer

❏ Choreographer

❏ Singer

❏ Photographer

❏ Writer

❏ Editor

❏ Broadcaster

❏ Librarian

❏ Translator

Service

❏ Chef

Career Lingo

Writers generally fall into one of three categories. Writers and authors develop original fiction and nonfiction for books, magazines, trade journals, online publications, company newsletters, radio and television broadcasts, motion pictures, and advertisements. Editors examine proposals and select material for publication or broadcast, and review and revise a writer's work in preparation for publication. The third area is technical writers who develop technical materials such as equipment manuals, appendices, or operating and maintenance instructions. The number of online publications and services is growing in volume and sophistication, and that's good news for writers and editors. Check out the American Writers and Artists Institute website and learn more about copywriting and travel writing.

Analyzing Orientation Jobs

People with the Analyzing orientation gravitate toward working alone or in small groups in laboratory or academic settings where they can solve problems and run experiments. They are comfortable using data skills in such occupations as medical technician, computer programmer, engineering, and science. Place a check mark in front of those jobs that you would like to research further.

Management, Business, Finance

❏ Research and Development Manager

Professional

❏ Computer Programmer

❏ System Analyst

❏ Computer Scientist

❏ Aerospace Engineer

❏ Biomedical Engineer

❏ Chemical Engineer

❏ Computer Hardware Engineer

❏ Nuclear Engineer

❏ Chemist

❏ Physician

❏ Biochemist

❏ College Professor

❏ Math Teacher

❏ Science Teacher

❏ Mathematician

❏ Statistician

❏ Biological Scientist

❏ Medical Scientist

❏ Medical Researcher

❏ Biologist

Producing Orientation Jobs

People with a Producing orientation enjoy using their hands and seeing the results of their labor. They generally like working outdoors and are good with tools, construction work, and repair occupations. Producers like to work their thing skills. Typical jobs for Producers are mechanics, veterinarians, and carpenters. Place a check before those jobs that catch your interest for further exploration.

Management, Business

❑ Farmer

❑ Rancher

❑ Agricultural Manager

Professional

❑ Veterinarian

❑ Landscape Architect

❑ Vocational Teacher

❑ University Extension Service Staff

❑ Professor of Agriculture

❑ Professor of Environmental Studies

Construction Trades

❑ Brick Mason

❑ Stonemason

❑ Carpenter

❑ Installers

❑ Cement Masons

❑ Drywall Installers

❑ Painters

❑ Plumbers

Farming, Fishing, Forestry

❑ Agricultural Worker

❑ Forest Worker

❑ Conservation Worker

Installation, Maintenance, Repair

❑ Electrician

❑ Electrical Equipment Mechanic

❑ Electrical Equipment Installer

❑ Electrical Equipment Repairer

❑ Plumber

❑ Aircraft Mechanic

❑ Automobile Mechanic

❑ Heavy Vehicle Mechanic

❑ Installers

❑ Maintenance and Repair Worker

Production Occupations

❑ Assembler

❑ Machinist

❑ Tool and Die Maker

❑ Welding Worker

❑ Bookbinder

❑ Woodworker

❑ Power Plant Operator

❑ Metal Workers

❑ Stone Cutters

❑ Dental Laboratory Technician

Service

❑ Chefs

❑ Food Preparation Worker

Transportation and Material Moving

❑ Bus Driver

❑ Taxi Driver

❑ Chauffeur

❑ Sailors

❑ Ship Engineers

❑ Material Moving Occupations

❑ Railroad Conductors

❑ Switch Operators

❑ Rail Transportation Workers

Adventuring Orientation Jobs

The Adventuring orientation person likes to takes risks and enjoys competitive physical activities as well as teamwork. Adventurers are active, energetic, and confident in physically demanding and risky situations. Adventurers employ their physical skill in their work. Typical occupations for the Adventure orientation are athletes, military and police officers, and athletic coaches. Place a check mark in front of those jobs that interest you the most and you want to research further.

Service

❑ Military Officer

❑ Military Enlisted Personnel

❑ Police Officer

❑ Probation Officer

❑ Correctional Officer

❑ Firefighter

Professional

❑ Emergency Medical Technician

❑ Test Pilot

❑ Athletic Instructor

❑ Athletic Trainer

❑ Athletic Coach

❑ Professional Athlete

❑ Fitness Instructor

More About These Jobs

Look at all the jobs that you checked off and add them to the Career Ideas List section of your Career Profile Map in Appendix A. In instances where you have checked the same job listing as you did under your Temperament, place a check mark in front of the job. Add the new ones to your ongoing list.

Remember to look up any new jobs you placed on the list in the *Occupational Outlook Handbook* Index. For more on how to access this information, refer to the "More About These Jobs" section in Chapter 15.

The Least You Need to Know

- ◆ Looking at jobs that are in your areas of interest orientation can produce more options for you to explore in your pursuit of finding your perfect career.

- ◆ The seven interest orientations are Influencing, Organizing, Helping, Creating, Analyzing, Producing, and Adventuring.

- ◆ It is never too early to start looking up descriptions of jobs that fall in your interest areas. Use the *Occupational Outlook Handbook* to find out more about jobs that peak your interest.

17

Jobs That Fit My Skills

In This Chapter

- ♦ Look at primary job categories that match your skills
- ♦ Identify occupations that match your skills
- ♦ Find out where to get more information on jobs that match your exact skills

In Chapter 10, you identified the skills that you want to use or develop for use in your perfect career. Your skills fell in one or more of the three core skill groups of working with data, working with things, or working with people. Most jobs combine these skills in some way with a primary emphasis on one of the skill areas. For our purposes in this chapter, we will do a rough cut of the job categories and occupations within those that have an emphasis on working with data, things, or people. In preparation for looking at the job lists in this chapter, take out your Career Profile Map from Appendix A and look at the Skills section. Use these skills as a guide to looking at the jobs listed under the Data, Things, and People skill groups.

This third cut at looking at jobs that match your profile will give you some overlap with occupations you have already identified in Chapters 15 and 16. This is good! Again, it confirms some occupations that are meeting your requirements across temperament, interests, and skills. Be sure to place another check in front of those occupations already on your list. Additional occupations you discover from this cut on skills can be added to your growing list of options. Let's begin with a look at some possible jobs that match the skills you want to use in your career.

Data Skills

There are three ways of approaching working with Data skills: Analyzing, Ideas, and Creative. People who use Analyzing skills enjoy using their minds to figure out how to use data, how to organize it, and how to make it useful. Accountants, air traffic controllers, and office assistants use Analyzing skills. People who use Idea skills often work with data to present it to others in the form of ideas. For example, speech writers and advertisers put data together to articulate ideas that their audience will be able to comprehend.

If you prefer to work with data to create something from scratch, then you fall in the Creative skills area. Artists and people who invent or create new things out of data are found in the Creative category of Data skills. Place a check in front of the jobs that you find interesting so that you can get more information on them.

Management, Business, Finance

❏ Administrative Services Manager

❏ Computer and Information Systems Manager

❏ Engineering Manager

❏ Natural Sciences Manager

❏ Financial Manager

❏ Food Service Manager

❏ Funeral Director

❏ Lodging Manager

❏ Purchasing Manager

❏ Purchasing Agent

❏ Accountant

❏ Budget Analyst

❏ Claims Adjuster

❏ Appraiser

❏ Claims Examiner

❏ Claims Investigator

❏ Cost Estimator

❏ Financial Analyst

❏ Personal Financial Advisor

❏ Insurance Underwriter

❏ Loan Counselor

❏ Loan Officer

❏ Management Analyst

❏ Tax Examiner

❏ Tax Collector

❏ Revenue Agent

Office, Administrative Support

❏ Computer Operator

❏ Data Entry

❏ Information Processing Worker

❏ Financial Clerk

❏ Bookkeeper

❏ Gaming Cage Worker

❏ Procurement Clerk

❏ Bank Teller

❏ Information and Record Clerk

❏ Brokerage Clerk

❏ Credit Authorizer

❏ File Clerk

❏ Hotel Desk Clerk

❏ Human Resource Assistant

❏ Interviewer

❏ Order Clerk

❏ Receptionist

❏ Reservation Agent

Material Recording, Scheduling, Dispatching, Distributing

❏ Cargo Agent

❏ Courier

❏ Dispatcher

❏ Meter Reader

❏ Production Clerk

❏ Shipping Clerk

❏ Traffic Clerk

❏ Stock Clerk

❏ Weigher, Measurer

❏ Office Manager

❏ Office Clerk

❏ Postal Service Worker

❏ Secretary

❏ Administrative Assistant

Professional

❏ Actuary

❏ Computer Programmer

❏ Computer Software Engineer

❏ Computer Support Specialist

❏ System Administrator

❏ System Analyst

❏ Database Administrator

❏ Computer Scientist

❏ Mathematician

❏ Operations Research Analyst

❏ Statistician

❏ Drafter

❏ Engineering Technician

❏ Agricultural and Food Scientist

❏ Biological Scientist

❏ Medical Scientist

❏ Conservation Scientist

❏ Forester

❏ Atmospheric Scientist

❏ Chemist

❏ Environmental Scientist

❏ Geoscientist

❏ Physicist

❏ Astronomer

❏ Librarian

❏ Audiologist

❏ Chiropractor

❏ Dentist

❏ Dietitian

❏ Nutritionist

❏ Optometrist

❏ Pharmacist

❏ Physician Assistant

❏ Physician/Surgeon

❏ Podiatrist

❏ Nurse

❏ Respiratory Therapist

❏ Speech Language Pathologist

❏ Veterinarian

Health Technologist

❏ Cardiovascular

❏ Clinical Laboratory

❏ Dental Hygienist

❏ Sonographer

❏ Emergency Medical Technician

❏ Medical Records

❏ Nuclear Medicine

❏ Occupational Health and Safety

❏ Optician

❏ Pharmacy

❏ Radiologic

❏ Surgical

❏ Veterinary

Engineer

❏ Aerospace Engineer

❏ Agricultural Engineer

❏ Biomedical Engineer

❏ Chemical Engineer

❏ Civil Engineer

❏ Computer Hardware Engineer

❏ Electrical Engineer

❏ Environmental Engineer

❏ Industrial Engineer

❏ Materials Engineer

❏ Mechanical Engineer

❏ Mining/Geological Engineer

❏ Nuclear Engineer

❏ Petroleum Engineer

Artist

❏ Painter

❏ Illustrator

❏ Sculptor

Designer

❏ Web Designer

❏ Interior Designer

❏ Fashion Designer

❏ Graphic Designer

❏ Floral Designer

❏ Commercial and Industrial Designer

❏ Merchandise Displayer/Visual Merchandiser

❏ Set and Exhibit Designer

Media and Communication

❏ Announcer

❏ Broadcaster

❏ Sound Engineer Technician

❏ Interpreter, Translator

❏ News Analyst, Reporter

❏ Photographer

❏ Camera Operator

❏ Writer

❏ Editor

Sales

❏ Cashier

❏ Insurance Sales Agent

❏ Real Estate Broker

❏ Sales Engineer

❏ Securities Agent

❏ Travel Agent

Service

❏ Dental Assistant

❏ Medical Assistant

❏ Medical Transcriptionist

❏ Pharmacy Aid

❏ Physical Therapist Aid

Thing Skills

Thing skills are found in a couple of areas. People who like to work with concrete things such as materials, metals, tools, and plants are in the area we call Producing skills. You are using materials to produce an end product—a garden, a house, a bridge. The second area, Adventure skills, is focused on using physical ability as the basis of your skill. Athletes, fitness trainers, and military personnel fall into this category. Put a check in front of those jobs that you think would match your skills and are of interest for more research.

Construction Trades

❏ Boilermaker

❏ Brick Mason

❏ Stonemason

❏ Carpenter

❏ Carpet, Floor, Tile Installer

❏ Cement Mason

❏ Building Inspector

❏ Construction Equipment

❏ Operator

❏ Construction Laborer

❏ Drywall Installer

❏ Electrician

❏ Elevator Installer

❏ Glazier

❏ Hazardous Materials Removal Worker

❏ Insulation Worker

❏ Painter, Paperhanger

❏ Pipe layer

❏ Plumber

❏ Plaster/Stucco Mason

❏ Roofer

❏ Sheet Metal Worker

❏ Iron and Metal Worker

Farming, Fishing, Forestry

❏ Farm worker

❏ Farmer

❏ Ranger

❏ Graders and Sorters

❏ Agricultural Equipment Operators

❏ Fisherman

❏ Fisher Vessel Operator

❏ Forest/Conservation Worker

❏ Logging Equipment Operator

Production

❏ Assembler

❏ Food Processor

❏ Metal/Plastic Worker

❏ Computer Operator

❏ Machinist

❏ Machine Setter

❏ Tool/Die Maker

❏ Welder

❏ Bookbinder

❏ Prepress Technician

❏ Printing Machine Operator

❏ Woodworker

❏ Power Plant Operator

❏ System Operator

❏ Precious Stone Cutter

Professional

❏ Athlete

❏ Coach

❏ Umpire

❏ Dancer

❏ Choreographer

❏ Musician

❏ Singer

❏ Actor

Service

❏ Chef

❏ Cook

❏ Food Preparation Worker

❏ Bartender

❏ Building and Grounds Worker

❏ Pest Control Worker

❏ Recreation Director

❏ Fitness Trainer

Transportation, Material Moving

❏ Aircraft Pilot

❏ Air Traffic Controller

❏ Bus Driver

❏ Tax Driver

❏ Chauffeur

❏ Truck Driver

❏ Delivery Service Driver

❏ Locomotive Engineer

❏ Rail Yard Engineer

❏ Railroad Conductor

❏ Switch Operator

❏ Yardmaster

❏ Ship Engineers

❏ Deck Officers

❏ Marine Oilers

❏ Sailors

❏ Pilots

❏ Material Moving Worker

Installation, Maintenance, Repair

Mechanics, Installers, Repairers

❏ Computer

❏ Office Machines

❏ Automated Teller

❏ Electronics

Installation, Maintenance, Repair

Mechanics, Installers, Repairers

❑ Home Entertainment

❑ Equipment

❑ Telecommunications

❑ Equipment

❑ Aircraft

❑ Automobile

❑ Automotive Service

❑ Technician

❑ Diesel Service

❑ Heavy Vehicle

❑ Small Engine

❑ Coin, Vending

❑ Heating/Air Conditioning

❑ Industrial Machinery

❑ Telephone Line

❑ Maintenance and Repair Workers

❑ Millwrights

❑ Precision Instrument

People Skills

These are the skills we use to influence others and to be of help to others. Managers, supervisors, and salespeople are primary examples of occupations that directly relate to the use of influencing skills in working with people. Counselors, human resource personnel, teachers, and customer service people use primarily helping skills. Almost all occupations require some type of People skills; however some occupations have those at the top of the list. Place a check in front of those jobs that seem to fit your skills the best and are of the most interest to you.

Management, Business, Finance

❑ Advertising Manager

❑ Marketing Manager

❑ Public Relations Manager

❑ Sales Manager

❑ Promotions Manager

❑ Education Administrator K–12

❑ Education Administrator Higher Education

❑ Human Resource Manager

❑ Corporate Trainer

❑ Labor Relations Specialist

❑ Industrial Production Manager

❑ Medical and Health Service Manager

❑ Property Manager

❑ Community Association Manager

❑ Executive

❑ Loan Counselor

❑ Management Analyst

Professional

❏ Psychologist

❏ Social Scientist

❏ Clergy

❏ Counselor

❏ Social Worker

❏ Human Service Worker

❏ Lawyer

❏ Teacher K–12

❏ Teacher Aid

❏ College Professor

❏ Instructional Designer

❏ Announcer

❏ Performer

❏ Broadcaster

❏ Occupational Therapist

❏ Art Therapist

❏ Dance Therapist

❏ Recreational Therapist

❏ Speech Pathologist

❏ College, University Student Life Staff

Sales

❏ Real Estate Broker

❏ Sales Agent

❏ Retail Salesperson

❏ Sales Supervisor

❏ Travel Agent

❏ Financial Planner

❏ Stockbroker

❏ Insurance Salesperson

Service

❏ Childcare Worker

❏ Personal and Home Health Aid

❏ Flight Attendant

❏ Cosmetologist

❏ Hairdresser

❏ Barber

❏ Customer Service Representative

❏ Call Center Representative

More About These Jobs

First of all, take all the jobs that you checked and add them to the Career Ideas List section of your Career Profile Map in Appendix A. In instances where you have checked the same job listing as you did under your Temperament or your Interests, place an additional check mark in front of the job. Add the new ones to your ongoing list.

Remember to look up any new jobs you placed on the list in the *Occupational Outlook Handbook* Index. For more on how to access this information, refer to the "More About These Jobs" section in Chapter 15.

The Least You Need to Know

♦ The three core skill areas are working with data, working with things, and working with people.

♦ There are three ways of approaching Data skills: Analyzing (figure out how to use and organize data), Ideas (work with data to present it to others in the form of ideas), and Creative (work with data to create something from scratch).

♦ Thing skills are found in a couple of areas: people who like to work with concrete things to produce an end product use Producing skills, and people with Adventure skills focus on using physical ability as the basis of their skill.

♦ Almost all occupations require some type of People skills involving the use of influencing skills and helping skills.

18

Education and Training Resources

In This Chapter

- ◆ Decide whether or not you want to get a degree
- ◆ How to find the right college for you
- ◆ Look at alternatives to going to college

By now, you have a good idea of the types of skills and knowledge that you would like to use in your perfect career. For those of you who don't have the skill or knowledge base that you need to pursue a job right now, it's time to consider your options. Among the educational options that provide you with degrees are a two-year Associate's degree; a four-year Bachelor's degree; a Master's degree; a Doctorate degree, or a professional degree. Then there are post-graduate internships and certification programs. There are also many options for those of you who don't want a degree but need to further your skills and knowledge. These options include certifications and licenses, apprenticeships, workshops and seminars, and home schooling. All of these options and more will be explored in this chapter.

After you decide the type of education you need to acquire your desired skills and knowledge, then you need to find the right place to acquire it. How do you find the right program for you? Where do you go to look at your options for schools, training programs, and certifications? Good questions—the answers are coming up soon.

Do I Want More Education?

In making decisions about the type of education and training we want to acquire, we often are faced with difficult realities in our lives. It's necessary to face these issues and take the time to sort out the answers for ourselves. Here are some issues that most people struggle with:

Financial considerations. For most of us, the question arises, "How am I going to pay for this education?" It is important to understand that there is a wide range of costs among the various types of schools and programs that are available to you. There are also financial-aid packages that can be repaid over a long period of time at very low interest rates. Or you may be eligible for financial aid through scholarships or your ability to qualify for certain educational aid. You may also be in a position to borrow money from a family member.

Responsibilities. Life's everyday responsibilities come into play when others are financially or emotionally dependent on us. If you are the major provider for your family or you are taking care of someone in your family, then these realities may influence your educational and training choices.

It's important to remember in these situations that education and training comes in many forms. Among them are night or weekend classes, online self-study programs, as well as continuing education classes and seminars. Because so many people cannot afford to stop working, there are programs designed specifically for you. Remember that your education and training can benefit everyone in your circle of responsibility. It's important to engage members of your family and support system in figuring out ways to divide those responsibilities differently so you can pursue or further your education.

Motivation. Researching and finding the right education for you takes time and effort. Most people get discouraged because they don't know where to start looking. And unfortunately, many people choose staying in a boring job that makes them unhappy over rolling up their sleeves and finding their way to happiness. You are reading this book, so you are already motivated—keep it up and follow the tips you will receive for finding the education you deserve.

Lack of knowledge about educational options. Some people cannot see themselves in a traditional college setting. The fact of the matter is, there are many different types of college settings. Some are more traditionally Ivy League in dress and campus climate. Others have a more experimental and rebellious environment, allowing for individual style and character. There are colleges that lean toward classroom learning and others that have more practical, hands-on learning. So, don't count out a degree until you check into schools that might meet your needs. Another factor to consider is that no matter what your chosen occupational field, you will need education, and some of that, if not all, can be credited courses. You can work toward a degree over time through the courses you need to take along the way. This gives you the option of getting a degree down the road. Look into this—don't overlook opportunities to build up credits.

Goals. You have an incredible amount of information on your work and life goals by now. You know the amount of money you want to make, the lifestyle you want to life, and the skills and knowledge you want to use. The next step is looking at the advantages and disadvantages that different educational avenues will provide against your goals. Be as realistic as you can about the kind of education that is going to position you best for your future and give you the best options. Remember to stretch yourself into your learning zone—take a calculated risk to develop your skills and knowledge.

If you are wondering, "Do I really need to go to college to do what I love to do?" The answer is, "It depends." The first thing you need to do is look into what the educational and training requirements are for occupations you are thinking about going into. Next, consider your long-term goals. If you pursue a career that does not require as much education, will it be one that you can advance within, maintain your physical ability to do, and be satisfying for a long period of time? You know that furthering your education usually ends up in more money in your pocket and more opportunity within your field. So, whatever you do, keep up your education in the field you choose.

Do You Need More Education?

Don't be left out in the cold because you didn't find out what you need to do to be employed in your perfect career. Knowing what is required sometimes means that we decide on other options that don't require quite so much education (for example, becoming a paralegal instead of a lawyer). Or you may want to break a career field down into manageable steps that can be taken over several years. If you are interested in becoming a psychologist, you may want to start with a four-year degree in psychology or counseling, work in a human service area or human resource area in business, then get a Master's degree that prepares you for licensing, and eventually go for your Doctorate. For many of us, breaking down a career field like this lays out the requirements of our fields of interest, and we can begin to put our road maps together. It also lets us know exactly what types of education we need to have in order to be in our fields of interest.

Get Specific

There is an easy way to find out what degrees and/or training is needed for any job you are interested in. Get online and follow these steps:

1. Go to CareerInfoNet at www.careeronestop.org.

2. In the upper-right corner of the page, click on "Site Map."

3. Scroll down to the "Career InfoNet" section of the site map and click on "What It Takes."

4. Scroll down the menu on the left and click on "Education & Training."

5. Choose the State you want to search in (for example, Arizona) and click the Search button.

6. Choose an occupation group from the list of Job Families (for example, Community and Social Services) and click the Search button.

7. Choose a specific Occupation (for example, Health Educators) and click the Search button.

You are now looking at a screen that gives you an overview of the occupation and specific information on educational and training re-quirements including where you can find specific training.

Insider Tips

For those of you who still don't like to use computers, go to your local library and use the *Occupational Outlook Handbook* (Jist Publishing, 2004). This resource has information on the training and education required for more than 250 occupations.

Get Paid

According to the U.S. Census Bureau's most recent studies done from 1997–1999, the average annual earnings of workers 25 to 64 by educational attainment are as follows:

Education	Annual Salary
Doctoral Degree	$89,400
Professional Degree	$109,600
Master's Degree	$62,300
Bachelor's Degree	$52,200
Associate's Degree	$38,200
Some College	$36,800
High School Graduate	$30,400
Not High School Graduate	$23,400

Remember that these are averages and that there are always exceptions to any of these figures. A high school graduate with certifications and licensing can be making $60,000 a year in some professions. A Ph.D. can be making $30,000 a year because they have to teach part-time due to limited positions in their field.

Finding the Right College

For those of you who are deciding to go on to school for an Associate's degree, a Bachelor's degree, a Master's degree, or a Ph.D., this section is for you. You will begin by thinking about some of the factors that may come into play in making your decision about the best match for you:

♦ **Cost (tuition, financial aid).** Consider what your boundaries are for how much you can afford to pay out of pocket. Then find out what financial-aid packages are available at colleges or universities in which you are interested. Consider whether they have work study programs for undergraduates or teaching assistant positions for graduate students.

♦ **Location.** Does the location of the school matter to you? If so, you can do a search that takes that into consideration.

♦ **Size.** Do you like to swim in a small pond or a large one? This is often a major factor for undergraduates who feel more comfortable in one or the other. Graduate programs are usually smaller, and you feel like you are on an island no matter what the size of the school. In other words, your focus is with your peers and your program.

- **Extra-Curricular Activities.** This is especially important to some undergraduate students. If you play sports, like to be in plays, or enjoy being in student organizations, then you can search for schools by activities. Often talking to your coaches or teachers at your current school about colleges and universities that would give you the most opportunity to participate in activities of your choice is a great idea. Often they can help you decide which schools might be best for you.

- **Majors, Programs, Options.** Please don't forget this one. If you are an undergraduate, then you may want to attend a school that has at least two majors that interest you. Just in case you find that your first choice isn't right for you, other options will be available. As you progress in your education to getting a Master's degree or Doctorate, your program becomes one of the major decision-making factors. All these programs usually have a bit of a different concentration or approach to the subject matter so you want to find a good fit for how you learn and what the major focus of the degree program is.

- **Grades.** Not every school is going to be an option, depending on the grades you have already achieved before you apply. You can do searches that will tell you what schools are accepting students in your grade point range.

- **Student/Faculty Ratio.** Often this is related to the size of the school. Big universities tend to have larger classes, especially at the freshman and sophomore levels. If you are looking for more contact with faculty right away, you can do a search to find the right ratio of students to faculty for you.

- **College Standing/Reputation.** There is no right answer to what a "good" college is. It's more what you want and how it fits with your life goals. Some people only want to attend the Harvards of the world, which means they start preparing at a very young age to keep those grades up. There are many good colleges out there. If you want to know the recommendations for the best colleges and graduate schools, go to *U.S. News and World Report*'s College and Careers Center to look at the rankings.

- **Student Body Profile.** For some people, the atmosphere of a campus and the type of people who are drawn to that school are very important. This may come in the form of the amount of diversity in a student population. Or it may be more about how preppy or laid back the dress and attitudes of students and faculty might be. This is something you can find out more about by visiting the campus and meeting with students who attend.

Coach Wisdom

What if your grade point average is poor? Don't despair. Here are some suggestions: 1) Take some college classes to demonstrate that you can do the work and get good grades; 2) Consider re-taking classes that are important to your current direction to demonstrate that you are now ready to do the work and can get the grades; 3) Go to a 2-year college, get good grades and transfer to a four year college; 4) Look for colleges that will accept lower grade point averages and still have a good reputation.

The next step for you is going to some of the resources available to look up colleges that match your needs and preferences on most of the preceding items. The following is a recommended list of resources:

- ◆ CollegeNet (www.collegenet.com) is a multifaceted site. It has a search component where you can narrow your search for college that meet your criteria. Click on "College Search" and put in your preferences for a list of colleges that meet your criteria. This site also has financial aid and scholarship information and allows you to apply to colleges online.

- ◆ Peterson's (www.petersons.com) is a well-established guide that allows you to search for colleges, graduate schools, and online educational options for adult learners. It's easy to put in your preferences and to access a list of schools and programs that meet your needs. Peterson's also has financial aid information.

- ◆ GoCollege (www.gocollege.com) has a search tool to find colleges that match your preferences, a virtual tour of colleges, scholarship information, answers to common questions that parents and students ask about going to college, a place to ask the expert questions, distance learning information, connections to campus radio stations, and free practice tests for the SATs and ACT.

- ◆ Historically Black Colleges and Universities (HBCUConnect.com) has a complete listing of colleges, scholarship and financial-aid information, tips on taking the ACT and SATs, and more

- ◆ UnivSource (www.univsource.com/womens) has a full listing of women's colleges in the United States.

- ◆ Canadian Colleges (www.aucc.ca) has links to all the colleges, graduate programs in Canada, and financial-aid information. Yahoo! Directory Canada Colleges and Universities also has listings of schools in Canada by regions as well as technical and community college listings.

- On-line Distance Learning, Yahoo (dir.yahoo.com/education/distance_learning) has an excellent listing of accredited schools offering on-line degrees.

After you have identified your colleges or graduate programs of choice, you can ask them to send you a catalogue, financial-aid and scholarship information, and an admissions packet. Or, you can use CollegeNet to apply online.

Educational Alternatives

Besides going to college for a degree, you have many other ways to develop your knowledge and skills. Many occupations require you to have explored these training alternatives to be eligible for employment. Becoming a plumber requires an apprenticeship. Carpenters can gain knowledge in a vocational school or in informal or formal apprenticeships. Many certifications are available (and sometimes required) for fitness instructors and auto mechanics. Nurses and teachers in some states need to acquire a certain number of credits yearly to keep up their licenses and teaching certificates. And this is just a small sample of the wide world of educational requirements! Let's get started with a listing of where you can find the type of education or training your occupation requires.

Certifications and Licensing

The terms "certification" and "licensing" are often interchangeable; however, the Council on Licensure, Enforcement and Regulation (CLEAR) gives the following definitions:

- Licensure is the most restricted form of professional and occupational regulations. It gives a person the right to practice and requires meeting state standards before practicing.

- Certification is a less restrictive classification. When you meet the qualifications for a certification, the state will grant you the right to use the certification title. You can practice your occupation without a certification, but you are not allowed to use the title.

If you haven't already looked up your occupation to find out what type of certifications and licensing are required, start by looking up the occupational description in *Occupational Outlook Handbook* (Jist Publishing, 2004) or go to www. CareerOneStop.org where you can look up your particular occupation.

For more detailed information on licenses and certifications in the United States and Canada, go to the Council on Licensure, Enforcement and Regular (CLEAR) site at www.clearhq.org.

Apprenticeships

An apprenticeship involves learning a skilled trade through on-the-job training, classroom instruction, or both. Apprenticeships are sponsored by employers, employer associations, and unions. You need to be accepted into these programs in order to be an apprentice. Typically, apprenticeships pay you while you are learning. An excellent source of apprenticeship information in the United States and Canada is at www.technicaljobsearch.com. When you are on this site, click on "Job Banks" in the left-hand menu, click on "Entry Jobs," and then click on "Apprenticeships." This page will list all types of information regarding apprenticeships, forums, programs, certifications, and more.

Another source of information is the Apprenticeship Training, Employer and Labor Services site developed by the U.S. Department of Labor (www.doleta.gov/atels_bat). This site gives you up-to-date information on apprenticeship programs.

Vocational and Technical Schools

Vocational and Technical Schools can prepare you for a number of different occupations, from any of the trades, to being a culinary expert, to automotive mechanic, to flight attendant, to realtor, to any form of technology, and so on. Some of the sites recommended by the U.S. Labor Department are:

- Trade-schools.net has trade and vocational schools by occupational area, a search tool to look up schools on your own, and a list of occupations and descriptions for those areas that benefit getting education through trade and vocational schools. It covers selected schools in the United States and Canada.

- VotechDirect.com is a search tool that links to vocational and technical schools by degree or location.

After you identify what the educational and training requirements are for your field of interest, you may decide that a vocational or technical school is for you.

Seminars and Short Courses

If you want to learn about anything, there is always a course on it somewhere in the world! You can start with your local community colleges and universities. They offer a variety of types of courses from continuing education; to professional development (that your employer may send you to); to credited courses, workshops, and seminars. Your local community probably has a leisure services organization that offers short courses in all types of categories from dancing, to art, to calligraphy, to writing.

Then there are courses of all kinds on the web. Short teleclasses of one to four sessions are common. You may run across advertisements for teleclasses on individual websites. Type "teleclass" and check out the list that comes up or type your occupational interest + teleclass and find a wealth of knowledge. Teleclasses are popular for life-coaching topics—go to www.teleclass.com for a listing of free and for-fee teleclasses on this topic. They are also popular in the real estate investing business and many others.

Insider Tips

Newspapers run ads for-free and for-fee workshops and classes on a weekly basis—check these out. You can usually find these in the weekly calendar listing of local events that come out on Thursday or Friday. You can also check the Leisure section of most newspapers for daily listings of events.

For those of you who want to educate yourselves, there is still the option of reading books and listening to tapes. If you want to increase your learning by talking with others, you can always form a study group to discuss and apply the concepts you are learning.

The Least You Need to Know

◆ It's important to understand that in today's world we all need to be life-long learners. Keeping your skills and knowledge up-to-date in whatever occupation you chose is absolutely necessary to remain viable in the workforce.

◆ You need to research occupations you like to understand each one's educational and training requirements. Go to www.careeronestop.org and choose the General Education category on menu to find out requirements.

◆ Finding the right college for your specific situation has been made much easier with the search tools available on several websites.

Part 4

Learn More About Your Dream Career

This section is going to help you to do more research on what the perfect career match really is for you. Some of you will be ready to get more specifics by using the Internet, interviewing people in jobs you want, working with a coach or mentor to conduct your research, or using multi-cultural resources. Did you think you were done just because you have a few careers that match your profile? No way! An important part of this process is researching your two or three top career choices to make sure they are really for you. Some of you will want to try out a job, so we look at ways you can do this in a strategic way. Others might be thinking about running a small business. If that's the case, we have information for you on that as well as stories of people who have multiple streams of business. Last but not least, we send you on your way with a plan of action for securing your perfect career.

Resources on the Internet

In This Chapter

♦ Learn the basics of searching the web

♦ Know where the best places are on the web to find out more about your short list of career options

♦ Check out job sites and employer information on the web

♦ Discover other resources for gathering data about careers

Learning to use the World Wide Web to support your career exploration is critical. The next step in your career journey is to find out as much as you can about the occupations and career areas that you have selected—your short list of careers. Think of this part of your search for your perfect career as a fun project. You need to find out as much as you can, from as many sources as possible, about all aspects of the two or three career areas you have decided to explore. Here is a checklist of what you are looking for:

♦ Nature of the work. What are the responsibilities and tasks that you will be doing on this job?

♦ Working conditions. What is the work environment like? Where do you work? Is it stressful or not?

◆ Employment. Where are you employed? What type of industry employs you?

◆ Training, qualifications, and advancement. What do you need in order to attain a position in this occupation? What are the advancement possibilities?

◆ Job outlook. How fast or slow is this occupation going to grow? Why is it in a growth or decline pattern? What is the longevity of this occupational group?

◆ Salary and earnings. How much money will you make? What is the range? Is it different if you work in different settings?

◆ Related occupations. Are any of the occupations of interest to you that require similar skills?

Insider Tips _____

Use this Career Comparison Chart to take notes on what you find from research you do on the web and then carry it over into Chapter 20 for your in-person research phase.

Use the Career Comparison Chart that follows to take notes on the information you find on each of the categories. Give each career selection an overall rating of either Great Match/Good Match/OK Match/Forget It. When you have completed this phase of your research you can see how each career option matches your requirements for your perfect career.

Career Comparison Chart

Category	Career #1	Career #2	Career #3
Nature of Work	_____	_____	_____
Working Conditions	_____	_____	_____
Employers	_____	_____	_____
Training Required	_____	_____	_____
Job Outlook	_____	_____	_____
Salary	_____	_____	_____
Overall Rating	_____	_____	_____

With this information, we are going to start your research on the World Wide Web. We will use the Internet to do some in-depth understanding of these career areas first. I apologize up-front to those of you who are well-versed in computers—this will be a very simple tutorial!

Five Essential Websites

The following websites are the premier sites for finding out more about any occupation:

- ◆ Occupational Outlook Handbook (www.bls.gov)

- ◆ Career Guide to Industries (www.bls.gov/oco/cg/home.htm)

- ◆ O*Net (www.onetcenter.org)

- ◆ CareerOneStop (www.careeronestop.org)

- ◆ JobProfiles.org (JobProfiles.org)

Insider Tips

A book called *The Occupational Outlook Handbook* (Jist Publishing, 2004), from the U.S. Department of Labor, is updated and printed every two years. It provides one- to two-page descriptions of more than 270 major jobs, covering more than 90 percent of the labor market. *The Career Guide to America's Top Industries* (Jist Publishing, 2004) is also available at your local bookstore.

The first three sites on this list have been developed by the U.S. Department of Labor. The Department of Labor is responsible for the system of job classifications, keeping up with any trends related to jobs and employment and generally providing the government and the public with information about jobs.

If you are the type of person who is great with computers and likes to go right to the site and do your own guided tour—go right ahead. For those of you who need a little more help with collecting information, I will point you in the right direction. All of these sites have a fantastic amount of information, so it can be a little daunting if you don't know what you are looking for. Each site is described in the sections that follow.

Occupational Outlook Handbook (OOH)

The Occupational Outlook Handbook (www.bls.gov) is part of the Department of Labor site and contains all types of information on jobs, economy, social security, employment statistics, and so on. You might want to save this one in your favorites for future reference. Scroll down to "Occupations" and click on *Occupational Outlook Handbook*. This will take you to the site where you can look up all the information on your career comparison chart. Read the instructions to see how you can either browse jobs in an *occupational cluster* or do a search for a particular job title. Looking over the jobs in the occupational clusters, such as Sales, will give you ideas about all the industries and types of sales that are available in this wide world of work.

Career Lingo

Occupational clusters refer to groupings of occupations under one title. For instance, the Sales and related occupations cluster encompasses the following jobs: cashiers, counter and rental clerks, demonstrators, product promoters, and models, insurance sales agents, real estate brokers and sales agents, and so on. It is a classification system that helps job seekers, employers, and job experts to display and communicate information. Changes to the titles and content of these clusters have recently been made by the U.S. Department of Labor and can be found on the O*Net site at www.onetcodeconnector.org.

Career Guide to Industries

The Career Guide to Industries (www.bls.gov/oco/cg/home.htm) provides information on available careers by industry, including the nature of the industry, working conditions, employment, occupations in the industry, training and advancement, earnings and benefits, employment outlook, and lists of organizations that can provide additional information. It discusses 42 industries, accounting for more than three out of every four wage and salary jobs in 2002.

The Career Guide to Industries is a companion to the *Occupational Outlook Handbook*. For some of you, this might be a good way to expand your thinking about careers in industries in which you think you might like to work. You will find the Career Guide to Industries on the Occupational Outlook Handbook website at www.bls.gov/oco/home.htm. On the right side of the screen, under the list of occupational clusters, you will see the "Career Guide to Industries" link. Click on this, and it will take you to the page where there are instructions on how to search this information.

O*Net

O*Net stands for the Occupational Information Network. It is a comprehensive database that provides information about jobs and about worker requirements for these jobs. Information related to the job itself involves the work activities, work and organizational context, outlook, wages, tasks, kinds of tools or equipment used, and so on. Worker requirements involve skills, knowledge, experience, education, abilities, interests, work styles, training, licensing, and so on. This is a very useful website for researching your top career choices to find out more specifics on what is involved in these jobs and what would be required of you. You can access O*Net at www. onetcenter.org.

The following are some specific ways to use O*Net to help you in your career exploration:

◆ **Occupation Descriptions.** From the www.onetcenter.org website, click the "O*Net OnLine" link (the second main tab link from the left). This will take you to the O*Net OnLine welcome page. Look up a particular job by clicking on "Find Occupations" and enter the job title for which you are looking. You need to use a job title that is in their system. If you don't match anything, then look at the job titles in the "Browse By Job Family" drop-down list and pick the one closest to what you are searching for. Click the Go button, and you will get information that can help you fill in your *Career Comparison Chart* (a few sections earlier in this chapter). Click the link to the specific job title. Click on the "Summary" link to get an overview of the job, "Details" to get a full description of all the Career Comparison Chart categories, or "Custom" to create a custom report for a particular job. This report will show you the importance of each of the O*Net categories. This is a very cool way to see all the job requirements and get a good overview of what this work would be like and the context you would be doing it in.

> **Insider Tips**
>
> The Department of Labor's O*Net site is the latest in their contribution to helping workers, employers, and employment specialists to operate within a common model. This content model provides a common understanding of terms, job information, job listings, job search tools, and much more.

◆ **Occupational Listings.** From the www.onetcenter.org website, scroll down to Products on the left hand listing, click on "Occupational Listings." When you get to the Occupational Listings page, click on "Occupational Definitions, Sorted by Code." This is a great way to look at all the different job families and get quick descriptions of jobs under those you think are interesting to you. One of the things you want to do is expand your knowledge of the jobs that are out there in your field of interest.

O*Net has grouped occupations into different categories from the ones that you will find in the *Occupational Outlook Handbook*. There are more categories or job families in O*Net, and they group jobs in a way that is easier to understand. Here are the following job families for O*Net: Management; Business and Financial Operations; Computer and Mathematical Science; Architecture and Engineering; Life, Physical and Social Science; Community and Social Services; Legal; Education, Training and Library; Arts, Design, Entertainment, Sports, Media; Health Care Practitioner and Technical; Health Care Support; Protective Services; Food Preparation and Serving Related; Building and Grounds, Cleaning and Maintenance; Personal Care and Service; Sales and Related; Office and Administrative Support; Farming, Fishing, Forestry; construction and Extraction; Installation, Maintenance, and Repair; Production; Transportation and Material Moving; and Military Specific.

CareerOneStop

CareerOneStop at www.careeronestop.org is a site that is produced by a federal-state partnership and is funded by grants to states. Career One Stop follows the U.S. Department of Labor vision for America's Labor Market Information described in O*Net. This site has a collection of electronic tools that offers unique solutions to perspective job seekers, employers, and the public workforce community. You can also connect to your state CareerOneStop services through this site. The tools are divided into three categories:

◆ America's Career InfoNet is where I want you to concentrate right now. This site is for career seekers who want information on wage and employment trends, occupational requirements, state-by-state labor markets, employer contacts, licensing and certificate requirements, and more. Our recommendations are going to be in this area of the site because it fits with where you are in your dream career search.

◆ America's Job Bank, which is a job market where job seekers can post resumes and look for their dream job and employers can post jobs and search resumes.

◆ America's Service Locator directs you to services in your area that include unemployment benefits, job training, youth programs, seminars, education opportunities, disabled or older worker programs, and more.

We suggest that you go right to the CareerOneStop site map by clicking the "Site Map" link in the top-right corner of the page. When you get to the site map, here are our recommendations for some unique resources on this site:

- Click the "General Outlook" link. You are asked to identify the level of education of the types of jobs you want to look at. Then you are given a list of the fastest growing jobs at this educational level with information about salary category for each job. You can also click on the job titles to get more detailed information by state. The detailed information also has links to career videos, education/licensing/certificates required, and the outlook for this job.

- Click the "Jobs & Employers" link. Follow the links to find out what actual jobs are posted for a particular job category in a particular state. This is a great way to see what is involved in an actual job.

- Click the "Licensed Occupations" and "Certification Finder" links. Both sections are wonderful for scanning the types of jobs that require one of these qualifications for employment. These lists can expand your thinking about what career areas you might want to prepare yourself for. The Licensed Occupations and Certification Finder links are described more in-depth in the section "Get Specific" in Chapter 18.

- Click the "Skills Profiler" link. This is a great tool. It has three pieces to it. The first is the Skills Identifier where you identify your specific skills. The second is the Skills Explorer that matches your skills to occupations that use your skills. This is wonderful for identifying more occupations for you to consider. The third tool is the Skills Gap Analyzer, which analyzes the gap between your skills and the skills needed in a particular job. So, if you have your dream job in mind, you can check out how close you currently are to being prepared for it. This is definitely a top of the list resource for you.

- Click the "Resumé Tutorial" link. Even though this is a step away from the research we are encouraging you to do at this point—having a resumé never hurts. In fact, some of you may be job hunting at the same time as you are engaged in finding your perfect career. So this is a good tutorial that gives you the basics of resumé writing and links to sample resumés and cover letters.

There are lots of other helpful links on this site; spend some time surfing through CareerOneStop and see where it leads you.

JobProfiles.org

JobProfiles.org is a terrific site to read profiles of people in jobs you might want to go into. People share rewards of their jobs, stressful parts of the job, basic skill requirements, job challenges, and advice for the job seeker in that field. This site is highly recommended for you right now—go read profiles of people in the career areas you think you want to go into.

Where the Job Listings Are?

Even though this book on finding your perfect career is not focused on the job hunt itself, we would be remiss if we didn't address the growing number of job sites on the Internet. So, we will give you a list of the top sites for your future reference. Here are our recommendations for job sites with the most traffic:

> **Insider Tips**
>
> Only a small percentage of jobs are actually posted on each of these job sites. The jobs advertised on the job sites are predominantly in professional fields. Never rely solely on applying for jobs on job sites if you want to land a job anytime soon. Networking and who you know are still the number one avenue to getting a job.

- ◆ America's Job Bank, which can be found on the CareerOneStop website: www. CareerOneStop.org.

- ◆ CareerBuilder also includes newspaper classified ads and is one of the fastest growing job sites: www.CareerBuilder.com.

- ◆ JobBank USA has a large span of jobs and the capability to search in a variety of ways, including seeing job postings by companies participating in the site: www.JobBankUSA.com.

- ◆ Monster.com is well established as a job site and has just added a networking component to their job locator and their career planning tools section: www. Monster.com. Monster also has a Canadian job site at www.Monster.ca.

- ◆ The Riley Guide to International Job Opportunities has a comprehensive listing of Canadian job sites at www.rileyguide.com/internat.html.

Besides job sites there are all types of other resources you can tap into through the web, from employer sites, to professional groups and associations, to newsgroups, to networking sites.

Employer Sites

Many employers advertise jobs right on their own website. Besides that, you can learn a great deal about the organization by reading their mission statement, looking at their products and services, and reading about their senior leadership. Usually these sites have a way to contact them, so this could be your first contact with a company.

Professional Groups and Trade Associations

Professional groups and trade associations often post jobs in their fields on their websites. To find out the names of professional groups or associations, go to the Yahoo Directory Business and Economy > Organizations > Professional at http://dir.yahoo.com/Business_and_Economy/Organizations/Professional or go to www.Yahoo.com and do a search.

Specific trade associations and loads of information on the trades can be found at www.constructionweblinks.com. Click on the "Site Map" link and click on the "Trade Organizations" under the left-most Organizations heading.

Newsgroups

Newsgroups are another source of updated job listings. These can be somewhat frustrating because you have to wade through quite a bit of information to come across a newsgroup that may be useful to you. If you are interested in newsgroups, start by going to www.careers.org where you will find a comprehensive list of career newsgroup sites.

Networking Sites

Networking sites are great for meeting (either online or in person) people who are in careers you think you might be interested in or have decided to pursue. You can learn more about the career field from these contacts and sometimes this turns into job opportunities for you.

- ◆ ExecuNet (www.execunet.com) is an executive networking and career management service where you can network with professionals in your field. They also have listings of local meetings at CareerJournal.com calendar of career events.

- ◆ The Five O'Clock Club (www.fiveoclockclub.com) is an organization that you join to work with career counselors to help you find work. They also have a networking function. They have local and virtual meetings that you can find out about at their website.

♦ 40 Plus (www.40plus.org) is the nation's oldest nonprofit organization dedicated to helping currently available managers, executives, and other professionals over 40 years of age find jobs. There are chapters in the United States and Canada.

♦ The Layoff Lounge (www.layofflounge.com) provides jobs, networking, and resources for the unemployed. You can access information about meetings and online services at their website.

Career Lingo

The **six degrees of separation theory** maintains that the person you want to meet is only six people away from you through your network of people you know. For example, you (1) know Tom, Tom (2) knows Joe, Joe (3) knows Sandra, Sandra (4) knows Jane, Jane (5) knows Bob, and Bob (6) is looking to hire someone for the position in which you are interested.

Some of the newest networking sites are LinkedIn (www.linkedin.com), Ryze (www.ryze.com), Friendster (www.friendster.com), Spoke (www.spoke.com), EntreMate (www.entremate.com), and CareerChangeNetwork (www.careerchangenetwork.com). They all base their networking strategies on the *six degrees of separation theory*. The networks run on people introducing you to people they know. It is an interesting concept for researching career areas as well as for job hunting information.

The Least You Need to Know

♦ The World Wide Web is a great resource for learning more about your top choice careers; you just need to know how to search for what you are looking for.

♦ When you get ready to do a job search, or if you would like to see job ads for careers you are interested in, the following job sites are good ones: www.CareerOneStop.org, www.CareerBuilder.com, www.JobBankUSA.com, and www.Monster.com.

♦ Additional sources of information about jobs can be found on employer websites, newsgroups, as well as professional and trade associations.

Chapter 20

Interviewing Job Holders

In This Chapter

♦ Understand the benefits of interviewing people who are already in your dream job

♦ Prepare a list of great questions to ask in your interview

♦ Understand the three stages of the interview process

Where do we start? There are so many benefits to doing interviews with people who are holding jobs that you think you would like to have one day. The absolute best way to find out about your short list of dream jobs is by doing in-person interviews. We know that some of you are holding your heads right about now. You are asking yourself why you need to do this stressful thing. Try to relax; people love to talk about themselves, and that is all you are asking them to do. You are not asking them for a job. You are not asking for much of their time. You are not going to sell yourself to them in this interview. It's all about them having a chance to be a mentor for 30 minutes to an hour. And they get to reflect on their own career. That is something that people pay a coach to listen to, and you are doing it for free. You actually bring a nice benefit to people you are interviewing—think of that!

Interviewing Benefits

You can do interviews with jobholders of your dream job at any point in your life. Suppose that you are deciding what you want your major to be in college. What a perfect way to find out what actual job holders are doing and seeing where they work. You may be thinking about going into a trade, and you want to spend some time with people who are already working. Many people use these interviews as a part of their job hunt. They want to make sure that this is the occupation for them, and they want to see the environments people work in. This is a great project to do when you are in high school or getting any type of advanced training or degree. Write a paper on careers you think you would like to go into and use this interviewing method as your main source of information.

Let's get specific about how *you* benefit from doing these interviews:

- You can ask questions and find out more specifics about an occupation.

- You get to do a reality check on what you have been reading and researching about this occupation so far.

- You can learn how this occupation is done in different work and organizational settings.

- You learn how people prepared for this occupation—the training, education, and experience it took to get to this point in their career.

- You understand that there may be different routes to preparing yourself for this occupation—you have choices.

- You learn what different organizations are looking for in their employees and the needs organizations expect people in this occupation to address.

- You learn what excites and motivates people who are in these careers and see how well that fits your profile.

- You can narrow down your choice to the occupation that really matches your profile.

- You are developing your *network* of people in your career field and can tap into this at a later date.

- You can expand your network by asking the person you are interviewing to refer you to people in other industries, companies, and locations.

- You gain experience in talking about your career goals and interests in a relaxed environment.

♦ You may find out about openings for positions that are coming up or are currently available.

♦ You may be invited to apply for a position or submit a resumé based on the request of the person you are interviewing.

Career Lingo

We all have extensive **networks** of people we know and can access to gather information, provide referrals or support, and so on. It's interesting how we sometimes limit ourselves because we think that our network has to be people who are our best friends and family. Our network is huge—made up of all the people we rely on and know in our lives. Sit down and make a list of everyone you come into contact with over a three-month period. That includes people who provide services for you such as your doctor, lawyer, dentist, auto mechanic, accountant, lawn maintenance person, yoga instructor, and so on. It also includes people you provide services to through your work or life tasks. All of these people have the potential to provide you with excellent information that will help you in your career search. You just need to let people know what you are looking for and see whether there is a way for them to help.

Although you can get some of this information from the sources we talked about throughout this book, believe us, "there is nothing that replaces firsthand information."

Coach Wisdom

Kim was an excellent student. She did all her research on looking into the business careers that interested her. She took notes and had a spreadsheet of what she had found out about every aspect of those careers. She wasn't a person who had much experience in the world. She had lived in one community all her life, except for four years at a state school. So, she didn't have a great deal of knowledge about the world of work. She was working part-time at a retail chain in the Human Resource Department, and she liked how that job was stretching her and introducing her to new sets of skills. She knew she needed to look at other industries and other aspects of the business world. When she did her first information interview, she was amazed at how much she learned. She got to see whole different environments in which people were working. She was able to see some of the projects that she might work on some day and understand more about what she needed to do to prepare. These interviews were really going to help her pick out the right MBA program. She was getting loads of advice on the best schools.

Who Should You Interview?

You want to interview people who are in positions that you think you would like to be in—your dream career positions. You may have two or three careers or occupations you want to know more about. That is great. Just remember that you want to interview at least two people from each career area—and three or four is ideal. Never depend on the opinions and perspectives of one person in a career or occupation. Why?, because you get a more realistic view of your dream career by talking with more people who are in it. And you will find out more about how people prepared themselves for their occupations as well as why they chose to work in a particular industry. You want to see the range of your options in approaching and preparing for your career.

You also want to choose people who are working in industries and organizations in which you think you would enjoy working. If you are not familiar with most organizational settings, try to interview people in at least three settings to see which ones appeal to you the most. If you already know the type of organization you want to be in, then do all your interviews in those organizations. Even within industries, there are differences across them due to size, culture, climate, customer base, and so on.

Finding People to Interview

This is often what stops people from doing these interviews. They just don't know how to go about locating people. Yes, it takes a little work. But, it's worth it—right! Most people love to help others, so put on your optimistic hat and get ready to find your people to interview. Let's look at some great ways to generate people to interview.

Make a List of Everyone You Know

The six degrees of separation theory is really relevant here. Some people in your network will know just the right people with whom you should be in touch. You don't know everything about people in your network. You have no idea about what their brain and memory and experience will tap into when you ask for assistance in this. Be a believer, and it will happen. Here are some ideas for people who need to be on your list: current and former friends, family, current and former colleagues, previous bosses, neighbors, any professional people in your life such as doctors or lawyers or dentists.

After you have this list of people you know, tell them what you need. Send out e-mails, make calls and reconnect, announce your request at family functions and dinners, take a few colleagues to lunch and brainstorm other connections.

Everyone I know List

Write the names of the people you know in this space. Next to their names, indicate how you know them (family, friend from high school, friend from college, business acquaintance, friend's mother/brother/father/sister, and so on). After you have developed this list, go back and fill in contact information. Keep adding to this list as you think of new contacts or are given contacts from people on your list.

Name	How I Know Them	Contact Information
_____	_____	_____
_____	_____	_____
_____	_____	_____
_____	_____	_____

Keep this on-going list on your Career Profile Map in Appendix A.

Career or Alumni Office at Your College

Many campuses have an alumni database that they can tap into and give you the names and contact information for people in jobs you want to interview. Other schools have websites you can use to contact alumni. Go to your school's website first and see whether they have a way for you to be in touch with other alumni. Then give your alumni office or career center a call and see what they can do for you. If this doesn't work, contact your buddies from college and start asking them who they know.

Professional and Community Organizations

Your local Chamber of Commerce is fantastic. They know all the businesses in your community and know who runs them, so getting specific information as a first step is easy. And you can call any Chamber of Commerce and get the same good service. Try professional organizations for the career or trade within which your dream career falls. Contact women's organizations or special interest group associations on the web or in your community. Also look up information on the web for organizations in your career field.

Professional or Trade Association Meetings

These are meetings where people from a certain career focus come together. An example of this is people who are trainers in organizations belong to ASTD, American Society for Training and Development. There are local chapters across the country. If one of them is within driving distance for you, go and meet the people and set up some interviews.

Check Local Papers for Articles on People Being Promoted

Every paper usually has a feature article on people in different careers each week, so this is a possible source for you. And there are often feature articles on local professional and trades people. Keep your eyes open. This can be something you make it a point to do each day as you read the paper. Gather three names each week for three weeks.

Magazines and Journals

Magazines and journals are another source of finding people who are in careers you want to know more about. If you belong to a library, you can use their online service to look up recent articles on magazines and journals that relate to your career area. Or just pay attention to the types of magazines you like to read to see if they have information on people in your preferred career areas. You can find popular magazines and journals on almost all career topics from politics, to business, to health, to fitness, to sports, to science, and so on. Here are some magazines that feature people who run large and small businesses:

◆ *Fortune* **Magazine** does feature articles on CEO's and Senior Managers.

◆ *Fast Company* does feature articles on a whole range on business leaders in up and coming companies to large established companies.

◆ *Inc.Com* is a magazine for small business owners with loads of articles on owners as well as insider tips.

Three Stages of Interviewing

The three stages to follow in making sure you have a successful interview are

♦ Good Preparation

♦ The Interview

♦ Follow-up Steps

Each one will be described, and the steps outlined will be in the sections that follow.

Good Preparation

Good preparation includes making the appointment, having knowledge about the interviewee's organization, having done your homework on gathering information on your career area and dream occupation, and getting your questions ready for the interview.

Get ready to make an appointment ...

If you're networking and data gathering has paid off, you have the name and phone number for the person you will interview. If you don't have a phone number, look up the organization on the Internet yellow pages or Verizon super pages at www. superpages.com. When you don't have the name of a person, look up the organization you want to go to on the web. Look at the page on their directory that tells you about the people who are leading the organization. This will give you familiarity with the titles they use. You will also generally find a phone number for the organization, or you can use the super pages.

When you call the organization, you can tell the operator that you want to reach the manager of the specific department where your ideal occupation would be located. Or you can ask to be put through to the Human Resource Department where you can ask for the name and number of the manager in the department you are interested in. You will undoubtedly be asked what you are calling in regard to. Respond by saying that you are researching your career area, and want to set up a 20 to 30 minute interview with (name). If you can stop into the organization to set up your interview, that is even better.

After you get through to the right office, you will either speak to another administrative assistant, or you will get a voice mail. Have your "make an appointment" script ready. Introduce yourself, tell them that you want to make a 20- or 30-minute appointment to interview the manager about their career. Make it clear that you are not looking for a job—just information. Tell the person your available times for this meeting—give a few options. A good idea is to offer to schedule an appointment during their break time or lunch time with an offer to buy them a cup of coffee or quick lunch for their time and effort.

Coach Wisdom

What happens when you get turned down? This does happen once in a while. Don't take the initial "No" for their final answer. Tell them that you understand that the person is very busy. Ask whether there are times during the week that are better for the person. Assure them you will not take up a great deal of time and that the person will be contributing to helping you to make good decisions about your career choice. See if the person is open to e-mailing responses to your questions. If the answer continues to be no, then ask if there is someone else in the organization that you can speak with who is in a similar position. Whatever happens, remain positive and make your next call. Most people are very receptive to helping others by talking about their own career experiences. The only difficulty is usually taking time to do this.

You can write a note to arrange an interview, but it is much faster to make the call. You will have to do it as a follow-up to the letter anyway. And sometimes, the initial contact is more enticing and can get you better results. Because information interviews have become so popular in recent years, some companies and individuals are not as receptive. When this occurs, you might ask for a referral or whether they have other ways of introducing people to careers in their organizations. Most of the time people are very willing to help as much as they can.

Okay, the hard part is now over—you have the appointment ...

Prepare for the appointment by going on the company website and reading about their products and services and check out the news releases, mission, and values. You have already done some research on this career area and specific occupation using the sources in Chapter 19. Review this information and identify some areas that you want more information about in this interview.

By knowing about the field and the organization, you are putting your best foot foreword to the person you are interviewing. You have done your homework, and they will be appreciative and impressed with this. And you will be able to converse more easily with this knowledge.

Now you need to gather all your questions together for the interview ...

Remember you only have about 30 minutes, so select the questions that are most important for you to have answered. You may already have quite a bit of information from your previous research, so identify those areas on which you want more in-depth information. Also you definitely want to know what their advice is on preparing yourself for this occupation. And you want to know what they like the most and least about the job.

Here are a whole bunch of questions to choose from that were developed by The Career Center at Florida State University at www.career.fsu.edu. The following interview questions are *reproduced with permission of The Florida State University Career Center.* These are great questions and will give you a great picture of what this job and industry is all about as well as get some great advice. Remember to choose the questions that you believe are most pertinent to information you need or want:

1. (Background) Tell me how you got started in this field. What was your education? What educational background or related experience might be helpful in entering this field?

2. (Work Environment) What are the daily duties of the job? What are the working conditions? What skills/abilities are utilized in this work?

3. (Problems) What are the toughest problems you deal with? What problems does the organization as a whole have? What is being done to solve these problems?

4. (Lifestyle) What obligation does your work put on you outside the work week? How much flexibility do you have in terms of dress, work hours, and vacations?

5. (Rewards/Dislikes) What do you find most rewarding about this work? What do you like least about this work?

6. (Salary) What salary level would a new person start with? What are the fringe benefits? What are other forms of compensation (bonuses, commissions, securities)?

7. (Potential) Where do you see yourself going in a few years? What are your long-term goals?

8. (Promotional) Is turnover high? How does one move from position to position? Do people normally move to another company/division/agency? What is your policy about promotions from within? What happened to the person(s) who last held this position? How many have held this job in the last five years? How are employees evaluated?

9. (The Industry) What trends do you see for this industry in the next three to five years? What kind of future do you see for this organization? How much of your business is tied to (the economy, government spending, weather, supplies, and so on)?

10. (Advice) How well-suited is my background for this field? When the time comes, how would I go about finding a job in this field? What experience, paid or volunteer, would you recommend? What suggestions do you have to help make my resumé more effective?

11. (Demand) What types of employers hire people in this line of work? Where are they located? What other career areas do you feel are related to your work?

12. (Hiring Decision) What are the most important factors used to hire people in this work (education, past experience, personality, special skills)? Who makes the hiring decisions for your department? Who supervises the boss? When I am ready to apply for a job, who should I contact?

13. (Job Market) How do people find out about your jobs? Are they advertised in the newspaper (which ones?) by word-of-mouth (who spreads the word?) by the personnel office?

14. (Referral to Other Information Opportunities) Can you name a relevant trade journal or magazine you would recommend I review? What professional organizations might have information about this career area?

15. (Referral to Others) Based on our conversation today, what other types of people do you believe I should talk to? Can you name a few of these people? May I have permission to use your name when I contact them?

16. Do you have any other advice for me?

17. Other questions you want to ask:

_____

_____

Remember to select the questions that are most applicable to your situation. Always start with a question that gets the person you are interviewing talking and engaged. So, keep question #1! Then you might want to prioritize the rest of the questions based on what you really want to know and don't forget to add your own specific questions. In the next section, we will walk you through setting up and holding the interview.

The Interview

The actual interview requires doing the basics of presenting yourself well. Be on time by getting your directions off the website or map quest, calling the organization to ask where you can park and the exact location of the office you are visiting, and leaving a little extra time for getting lost! Dress appropriately. Depending on the occupation you are interviewing in, the dress code will vary. No matter what, it's important that you dress professionally—neat, clean, on the conservative versus the flashy side, moderate amount of make-up or hair gel, shoes you can walk in and are for work versus clubbing. You can always call the Human Resource Department and ask what the dress code is. If you are interviewing someone in the trades, you don't have to wear a suit, but it's okay to be more on the dressed up side than the person might be whom you are interviewing. Remember, you are the one making an impression.

Relax and shake the person's hand, introduce yourself again, tell them how much you appreciate their time. Let them know the purpose of the meetings and that you have a list of questions you want to ask them. And you want them to feel free to add anything they think would help you understand the occupation and career field. Tell them you are going to take some notes to help you capture the information that will be shared, unless they would prefer you not to do this. If you don't want to take notes or the person prefers you don't, then you can sit down right after the interview and write down what you remember (that will be plenty).

Stick to the time allotted for the interview, unless the person insists on taking more time, which often happens. At the end of your time with them, ask them whether they can recommend anyone else for you to speak with. These may be colleagues they have in different industries or organizations or even someone else in this organization that they think would be a good person for you to interview. Thank them again for their time.

Follow-Up Steps

First write a personal note of thanks for the interview. Indicate the highlights of what you are taking away for yourself from this interview—how it has helped you. You might include your resumé for the person to keep on file if that feels appropriate at this time. He/she may have asked you for one during the interview.

Next reflect on the information that you have received and how it is influencing your decision-making process about schools, majors, occupations, and organizations you want to work in, and so on. If you are deciding that another aspect of this career is beginning to seem more interesting, be sure you do interviews in that area going forward.

Make more appointments for interviews using the list of people you gained from this interviewee. The closer you do this to the time you saw the person, the more likely it is that you will do it! Be proactive—you are on a roll.

The Least You Need to Know

- ◆ The main benefits of talking with people who are in jobs you think you want to do are that you learn firsthand what people do on these jobs, how they prepared for them, what different work environments are like, and what advice they can give you to achieve your career goals.

- ◆ In preparing for an information interview, you want to tap into your network to get names of people to interview, know what to say when setting up your appointment, do your research on the occupational field and organization before you go to the interview, and prepare your questions.

- ◆ During the interview, you want to share the purpose of the interview, ask specific questions, engage in relaxed dialogue, thank the person for their time and investment in you, and get referrals for more interviews.

- ◆ After the interview, follow-up with a thank-you note, making appointments with referrals and summarizing your learning and applications for your decision-making about career directions.

Chapter 21

Coaches and Mentors

In This Chapter

♦ Learn the difference between a mentor and a coach

♦ Know where to find a mentor or a coach

♦ What to expect when working with a mentor or a coach

It's nice to know that you can reach out and find support fairly easily these days. All along in this book, we have talked about being able to sustain your motivation for the career discovery process as well as pursuing your career goals. There are two types of support that will help you at different stages of your career journey. A coach is someone who can help you through the career discovery process, preparing for your job or school search, and help you to reach your life or job-related goals. A mentor is someone who you can look to for guidance in growing and learning professionally in your chosen career field. A mentor can be your boss, another person in the organization you work in, or someone you find on your own. This person knows the ropes, has been in your profession or career field, and is there to guide you as you enter each new phase of your career.

Both mentoring and coaching used to be almost exclusively part of the succession planning or training programs in organizations. Over the past several years there has been an explosion of coaching organizations, coaching schools, coaching networks, and coaches of every kind. Today coaching is available to everyone, not just those in organizations. And mentoring is not far behind with the opportunities online to find a mentor that matches your needs.

What Is Coaching?

Just as mentors used to be found mostly in formal organizational settings, so did coaches. Coaching was generally done by organizational development consultants who came in to work with management staff in organizations. Over the past several years, many managers have taken training in how they can coach their own employees using the skills of active listening, feedback, and development planning. And, some organizations have made coaching available to all employees. The difference between mentoring and coaching is closely aligned, and coaches often do mentor or find mentors for people they coach. Mentors need to have the experience and knowledge base in a particular profession or occupation in order to guide a new entrant into a field or position. A coach's skill sets focus more on the process of helping you to reach your goals. Many training programs for coaches have emerged over the past several years. These programs focus on people skills and approaches to helping people to reach their goals.

Coaching is usually defined as the art of partnering with another person to help them to reach their goals, to expand their horizons, and to inspire them to achieve the future they desire. Coaching is a proactive way to approach moving toward your goals and keeping the focus on the future versus the past. It is unlike therapy in which a person often wants to understand their past in order to understand their present behavior and feelings. For those of you who still need support, encouragement, or motivation to continue your career discovery and search process, a good coach is just what you need.

Most coaches have a specialty area that they focus on because they do have some knowledge and expertise about that topic. Some examples of specialty areas are career coaches, small business coaches, fitness coaches, healthy eating coaches, weight loss coaches, leadership development coaches, divorce coaches, financial planning coaches, retirement coaches, and so on. Almost any life/work topic that you can think of can be a coaching specialty. Many coaches today call themselves life coaches, and they offer coaching in the whole range of life issues that, as human beings, we may want to set some goals around.

Coach Wisdom

Ange DiBenedetto is a life coach in Amherst, MA. She specializes in working with people who are starting up their own small businesses and need to build their confidence in themselves as well as the knowledge about how to proceed. The name of her specialty area is, "The Courage to Succeed." Most life coaches have specialty areas that appeal directly to the needs of a particular client population.

How to Find and Select a Coach

In order to find the right coach for you, you should complete three steps:

♦ Setting Your Goals

♦ Determining a Good Match

♦ Locating Your Coach

Setting Your Goals

You need to do a little preparation yourself before you go out and look for a coach. First of all, think about the goal that you want to achieve. Do you want to identify your perfect career? Do you want to create a business plan for your small business? Do you want to find a job that matches your Career Profile Map (in Appendix A)? By deciding what your goal is, you are already narrowing down the specialty areas that you want your coach to have. For our purposes in this book, you may be looking for a career coach or a small business coach. However, some of you may love the idea of working with a life coach to achieve some of your lifestyle goals such as health and fitness, building a support system, or having more fun in life.

Determining a Good Match

The next part of your preparation is thinking about the kind of coaching relationship that is going to work for you. Remember, a coach will partner with you to help you to reach your goals. So, what kind of a partner are you looking for? Do you want someone who will hold you accountable for taking action toward your goal on a weekly basis? Do you want someone who challenges you to step out of your comfort zone and take some risks? Do you want someone who is very understanding and accepting of who you are right now? At different points in our lives, we are looking for different interventions to help us achieve our goals. Here is a short list of things to consider in your coach:

- Knowledge and background in your field of interest

- Good problem solver

- Can connect me with local networks in your field of interest

- Can provide resources to further your knowledge about you career area

- Affirms you

- Motivates you

- Compatible energy level with you

- Will challenge you to take risks

- Holds you accountable

- Can see you in person

- Has a good phone presence (if sessions are over the phone)

Now that you have thought through the kind of person you believe would make the best mentor for you, you can begin to turn your attention to finding this person.

Locating Your Coach

Now you are ready to locate your coach. An important aspect of this search is to find someone that both meets your list of criteria for a good match and has the type of credentials that make you comfortable. Many coaches have training through accredited coaching programs and through the International Coach Federation. And many coaches have degrees in counseling and related fields that have prepared them to work effectively with people in a helping relationship. Still other coaches are experts in their specialty areas and do not have any formal training as a coach. All of these options can be fine, depending on what you are looking for in your situation or your preference for the level of qualification in your coach.

If you are looking for a career coach, first look in the telephone directory under Career and Vocational Counseling. There is usually a short list of local providers. Another place for local providers is in your local newspapers and newsmagazines. Call each one of the telephone listings or ads that appeal to you and interview them. Tell them your goals and what you are looking for in a coach. Ask them about their services, their fees, and whether they have a website or a bio to which they can refer you. Often their websites will have testimonials from former clients. You can also ask them if they have clients who are comfortable and willing to act as a reference. This takes into consideration the fact that some clients would prefer to maintain a confidential relationship with their coach or counselor.

So many people today are coached over the phone. If you don't mind this, then you can expand your selection. Here are some sites you can go to for referrals and listings of coaches:

- International Coach Federation at www.internationalcoachfederation.com where they have a referral service to link you with a coach that matches your needs and has been credentialed by this coaching organization.

- Coachville at www.coachville.com where you can find a listing of all types of coaches to meet your needs. You can also sign up for teleclasses through Coachville where you can receive group coaching. Coachville offers a free membership to anyone interested in the coaching field and has all types of resources for coaches.

- Peer Resources Network (PRN) at www.info@peer.ca is a terrific resource, and they have a listing of highly experienced business and personal coaches that meet ethical practice and service conditions.

Sample Coaching Exercise

The following is a sample coaching exercise developed for a local professional business women's organization. This can help you to see one way that a coach can help you to establish your goals.

Keep Your Eye on the Prize—Reach Your Goals

Your Business Mission. Rate your current satisfaction with your business results from 1 to 7, with 1 being very dissatisfied and 7 being very satisfied:

___ Profits

___ Sales

___ Markets

____ Customer Satisfaction/Retention

____ Supplier Costs/Relationships

____ Employee Productivity

Generate a list of goals for the next 60 days that will result in increasing your satisfaction with your results and further achieve your mission:

_____   _____

_____   _____

_____   _____

_____   _____

Choose two goals from the previous list that you believe have the most leverage for creating greater results. Write them here:

Goal #1: _____

Goal #2: _____

As you look at both of these goals, what "next steps" need to be taken to achieve these goals? Write these next steps here. List everything you can think of—these do not need to be in order:

Goal # 1 Next Steps: _____

_____

_____

_____

Goal # 2 Next Steps: _____

_____

_____

_____

What distractions are keeping you from focusing on your goals? What do you find yourself doing during the day that takes away from your primary business goals? Write these down here:

Goal # 1 Distractions: _____

_____

_____

_____

Goal # 2 Distractions: _____

_____

_____

_____

Can any of these distractions be delegated, outsourced, *bartered* for services, or simply eliminated? If so, circle those distractions now. Put the name of the person in your network (next to the circled distractions) that you will ask to champion your distractions!

Career Lingo

Barter means that you are exchanging one good or service for another. No money changes hands; just the goods or services are exchanged. This is a great way for small business owners to get services that they need without paying their precious money for them. An example of this would be from Rene, a life coach, who exchanged a coaching session to help Karen get more focused on her business goals and get moving for a lovely piece of jewelry that Karen made.

Take a few minutes to think about people in your network who would be able to do the following:

♦ Take your distractions and add them to their bottom line profit.

♦ Receive your services in kind.

♦ Be a resource to you to problem solve off-loading these distractions.

Write down the names of people in your network that you will contact in the next week that might be able to assist you:

_____   _____

What Is Mentoring?

Mentoring is when a more experienced and seasoned person agrees to aid a less experienced person in developing professionally in a particular field. This relationship can take place between a senior in college majoring in engineering and a first-year student who is just starting in that major. It can be a person just starting a coaching business being mentored by a well-established coach. Mentoring can take place in any profession and in any industry.

Stop-Look-Listen

You may contact Rene Carew with any questions or for a free 20-minute coaching session at Rene@AuthenticLife.com or by calling 413-253-5653. Feel free to visit online at www. AuthenticLife.com.

Often, we think of mentoring as being your own personal ongoing orientation to a situation. Usually, if someone was new to a company, they would be given a mentor who would show them the ropes. This would include understanding the company's culture and normative behaviors and expectations, how they do things there, what's rewarded and what's not, who the players are, what types of activities or projects gain the most recognition, and so on. For someone looking for a mentor in their perfect career area, you might want to know some of the same things and more. For instance, what are the best companies to work for, what interviewers will be looking for, what a good career path might be, how to handle yourself in different situations, how to market your business, what classes to take to get the best education, and so on. Here are some benefits to having a mentor.

♦ Learn from the experience of your mentor.

♦ Develop goals for your career or professional pursuit.

♦ Develop your skills.

♦ Build your confidence.

♦ Learn about your strengths and development areas.

♦ Problem solve situations.

♦ Get oriented to your new situation.

How to Find a Mentor

Although it's a great idea to have your own personal guide for learning all about your perfect career, where the heck do you go to find these people? Here are several ways you can find a mentor:

◆ Call your local Chamber of Commerce and ask whether they have created such a service. If they have not, tell them what you are looking for and see whether they can give you the names of a couple of people in the area whom they think would be open to being a mentor and would be good at it.

◆ Get involved in your local or professional organizations. Run for office or get on the steering committee. This is a great way to be mentored by those who have experience in your occupation.

Coach Wisdom

Doreen became a member of The Women's Business Alliance of the Pioneer Valley. She was intrigued with the invitation on the part of the current leadership to join the steering committee. Member after member told about their experience of being mentored early in their careers by others on the steering committee and how this experience had made all the difference in making their businesses successful.

◆ Contact your professional or trade associations and find out whether they have a mentoring program—many of them do.

◆ Introduce yourself to speakers at events you attend that are related to your career area. Examples might be a lecture at a college, a speaker at a luncheon for a professional or trade association, or a speaker at a conference you attended. Let them know you are looking for a mentor and ask whether they would have time to sit down to explore this idea with you.

◆ If you are enrolled in a university or college, go to your career office or ask your advisor whether they have a mentoring program set up with advanced students, faculty, staff, or community members.

◆ Read autobiographies and biographies of people who have been in your dream career. Mentors act as guides; they give you the lay of the land. So reading books about the lives of people who have enjoyed occupations that you are interested in, become mentors through their written words and experiences.

♦ Let your network of friends, family, and colleagues know you are looking for a mentor. Tell them exactly what you are looking for, and you will probably have some contacts to call in a couple of days.

♦ If you have retirement communities in your area, there will be many people there who would love to mentor you and share what they know from all their years of experience. Most retirement communities have a central club house or management office where you can inquire and tell them about your search for a mentor.

♦ Contact your college's alumni office, and they will be able to refer you to graduates who are in your field of interest. Many of them have more formal mentoring programs set up.

♦ Formalize the mentoring relationship with your graduate advisor or a valued professor in your program.

♦ Use online mentoring sites to find a mentor:

   ♦ Mentors Peer Resources at www.mentors.ca has an up-to-date listing of mentor services available on the internet as well as the ability to ask virtual experts questions.

   ♦ Advance Mentoring is a site that you can join to be matched up with a mentor based on your requirements for location, career area, and so on. Go to www. advancementoring.com

Mentor Qualifications

Not everyone can be a good mentor. Some people have loads of experience and information, but they don't have the communication skills or the patience to impart their knowledge to others. You are looking for someone who is willing to take the time and enjoys being able to help someone else to grow and learn in their chosen career field. Here are some basic characteristics that you want in a mentor:

♦ Experienced and knowledgeable. Look for a person who has been in your field for at least five years longer than you have. You want someone who has made their mistakes and learned from them, who knows how to guide you around the land minds in your field. You also want someone who is good at what they do and can teach you how to do the same.

◆ Walks the talk. Look for a person who will be a role model. You want to be able to learn from their example as well as their words.

◆ Committed to working with you. Look for someone who is willing to spend time with you. This means a person who will initiate meetings, follow-through on promises made, take the time to network you with other contacts, and take the mentoring role seriously.

◆ Gives feedback. Look for someone who will be honest and open with you about what they see as your strengths and development areas. Someone who is willing to give you advice on how to correct behaviors or develop skills that you need to be effective.

◆ Cheers you on. Look for a person with whom you can be real. You want to work with someone who not only challenges you to learn but also sees you through the low points and lets you know that they have been there, too!

◆ Adapts their style to your needs. Look for a person who is open to learning more about who you are, what you need, and how you need it. Being able to have a direct conversation with your mentor about both of your needs is critical. You might even consider having a contract that takes into consideration both parties: three-month goals, times to meet, how you communicate, how often you communicate, how you learn best, type of support and learning you are looking for, what the mentor has to give, and so on.

◆ Compatible. Look for a person you believe you can work with on an ongoing basis. This is a learning experience and if you don't feel at all comfortable with someone, it probably won't work. This is a more complex area because you may want to work with someone who is very different from you as part of your learning. This is fine—just make sure that you have basic respect and ability to communicate. Others may want to find someone more like themselves, trading the comfort of sharing and being open for being challenged. Think about what you are looking for right now in your mentor relationship.

Being a Good Mentee

There are a few important points to remember in being a good mentee. If you want to be able to keep your mentor, follow these eight simple rules:

1. Be respectful at all times.

2. Honor time and availability boundaries.

3. Actively listen to guidance and advice.

4. Accept responsibility for your actions.

5. Learn from your successes and failures.

6. Be willing to try new things.

7. Accept and understand the feedback you receive.

8. Be a proactive partner in growing in your profession.

Mentors are usually very special people. They are willing to give of their time, energy, and caring for new entrants into a career field. The most successful mentor-mentee relationships are those that are explicit. You both agree to a mentoring relationship, and you develop goals and a plan of action for carrying out the mentoring goals. Mentors are not any particular age. It's about a more experienced person helping a less experienced person.

The Least You Need to Know

♦ For those of you who want more support and one-on-one conversations about your career goals and your career field, consider getting a coach or finding a mentor.

♦ Coaches can partner with you to help you to reach your life or work goals. Prepare for getting a coach by deciding on your goal and what you are looking for in a coach. Then, go to your local telephone directory, newspapers, or Internet sites suggested in this chapter to find the right match for you.

♦ Mentors have knowledge and experience in your career field and guide you in your professional development and orientation to that field. Mentors are all around you, from your professors and advisors in school, to your bosses, to retired people in your community who were in your career field.

Chapter 22

Diversity and Multicultural Resources

In This Chapter

♦ Locate multicultural educational resources

♦ Discover the best places to work

♦ Consider the importance of the work environment in choosing an organization for which to work

♦ Support a diverse and multicultural workforce

Do you sometimes wish that you had more resources at your fingertips that would speak directly to your needs? Perhaps you are wondering what the best companies are to work for if you are a person of color, a woman, gay or lesbian, disabled, or you are over 50. This chapter will provide some basic resources and point you to even more resources that are available to you. You will also have the opportunity to consider your career in the context of your diversity.

Career Lingo

Multicultural promotes the value of different cultures coexisting within a single society. It is a vision of cultural diversity that is deliberately fostered and protected. Multiculturalism is also known as diversity or pluralism, which means that differences among people and groups are recognized, respected, and valued.

Our global society is bringing more and more diversity to our organizations. Many of you will find yourself working in other countries as well as working alongside new immigrants to your home country. Our new working reality in a global society is pointing more and more to the important need to understand one another's cultures. Many organizations have already begun to provide training in this area for both those employees going to work in other countries as well as for learning about the different cultures of one's co-workers. For those who have taken advantage of these experiences, there is nothing more creative or exciting than working in a *multicultural* work team. When the bridges are built to understanding one another's cultural practices, clearer communication emerges.

Finding the Right College and Financial Aid

Deciding which college to attend has been made a little easier with websites that let you put in your criteria for what you are looking for in a college education and experience. You may want to pay particular attention to the types of cultural, extracurricular, and social and service clubs available on a campus. If you are seeking a college or university environment that attracts a more diverse population, then look at the location of the school, the types of activities offered, and the demographics of a school. Here are some ideas and resources to help you in narrowing down your choice:

- ◆ Go to Peterson's Guide at www.petersons.com and put in all your criteria for what you want in a college.

- ◆ Call the alumni office and ask to talk with recent graduates from your diverse community.

- ◆ Visit the campus and talk with current students; see for yourself how diverse the student population is and the types of services provided.

- ◆ Get a list of student organizations, fraternities, sororities, social clubs, sports teams, cultural events, and so on from the student activities office on each campus.

◆ Yahoo Education has a listing of colleges that specialize in education for particular cultures or groups. To access information, go to www.yahoo.com/education and click on "By Cultures or Group" under the college section. Yahoo's education section has many resources for college information.

Peterson's and Yahoo also have information on financial aid. In addition to these websites, you can find scholarship and financial aid information on the following websites:

◆ www.CollegeData.com—has a free scholarship finder search as well as a college match system.

◆ www.FinAid.org—has a student profile–based, financial-aid resource.

◆ www.FAFSA.ed.gov—is a free application for federal student aid.

◆ www.AdultStudentGrants.com—has scholarship information for going back to school students.

◆ www.StudentAid.ed.gov—has federal student-aid information.

◆ www.TheOldSchool.org—offers specialized search services for minorities and women.

◆ www.NextStudent.com—has a scholarship search that matches your profile.

◆ www.NAGPS.org—is the National Association of Graduate-Professional Students and has many resources on loan consolidation, grant writing, and current issues for graduate students.

◆ www.FDNCenter.org—has specific grant-funding information for people with disabilities and also user aids to facilitate doing the search.

◆ www.UNCF.org—is the United Negro College Fund and has access to more than 7000 scholarships.

◆ www.HispanicFund.org—has merit and need-based scholarships.

◆ www.CollegeFund.org—is the site for the American Indian College Fund that awards more than 6000 scholarships.

You can also use the major search engines to input "scholarship AND your culture" to do a comprehensive search.

Finding Diversity and Multicultural Career Services

College and university student services are generally terrific places to locate people to help you to assess your career interests or work through the process with you. Many academic departments that correspond to your background often have career services specifically for a particular major. You can also try your career center, alumni office, or student services department to see whether they specialize in working with diverse populations—for example, gay, lesbian, bisexual and transsexual, African American, women, Hispanic, Asian, or the disabled.

Many websites have job search and related services. A few of these sites also have career assessment services:

- www.Diversity.com—has a career center that offers a free career evaluation and ongoing career assessment and counselor services for a fee.

Insider Tips

If you belonged to a fraternity, sorority, or service organization with a national base, give them a call and ask whether they have recommendations for career services.

- www.Monster.com—has a Diversity and Inclusion section that is in partnership with the NAACP and has links to a variety of diversity sites.

- www.quintcareers.com—is the Quintessential Careers website that has a full range of diversity resources to choose from—this is an excellent resource.

Finding the Best Places to Work

Finding the right organization to work for is key to being successful and happy in your work life. It is definitely worth your time to look into the make-up of companies you think you might want to work in before you take the leap of employment. Fortunately, for the larger organizations, you can access information on the best places to work:

- *Fortune* magazine puts out a yearly list of the 50 best companies for minorities including Asians, Hispanics, Native Americans, and Blacks.

- *Working Mother* magazine puts out a yearly list of the 100 best companies for women.

- *Latina Style* magazine lists the top 50 companies for Latinas and Hispanic working women.

- *AARP* magazine publishes a list of best companies for workers over 50.

- *Hispanic Business* magazine has a listing of the 500 best companies for Hispanics.

- www.HireDiversity.com has an updated listing of the most gay-friendly companies with feedback comments from people who are working or have worked in these companies.

- www.JobAccess.org powered by CareerBuilder.com provides a place where people with disabilities can seek employment, confident that they will be evaluated solely on their skills and experience.

- www.HireDiversity.com has information for all cultural groups—excellent resource.

- www.rileyguide.com/diversity has a great list of sites for all the cultural categories including indigenous and native peoples.

- www.careers.org has diversity information for cultural groups.

Any company that you work for, no matter how small or large, needs to be committed to equal opportunity for all employees. Although the government has laws that enforce this concept, look for organizations that actively recruit, train, and promote a multicultural workforce. Ask whether the organization has a values statement that represents core behaviors. Often this values statement will give you some insights into what types of behaviors are the norm in this organization. You can ask about the culture of the organization in terms of whether people work in teams, are collaborative or competitive, as well as how easy or difficult is it for new people to advance and be accepted. Find out as much as you can about how multicultural the leadership is within the organization. Ask whether they have a mentoring or coaching program within the organization.

Another terrific resource for researching the best jobs and work places is through the many organizations that have been set up as networks or resources for your particular cultural identification. There are far too many to list here, so we will give you some places to start. Remember you can do your own searches using words like networking, professional organizations AND diversity, or women, or Asians, and so on. Here are some websites to get you started:

- www.diversityworld.com is continually on the lookout for online resources that promote workforce inclusion of all people. They have affiliation and networking groups as well as all kinds of career information and support.

- www.quintcareers.com/diversity has lists of associations and networking links for all the cultural groups as well as other career resources for each group.

- www.hodesrecruitmentdirectory.com is the Bernard Hodes Group website. The Bernard Hodes Group specializes in helping organizations to become more multicultural. Even though the site is set up for organizations, it also has great resources for job seekers. Resources include best places to work, diversity newspapers and publications, and selected association lists.

Finding Help with Small Businesses

If you are thinking about running your own business, there are benefits available for minority and women-owned businesses. Some examples of the support that you can receive from the *Small Business Administration (SBA)* are the following programs:

- The SBA has an "On-line Women's Business Center" (www.onlinewbc.gov) to help businesses get started and offers ongoing support. You can find information about loans and financing, training, mentor roundtables, IRS tax information, and government contracts.

- An integral component of the Entrepreneurial Development network of counseling and training services of the SBA has established The Office of Native American Affairs (www.sba.gov/naa). This program assures that American Indians, Native Alaskans, and Native Hawaiians have full access to necessary business development and expansion tools available through this agency.

- The SBA (www.sba.gov/news) has recently joined forces with the United States Hispanic Chamber of Commerce to support Hispanic Small Businesses to succeed through training, education, and access to resources. For news release, go to www.sba.gov/news for the September 16, 2004, news article.

Career Lingo

The **Small Business Administration (SBA)** is a government agency established to strengthen the economy by aiding, counseling, assisting, and protecting the interests of small businesses. Small businesses can receive all kinds of information on how to start a business, finance a business, and help you decide on the legal status of a business for free or at a very low cost. It is a wonderful service for small businesses. Check it out at www.sbaonline.sba.gov.

My Cultural Work Environment Preferences

Take out your Career Profile Map and look at the section on your work environment preferences. As you look over what you have already said is a priority for you in a work environment, consider whether there are any other additions based on your cultural background. There are no rules about having preferences based on your cultural background.

Some of us like being the "only" person who is like me (a woman, black, Hispanic, Asian, has a disability, is over 50). On the other hand, many of us want to have a few other people around that are like you. The benefits to this include not having to be the only representative of your group, not standing out as much, not being as visible or having the pressure to perform above and beyond the norm because you stand out. In addition, it's great to have other people in your organization who have similar cultural backgrounds. This adds to some people's comfort level, and many times is an enhanced support network within the organization.

So the question for you here is how important is it to you to be in a multicultural work environment? This will help to guide you in researching information on demographics of organizations you are applying to as well as to guide your decision making.

The other aspects to consider are what the organization has to offer in terms of mentoring and coaching programs, orientation to the culture, and continued guidance in maneuvering in that culture, training programs on communicating across cultures for everyone in the organization, specialized training programs for diverse employees, access to continued training, advancement opportunities, and so on.

Make a little organizational matrix to assess how well each organization you look at is matching your particular needs:

Organizational Components	Has Them	Does Not Have Them	I Want in an Organization
1. _____	❏	❏	❏
2. _____	❏	❏	❏
3. _____	❏	❏	❏
4. _____	❏	❏	❏
5. _____	❏	❏	❏

continues

continued

Organizational Components	Has Them	Does Not Have Them	I Want in an Organization
6. _____	❏	❏	❏
7. _____	❏	❏	❏
8. _____	❏	❏	❏
9. _____	❏	❏	❏
10. _____	❏	❏	❏

Supporting a Multicultural Workforce

We are all part of the multicultural workforce that exists in many companies today. Beyond the workplace, we are citizens of our community, our neighborhoods, our country, and our world. The globalization of business is increasing everyday, and with this globalization our multicultural make-up is increasing.

Some of us are students of the world, and we learn very easily about other cultures. Still others of us may have grown up in one culture, with very little exposure to other cultures.

Part of the continuous learning that is going to become more standard in our organizational lives is the fact that we have to learn more about other cultures in order to do business of any kind. Here are some ways you can begin this journey:

♦ Find out what programs your organization offers that engage you in learning about other cultures.

♦ Take an assignment to another country and immerse yourself in learning their culture, their language, and their way of communicating.

♦ Read autobiographies and biographies of people from different cultures.

♦ Watch PBS (public broadcasting system) or TV programs on other networks about different cultures.

♦ Travel to other countries on vacation.

♦ Stay with families in other countries for a few weeks.

- Read books about culture. Check out www.journeyinlife.com for suggested readings from Dr. Jean Kim.

- Look for lectures at local colleges on cultures.

- Go to festivals put on by cultural groups in your community.

- Request that your organization do a staff development or training program on getting to know one another's cultures.

Whatever our situations, there is room for learning more about one another and increasing our ability to work together in collaboration, harmony, and hopefully joyfully!

The Least You Need to Know

- When you are looking for great matches in colleges and organizations to match your career profile, look up information on financial aid and scholarships for members of your cultural group.

- Look to your college career center and alumni office for diversity resources and then check out websites that have assessment services: www.Diversity.com, www.Monster.com, and www.quintcareers.com.

- Minority- and women-owned businesses can receive great support from the Small Business Administration, and there are benefits available in obtaining government contracts for minority- and women-owned businesses.

- As a member of the multicultural workforce, we all have access to educational and learning events and resources that can help us to be a productive member of our multicultural work teams and organizations.

- It's important to consider the types of organizational climate and support that organizations have for promoting and maintaining diversity. Look at organizational policies around recruitment, retention, and development.

Chapter 23

Do You Really Need a J-O-B?

In This Chapter

◆ Earn a living running your own home business

◆ Know where to get the training for going into business for yourself

◆ Understand what it takes to be self-employed

For all of you who have been looking at jobs in the corporate and not-for-profit sector and not quite seeing yourself in this picture—this chapter is definitely for you! If you have ever thought about being your own boss, increasing your income, spending more time at home, combining your career with raising a family, making your own schedule, or working in your PJs until noon, being self-employed might be a good fit for you.

According to the Small Business Administration, Office of Advocacy, there were about 22.9 million small businesses in the United States in 2002, and about 16.5 million of those businesses were run by "solopreneurs." A solopreneur is a solo-entrepreneur, someone who is in business for themselves, and most likely working out of their home. They can be consultants, coaches, decorators, real estate investors, artists, crafters, Internet businesses owners, writers, and so on. There are thousands of possibilities, and more and more people are looking into this lifestyle.

Getting Off the Fast Track

For many of us, the thought of continuing to work for others in either the profit or not-for-profit arena sometimes becomes stale. We find ourselves day-dreaming about the bed and breakfast we want to run someday. Or wishing we could come up with that great idea for making a good income doing something BESIDES what we have been doing everyday for years. And then there are those of us who knew we weren't cut out for 9-to-5 lives (or should we say 8 to 7 these days) from the day we started down that track. There are a million reasons why we might want to think about starting our own business.

Our favorite story of getting off the fast track comes from Dr. Valerie Young, who started her career in corporate life, and is now the proud owner of www. changingcourse.com. Changing Course is the premier website for helping you to look at alternative careers and business streams to fulfill your life dreams. Here's Valerie's story direct from her website:

> "For seven years I commuted 90 miles a day to a high-stress job that paid the bills but did not feed my spirit. Although I felt like I was living in a Dilbert cartoon, the demands of work and life left me feeling constantly caught between a 'clock and a hard place.' I used to fantasize about changing jobs. Whenever my job would get particularly stressful I'd think about doing a job search. But was trading cubicles, or bosses, or one set of organizational headaches for another really the solution? If I'd bothered to look a little deeper, I'd have understood that I yearned for much more than a new job ... or even a new career. You see what I really wanted back then was simplicity and balance, to experience the right livelihood, and a desire to be my own boss. Somehow I was always too busy putting out fires at work to attend to my own mid-life crisis. So my longing for career fulfillment and a more simple life was always put on hold.

> My wake-up call came on September 30, 1993, when my mother Barbara Young died unexpectedly of a heart attack at age 61. My mother died just five months before her much-awaited retirement. It was a sorrowful reminder that life really is too short and precious to defer something as important as our dreams. That started me on my journey to living the life I wanted and doing the work I love."

Today, Valerie has multiple sources of income that include career consultations, the changing course website and products, and her seminar business on helping women to feel as bright and capable as they really are!

Whatever your reasons for considering going into business for yourself, it does take a commitment and some know-how to position yourself for success. Let's begin by looking at the types of jobs people are doing from home.

Work at Home Job Ideas

Your creativity and imagination are the only limits to the possibilities for businesses that you can run out of your home. Let's begin with you, your interests, and your Career Profile Map.

You already know things about yourself and the type of skills you want to use along with your interests. Take a look at those and brainstorm some ideas for a small business you can run out of your home. Most of us know what we really want to do, we just have to get out of our own way.

> **Insider Tips**
>
> A great resource for generating ideas about small businesses that fit your profile is a two-hour power session with Dr. Valerie Young. Contact Valerie at www.changingcourse.com or just go there and see all the resources for learning about alternative careers and businesses.

Avoiding Work at Home Scams

The first caution that comes with working from home is to not rely on "get rich quick" schemes. Most people are attracted to ads that tell us we can make a million in a short period of time. Or when you receive the lottery e-mail that says you have won—even though you never entered—you get excited. Then there are the phone ads that promise exotic vacations and lifetime supplies. There is always a price to pay, and usually it comes out of your pocket if not just out of the time you spend reading and listening.

For up-to-date information on the latest frauds and scams, go to www.scambusters. org. They have a free newsletter and free tips. Here are some tips for avoiding work-at-home scams:

♦ Do your homework. Make sure you know with whom you are dealing. Look them up on their website, call and speak to the person in charge, ask for a referral to someone who has used their services. There is a Better Business Bureau site where you can see whether the company has passed a reliability check— www.bbb.com or www.bbbonline.com. If you cannot find the company or get anyone to speak to you, forget it! A legitimate company is always willing to give you information.

♦ Do ask about the refund policy. Most legitimate businesses will have a refund policy, and it will be in their advertisement.

♦ Do know the job requirements and market. Ads may ask you to pay upfront for software, for example, to start your own medical billing service at home, but they don't mention that most states require a certificate or license to perform certain types of work, as does medical billing. Look up job requirements in the *Occupational Outlook Handbook* or online at www.careeronestop.org. You can also call your state attorney general's office to inquire about qualifications.

♦ Don't pay before you do your research. Sometimes you get psyched for making some fast money or finally finding something that will save you from your 8-to-5 job. Hold off, take a day, do your homework, and then decide.

♦ Do something you love. Start with what you enjoy doing and go to a site like www.changingcourse.com that has thoroughly researched sources to help you start your business.

♦ Do take advantage of available services. If you want to get involved in starting a business that, for example, uses e-Bay to sell your items, go to the source and get a tutorial from them. You can also check with your local college or leisure services for short courses specific to your business interest or to refer you to more resources.

Starting a Small Business

Okay, so now you are seriously thinking about starting your own business and following your dreams. There are several aspects to getting a business started, and most businesses take about three years to really get off the ground and become profitable. So you have to be in it for the long haul. Here are some of the things you want to think about in forming your own small business:

♦ What business are you in? What is the core of your business? What problems or issues are you solving for other people? Whether it is a product or a service, you want to identify your niche in the market. It doesn't matter if many people are doing what you do—what are you doing the best?

- Who are your ideal customers or clients? What market are you going to target? If you are all over the place, forget it. You don't want to be all things for all people. You want to be *the* product or service for *these* people.

- How do you market your business? How do you let your market know who you are, what you are offering? Where do you market? How do you tap into and grow a network that is going to market for you and with you? What types of marketing materials do you need to have? Do you need a website?

- What financial investment do you need to start your business? How do you raise the money to start your business? How do you start your business on a shoe-string? What about your credit rating? How do you set up a business account? Do you need a bookkeeper? What types of records should you keep? What are the tax advantages?

- Are there legal issues you need to consider for your business? Can you use your personal tax identification number? Do you need liability insurance? What are you responsible for if you have employees?

- How do you put together a business plan that takes into account all of the previous questions, your time lines, and your income projections?

We know, you are probably asking where you go to find out about all of this. Along with the numerous online resources listed in the section, "Five Essential Websites," in Chapter 19, here are a few suggestions:

- Start with the SBA, your Small Business Administration. They have workshops for small business owners—or people thinking about becoming small business owners. Go to the www.sba.gov main website. They have online courses and local courses that are reasonably priced. If you are a woman-owned or minority-owned business, check out the possible benefits to your business.

- Yahoo has a small business directory with links to many sites that specialize in small businesses. Do a search, using the following wording: Small Business Directory AND Yahoo. Yahoo's Small Business Directory will come up as one of the first web sites.

- Many professional organizations offer courses on business planning and marketing. Check out the professional organization or association that is closest to your interests.

◆ Go to www.careeronestop.org and go to the Career Library where they have a listing of professional and trade associations by occupation. The idea here is to check out your national and local associations in your field of interest.

◆ Join a local association of small business owners who provide speakers and training sessions. Your local Chamber of Commerce can give you information on local professional organizations.

Insider Tips _____

Coachville is an organization for all kinds of coaches—life coaches, career coaches, small business coaches, and mentor coaches. Thomas Leonard started this organization a few years ago, and it has more than a million members worldwide. They have specialized training programs that are offered all over the country; offered at a reasonable price; and full of important information on marketing, planning, developing your business, and so on. Go to www.coachville.com to learn more about this organization if you are a coach or want to find a coach.

Self-Employment Success Factors

In order to be successful in your small business, there are a few things you will want to consider. Among them are setting up a decent home office space that welcomes you and promotes doing business. The next order of business will be to consider the hidden or least desirable elements of running your own business. And last but not least, are 10 secrets on how to be successfully employed.

Creating a Home Office

We will begin with the space itself. If you are thinking about setting up a desk in the corner of your living room—just out of the traffic area—I advise against it. Your office space needs to be, as much as possible, a separate space that you can go into and that others do not feel free to go into unless invited. For those of you who have to start in the corner of a room in your house, try to choose one that is out of high traffic. This may be your bedroom, or a space in the basement or attic area. If this space also has other uses, here are a few suggestions:

◆ Make a schedule for when this space becomes your office with ground rules about entering unannounced or calling you away for other concerns.

- Get an inexpensive screen or room divider that you can use to close off your office space.

- Rearrange some furniture, using taller bookcases to divide your section of the room.

- Literally put on your work hat. Like "gone fishing," only this hat is "gone to work" to help you to change your mind set about what you are about to do and warn others that you are not your available self right now.

Coach Wisdom

For those of you with little children who may vie for your attention (even though you do have your work hat on!!), here are a few suggestions: 1) Hire a babysitter or a nanny for specific hours every day or several days a week; 2) Take your children to a day-care program for the hours you will be working; 3) Do an exchange with a neighbor or friend for one or two days a week to free up time for one another.

As you consider the space you want to use for your office, see whether you can incorporate as many of the following as possible:

- Good lighting. Make sure you can see what you are doing and the atmosphere picks you up versus makes you want to take a nap. Think about inexpensive track lighting for this.

- Good air flow. A room with a window that you can open or put an air conditioner in is ideal. You can get some air, of the right temperature, no matter what time of year it is. There is nothing worse that going to work in a hot and stuffy office with nothing to look at but the walls around you.

- Enough room for a computer desk, a writing surface, a desk chair that is ergonomically correct (saves your back), an extra chair for clients or guests, a place to keep your files, books, and all the important resources you use in your business. The computer desks they make today are great because they save you space and you have a place for your computer, your printer, paper, and so on. You can probably find one for cheap in the want ads section of your local paper.

- Consider your electronic and communication needs—do some research to see what types of packages your phone company or your cable company have for installation and price the monthly charges for an extra phone line, high-speed computer connection, and fax line. Look for the best deal—they keep getting better and more consolidated.

◆ Then there are the basics that go with your marketing plan: a great message on your voice mail or answering machine, a business card that you can give out to clients, potential clients, friends, people in your network, and on and on. You will need to outfit your office with pens, pencils, pads, stapler, three-hole punch, paper clips, post-its, paper or electronic calendar, and address holder—and anything else you use in your trade.

The most important things about creating a home office are that you have made it inviting to go into, you are not distracted by other goings on in the house, and you have the resources available to support your work.

Coach Wisdom

Gisele painted her office a lovely lilac/purple color. She always wanted an office this color, and now she has it. She enters her purple room and feels safe and warm and ready to switch gears and do her work. Fabric can do wonders for chair coverings or to make a wall hanging. Beautiful pictures from magazines of your choice can be framed very inexpensively. How about a couple of inspirational poems that sit right in front of you while you work?

The Hidden Realities

Now you are all excited about starting this new venture, you need to prepare for some hidden realities of being in business for yourself. They are not insurmountable, but it helps to know what to expect:

◆ **Marketing costs.** Although you don't need a whole bunch of money to start some businesses, you do need to get your product or service out there to your market. And networking is one of the best ways to build people's confidence in you and your business. Some costs associated with this may be: membership in your Chamber of Commerce; membership in local, regional, or national professional groups or associations; networking and business exchange events. All these groups add up to a several hundred dollars a year. And then there are the advertising costs to get product and service recognition. These may include ads in papers, business journals, or magazines. We advise that you take a marketing course right away and find the free ways to advertise yourself, such as being a speaker at an event or being interviewed for an article in a local paper.

◆ Living without a paycheck. This is a whole different way of living. You used to know just how much money you were going to get every week or every month. Now, you are going from sale to sale of your product or service. And, sometimes you don't get your money right away. People may say, "I forgot my checkbook, is it all right if I pay you next week?" Or you may be sending an invoice to your clients or customers, and some of them may not pay for a month, two months, or even three months. So, you get the picture. You need a slush fund. Most people prepare for this with savings they can use and replenish when they get paid. Others take out a home equity line of credit and have money on hand to pay the bills on time. You must keep up your credit, so don't fall behind on bills. Being in business for yourself means you are your credit—so keep it looking good. Again, we would advise taking a workshop right away on how to manage your money and how to bill your clients and customers. You can anticipate all the delays and figure out how to set boundaries with clients as well as get your slush fund in order.

◆ Health insurance and retirement. You are now responsible for your own coverage. Look for ways to get a group rate for your health insurance. Call your Chamber of Commerce or look into what your professional associations might provide here. If you have an insurance carrier for other policies, contact them and see whether they have a discount rate since you already have policies with them. Barter with a financial planner to help you think about ways to set aside some money for retirement, or how to make the retirement fund you already have work better for you. Go to www.changingcourse.com for other solutions to finding health insurance you can afford.

◆ Focusing your energy. This can be very tough for people who have not been used to working from their home. There are so many distractions. You can trim those trees, do that laundry, "oh that kitchen needs a good cleaning!", and so on. You will have to develop a routine that works for you. If you have children to get off to school, start your workday after they leave. Get up earlier and straighten up and do the dishes or put in a laundry load. Try not to take time out of your work day to do household chores.

> **Insider Tips**
>
> One of your benefits from working at home is you do get to reward yourself! Go for a walk mid-morning to get your exercise and get those endorphins going. Tape your favorite program and watch it over lunch or on breaks.

For some of us it takes a little time to adjust to the freedom that comes with working from home. If you keep your eye on the prize of growing your business, then this focus will help to pull you into a work mode more quickly.

Being Your Own Leader

The number one reason small businesses fail is because there is no preparation for being your own boss! For those of you who have worked in organizations, you will be familiar with Jason's story. Jason and his co-workers spent hours complaining about the lack of leadership that their supervisor provided. If they were running this business, they would be letting employees know what a good job they were doing. They would pat them on the back and give them tickets for the ball game to reward them for such good work. They complained that the "boss" just didn't care about the business. He never shared the vision of where the company was headed or how they contributed to making it happen. They all agreed that if they had the chance, they would do it differently.

Well, just as leaders, managers, and supervisors in organizations usually aren't given the preparation to be leaders, neither are we as small business owners. So, here's a list of top tips for being your own leader:

◆ Keep your Vision Summary (refer to Appendix A) in front of you—in your planner, on your refrigerator, on the wall of your office. Step into your Vision Summary and experience yourself already there—picture yourself living the life you want to live, doing the work you love. Write down all the benefits you will experience when you are living your vision.

◆ Set up an R&D (research and development) Group. These can be people in your network that you know you can run ideas by. It can also be a new group that you set up specifically to support one another in brainstorming and evaluating new ideas for your business. You can use this group to explore marketing, new products or services, and pricing.

◆ Set up an accountability system. It's lonely and isolating to be in business for yourself, so establish a way to check-in, report, let someone else know what you have accomplished each day. This could be a coach, a buddy, a partner to check in with. Some people set up a once a week 40-minute call with one other person to go over goals for the week, problem solve, and report on progress.

◆ Reward yourself. For example, if you finish this project by the end of the week, you should reward yourself. What will stimulate and drive you through the doubt, the complexity, the "not so" favorite tasks?

♦ Affirm yourself. Keep a journal of your successes, your learning, and your ideas to remind yourself how good you really are, what you do well, and the results you are getting. When you have a lull in the day, say an affirmation that reminds you of who you are or are striving to become.

♦ Exercise and eat healthy. This is absolutely necessary. In order to keep your mind clear, your energy flowing, and those good endorphins stimulated, you need to make this a priority.

♦ Know your strengths and your weaknesses. Delegate those things you don't do well to others (for example, hire a virtual assistant, a web designer, a writer, an accountant, a marketing coach). Don't bog yourself down by trying to be an expert in every aspect of your business; grow your strengths, that's where your passion lies.

♦ Listen to yourself. Pay attention to your own intuition, feelings, and thoughts. Use them as guides for what you need to focus on and take action on. There are opportunities as well as areas of resistance and unfinished business that can nag at us and pull our energy down if we do not address them. So, don't waste time—listen to yourself!

♦ Be a continuous learner. Get better, deeper, and more knowledgeable about your areas of expertise. Learn a new skill, take an art class; satisfy your need to know more about interior decorating, real estate, or woodworking. This will keep your brain active. By meeting new people and stimulating new thoughts, you will get ideas that will bounce back to your primary business—it all works together.

♦ Get a coach who will call out *the leader in you* on a weekly basis! A friend asked whether Sue thought she needed a coach, and Sue's reply was, "yes, I could certainly use one to keep up my motivation; *but*, I don't have the money right now." Then Sue went to the mall and spent $100 on the sales! Okay, Sue, where are your priorities?

So, for those of you who are thinking about starting your own business or streams of business, you have many things to think about. Take a few minutes to summarize your own thoughts and feelings about going the small business route. Choose a number between 1 and 7 that gauges your interest in pursuing your own business—with 1 being "not interested at all" and 7 being that you are "extremely interested." Then, write down your summary of your thoughts and feelings.

Interest in Starting Your Own Business (1 – 7): _____

Summary of Thoughts and Feelings:

_____

_____

_____

_____

_____

The Least You Need to Know

◆ There are many alternatives and resources for those of you who want to be in your own business. Many small businesses are run right out of homes.

◆ The best way to avoid work-at-home scams is to take your time and do your research to find out whether you are looking at a legitimate business.

◆ Being in business for yourself means you have to figure out what business you are in, who your ideal customers are to whom you want to market, how to go about marketing, and how much of a financial investment you want or need to make.

◆ Running a successful business has three major components: setting up a workable home office, understanding the hidden realities of being in business for yourself, and learning to be your own boss and taking on the leadership that will motivate you and sustain your business.

24

Multiple Business Streams

In This Chapter

♦ Tap into why multiple streams of business might work for you

♦ Figure out which streams of business to use in your start-up phase

♦ Find out what others are doing

For those of you who are considering going into your own business, you may want to consider having multiple streams of business. Multiple streams means that you have more than one profit center. You have more than one way of making money! We know that most big businesses have more than one profit center, but we often think of small business as having just one. Even though most businesses are known for a primary product or service, if you look closely, you will see the other streams. Businesses have become savvy about not relying just on one means of economic health. Given a changing economy, changing needs and wants of consumers, and new consumer bases businesses have to be thinking ahead and thinking more broadly about their success strategy. The same applies to small businesses.

Why Multiple Streams

Let's look a little more closely at some reasons why you might consider having multiple streams of business. The reasons can range from liking more variety in your work, to having an economic need, to using your creativity to grow your business, to just being in the right place at the right time. Before you read some stories about people who have put together their own successful streams of business, let's take a look at why you might even consider it.

Coach Wisdom

An example that almost all of us would be familiar with is McDonalds. What is McDonalds known for—the hamburger and fries, right! For many years this was the center of their business. Slowly, the realities of health-conscious customers began to seep in—first came the chicken, then the salads, now a whole campaign to meet the needs of their eating healthy consumers. During this transition time, McDonalds took some hits in their income because they stuck to their basic stream of business too long.

Variety

For those of you who want to be in business for yourself, but you can't see yourself concentrating on just one service or product—think about multiple streams of business. Perhaps you have several things that you love to do, to make, or to sell. Or maybe you just get bored with spending all your time on one product or service. There is a high percentage of people like you in the world—people who like and need variety in their perfect careers.

Economic Need

Some streams of business only bring in a certain amount of profit. It might be because you can see only so many clients a week before you fall over from exhaustion. Or it might be that your market for one particular service or product is limited to a certain profit margin. Why wouldn't you just get into something more lucrative rather than staying with a limited profit center? Well, many of us love what we do and don't want to just go where the money is. We need to be able to do what we love and also figure out more ways to increase our income when that is what we desire.

Growing Your Main Business

Now, multiple streams are great for growing your business and allowing your creativity to run wild. See yourself having your main business up and running, or maybe you have two streams going. You are "in the business," meaning you are gaining knowledge, making contacts, growing your expertise. Now, you see more opportunities and generate more ideas for ways to expand, or grow into different aspects and streams of business. These may all be related to your core business, but they are separate profit centers.

Open to Possibilities

Your *entrepreneurial* self is alive and well in this scenario. What happens to most of us as we get more experience in our own businesses is that we become more entrepreneurial. That means, we are looking for opportunities to grow, develop, try out new business streams. These may be streams we would never have thought about before, but they come across our path, and WOW, we see the possibilities. Sometimes it's just being in the right place at the right time. We call that luck, but often it's because we are open to something new and maybe very different.

Career Lingo

Entrepreneurial is being willing to take risks to make a profit. Most entrepreneurs see opportunities and are willing to step out of their comfort zones to pursue the chance to make a profit.

Tips for Identifying Your Profit Centers

There are some practical things to think about in getting your multiple streams of business going. For our purposes in this exercise, let's call your multiple streams, "profit centers." You want to start thinking in business terms!

It is understandable that the beginning phase of going into your own business can be scary for many people. Chapter 23 gave you some resources for getting started, so we won't review those here. However, there are a few more tips we would offer you for thinking about your profit centers.

These tips have been adapted from *Making a Living Without a Job: Winning Ways for Creating Work that you Love* by Barbara J. Winter, Bantam Books, New York, 1993.

◆ Figure out what you love to do. Brainstorm a list of businesses that you could be in given what you know about yourself. Now, pick one stream of business you know you would be happy doing and put that at the top of the list. Then choose your top five in priority order. If you only have two or three that you really want to do—that's fine.

◆ Estimate how much it would cost to put each one of your priority businesses into motion. You may have to do some research for this. Do some interviews with people who are in this type of business. Make an appointment to see someone at the SBA (Small Business Administration) to help to give you an idea. Go on the Internet and look up information on wholesale costs of products, inexpensive marketing tool costs, and so on. Consider bartering with local merchants for some of your start-up costs.

◆ Estimate how much of a profit you can make from each of your profit centers in the first year. Many of us already have a sense that some streams are going to be higher profit margins than others. What you are looking for here is a realistic view of your profit margin in your start-up period.

◆ Take a look at the analysis you have done to select those streams of business that will cost you the least to get up and going and bring in the most profit. In making your selections, you need to know how much income you need for this next year. It usually takes two to three years for a new business to bring in a better profit, so keep that in mind. Don't get discouraged, there is much more support for you out there in terms of learning to market and financing your businesses. This is just a way to get you started in thinking about what you really want to do and which streams to get started *first*.

Use the table that follows to do some figuring about your profit centers. Use this to do some brainstorming of all the possible businesses you could be in. Then use the second column to prioritize those businesses. Based on information you collect, use the third and fourth columns to estimate how much it would cost to start these businesses and what you can expect from a profit for the first year. The rule of thumb is to choose the business that will make the most profits and cost the least amount of money to start up.

Top 5 Possibilities for Business Streams	Prioritize Businesses	Cost of Start-Up	First Year Profit
_____	_____	_____	_____
_____	_____	_____	_____
_____	_____	_____	_____
_____	_____	_____	_____
_____	_____	_____	_____

Multiple Stream/Profit Center Stories

It's always good to hear about how other people are working their multiple stream businesses. It gives you an idea about the range of different ways you can approach your own business. And it lets you see that there are real people out there making a living doing what they love in their own businesses.

Ange's Story

Ange has her doctorate from a Counseling Psychology program. She has been a therapist in private practice for more than 15 years. Ange has a steady practice of around 15 to 20 clients a week, and she thoroughly enjoys her clients. Ange is an advocate for people. She not only is the person to turn to in times of crises, she creates opportunities for people to use all the resources available to them to help them to live happy and healthy lives—and to feel good about themselves.

A couple of years ago, Ange decided that she would like to expand her income base. She had several reasons for wanting to do this at this point in her life. She and her husband were thinking long range about their retirement income, and she wanted to be able to increase her income substantially. Also at this point in time, the number of clients she was seeing each week had reduced to a handful. As most people who are psychologists or therapists of any kind know, this is quite common at different points in one's practice. Ange had depended on her network, word of mouth, and client referrals to keep business up. Now she was experiencing a time when she felt like she had to start over. Given her goals of increasing her income, this actually became a time of opportunity for her. She started to think about expanding her business into other areas. The whole life-coaching movement was taking off, and Ange decided to look at this work as one way to broaden her client base.

Ange joined a coaching support group. The support group members attended several low-cost conferences and marketing seminars put on by Coachville (www.coachville. com). Ange began her multiple streams of business by identifying three new streams of business that she wanted to develop:

1. Attracting life-coaching clients. Clients who were struggling to reach their goals and needed a coach to help them to take action and achieve their goals. This was right up Ange's alley. She is all about taking action to reach goals!

2. The courage to succeed. This stream of business centers around helping people who are just starting in their businesses and are in need of building their confidence in themselves as well as taking action to develop their businesses.

3. Self-care. This is a stream of business that focuses on how to take care of oneself. The focus is living a healthy life and all that entails—eating right, maintaining fitness, regular check-ups, and lowering stress.

As she progressed in developing her new streams of business, she also built up her therapy clients. She now calls herself a "theracoach" because she does some of both with her clients—a new *nitch*! Along the way, she was asked to become a visiting professor at a local university for two years. So in addition to her clients—back up to 15 to 20 a week—she was also teaching two courses.

So, where are we? We are at five streams of business right now with therapy, life coaching, courage to succeed, self-care, and teaching. So, she added a sixth stream—real estate. With the income from her teaching position, she has bought two rental properties. This interest grew out of her extensive knowledge about construction and "fixing a place up." Along with her husband, she was able to buy two very productive properties.

All of her streams of business come out of interests, skills, and goals that are particular to Ange. She took her background in therapy and combined it with coaching. She took her commitment to helping people who are in need and grew that into programs that teach people to honor themselves and take action on their own behalves. She took her talent and interest in construction and working with her hands and combined that with her desire for a more stable retirement income. Voilà—real estate investor! For more information about Ange's businesses, go to www.Dr-Ange.com.

George's Story

Georgeanne is a multi-talented woman. She studied to be an architect and worked in this profession until she had her first child. Along with working full-time as an architect, she also began to invest in real estate. During the year that she stayed home with her son, she began to explore all her areas of interest. She knew that she did not want to go back to work full-time as an architect. Although she thoroughly enjoyed the creative design aspects of this work, she was not as thrilled with the implementation and construction phase.

As George began to work with her life coach, she knew that her perfect career would be as an international speaker, traveling to different parts of the world. This combined her love of presenting and speaking to groups and her desire to be in a variety of cultures and experiences. This became her long-range goal, and she needed to fill in the specifics. Like—what would she be speaking on? What was the subject area? She started with exploring what her other top priorities were in terms of creating streams of business. She came up with the following:

- ◆ Real estate investing. She had already bought a couple of properties and saw this as a good way to produce income that could support her other streams of business. She loved learning about investing and read every book on the subject. She signed up for a real estate mentorship program that would help her to learn through the actual experience of buying real estate.

- ◆ Inventor. George's creativity comes out in so many ways. One of them is inventing. Since her little boy had been born, she had been coming up with ideas for more convenient carriers and other baby products. She attended a Dreams Can't Wait workshop sponsored by Changing Course (www.ChangingCourse.com) where she met a woman who helps women inventors to get prototypes made of their products.

- ◆ Public speaker. Here George had two areas in which she had expertise. Her first love was speaking on the topic of how to become a real estate investor. She was very committed to helping people to believe in their ability to be an investor even if they were living on a low income. Her workshop was not only about the how to's of real estate investing, it was about believing in and empowering yourself to make a good living. Her second area of expertise was speaking on interior design. Through her work as an architect as well as her natural creativity, she was really good at helping people to look at a space and turn it into their dream room at a low cost. She started out by giving a short talk on both these topics to her local Mocha Mom's group—a group that provides all types of support for stay-at-home mothers of color. Out of this talk, she had several requests for interior design consulting. This was the beginning of her build-up to international speaker!

♦ **Architecture design projects.** Because she loved this aspect of the architecture business, she wanted to continue to explore ways to work on the front-end design projects. So far, she has combined her love of real estate investing with design work. She is exploring a relationship with some real estate investors to help them to design spaces for properties they have bought. This will also increase her learning about the investment side of the business.

♦ **Interior design.** While she is good at this and enjoys giving talks on it to help others to be able to do it at a low cost, she was finding out that most people wanted her to do it for them. After taking on a few projects, she is putting this business on the back burner for a while since it takes too much time and has aspects to it that are not on her priority list of jobs she loves to do.

Of all the streams of business, George is concentrating most on real estate investing. With the arrival of her second child, she will probably invent more products, and this could be a great second stream that produces a high income. As she progresses in building up her expertise and profit margins, she will be able to give more time to speaking engagements—and perhaps even writing as a way to become more visible. She has the basics going. Let's wish her well!

The Least You Need to Know

♦ There are many reasons that multiple streams of business might be for you. You may need variety, more income, want to grow your business into new areas, or want to become more entrepreneurial.

♦ Starting your multiple streams of business begins with deciding what your top priority streams would be, figuring out start-up costs for each one, and looking at expected profits for the first year. Based on all this information, you have a better chance of selecting your first stream based on low cost and high profit.

♦ The advantages of having several streams of business are many. You can address all your interests through your different businesses, you can do what you love AND make money, and you are constantly challenged and never bored!

25

Try Out a Job

In This Chapter

♦ Learn to think strategically when looking for transition work

♦ Try out a job in a few different ways

♦ Consider job relevance to your transition situation

Trying out a job comes in many forms. You can moonlight your way into a new career. You can reduce your current work to part-time and pick up a part-time position in your new occupational field. Then there is doing temp work, but only in your occupational area. Even some internships pay for you to learn on the job. And, you can do volunteer work that is in your career area. This is all about thinking strategically about how to transition from your current work situation to your desired work situation. Or for those of you who are not working yet—from wherever you are in your life to your new career. *Strategic thinking* is all about keeping your focus on your goal, making decisions, and taking actions that are going to move you closer to your goal.

You don't want to just take a part-time job because you can't stand your current job any longer. The part-time job you take needs to be a step toward your new career. The key is not to let your fears drive your decisions. Fears are signals. They help us to look at what we need to pay

Career Lingo

Strategic thinking means that you keep your focus on your goals and all your actions and decisions are ones that move you toward accomplishing those goals.

attention to. Perhaps it's the amount of money we have to earn to support ourselves. Maybe it's not feeling totally or even slightly competent in your new occupation. Whatever the signals are, write them down. Then start thinking strategically about how you can address these while making movement toward your goal.

Peter Senge wrote a book a few years ago, *The Fifth Discipline* (Currency, 1994). In this book he talks about the learning organization—the organization that is always open and proactive about learning. He proposes five disciplines to help people in organizations to open themselves up to and practice being a learner. One very relevant thing for us that he talks about is changing our mental models, changing how we think about our options. Senge encourages us to think in mental models of win-win. How can we further our career goals while still making a salary we can live on? This sets us up for thinking about solutions very differently from a mental model that says, "I can either make a decent salary, OR I can start doing the work I love to do." This second way of holding our thoughts says we can have one or the other. That does not allow us to be strategic in our thinking about how to move toward our career goals. So in the spirit of thinking strategically, be a learner and think in win-win scenarios that move you closer to your career goal.

Benefits of Trying Out a Job

Let's take a look at some of the benefits of trying out a job through moonlighting, part-time, temp work, internships, or volunteer work.

- ◆ On-the-job training. For those of you who don't have much to show on your resumé for background or experience in your perfect career area, then this is a great way to do that.

- ◆ Exposure to organization culture. Some of you may still be wondering whether this is really the career direction or work for you. There is no better way to find out than to spend some time in the setting you would be working in on a more regular basis. You can also work for different organizations so that you can compare cultures and see whether there are some that you prefer more than others. Never make your decision based on the experience with one organization! Organizations are like people—we all have different personalities.

◆ Permanent position. Of course there is always the possibility that any of these work options can lead to a permanent position. Seventy percent of getting a job is based on who you know. So, you are getting known when you work for someone on a part-time or temporary basis. You have the chance to demonstrate your self-management skills and your competencies as well as to show that you are a quick learner.

◆ Flexibility and lifestyle. Some of these options like part-time, temp work, or volunteer work may meet your lifestyle needs. Many people need or want the flexibility of schedules to match their current lifestyle needs. The different stages of our lives bring different needs. The beauty of these options is that you can still work at something you love to do and meet your lifestyle needs.

◆ Building your reputation. All of these job options help you to start building a reputation in your ideal career area. You are getting to be known for your skills and experience in this new field. The word is getting out, and your networks are growing. This brings more business and employment opportunities to your door step.

Coach Wisdom
All of the "try out a job" options in this chapter have their pros and cons. Don't be put off by your financial need, the time it takes to get into a new and perhaps additional job, or anything else that might cross your mind. Get into a mindset of researching the options that you find most appealing and fit your situation the best. Don't assume you know how much a part-time job pays—find out. Don't assume you can't start your dream job on a part-time basis—look at how others have done it and strategize!

Job Options

Now, back to some specific options for those of you who want to or need to work while you transition to your ideal career. And of course, these are strategic solutions.

Moonlighting

Moonlighting is a great word—working by the light of the moon. Traditionally people have worked a second job to pay the bills, do what they love to do but can't get paid for, help out with the family business, and so on. Today, moonlighting might mean going to a second workplace after you leave your primary one, or it could mean working at something different on the weekends, or it could mean working out of your home in the early mornings, evenings, and/or weekends.

Choosing to moonlight means you are keeping your day job (or night job) and taking on a second job. There are a few cautions here that you need to take into consideration:

1. The first is to make sure that there is not a conflict of interest with your primary work. Generally, you can't be doing the same work for another company while still employed by your primary employer. You need to make sure that what you are doing does not pose a conflict of interest. You can speak with your employer about this to make sure.

2. Another area to pay attention to is the amount of time you want to put into a second job. For some of you, this is a way of life. Artists have traditionally taken jobs that support them while doing what they love after hours. However, if this is new to you, take your time and consider the effects this will have on your lifestyle. You want to make this manageable so you can really start your transition into your perfect career. If you burn yourself out, you will be defeating the purpose and probably won't continue your transition. Something will have to go, and it often is the work you love to do.

Many people who are starting their own home-based businesses begin by moonlighting. If you are providing a service, you can schedule clients in the evenings or on weekends. If you sell a product, you can schedule sales calls or meetings in the evenings or on weekends. Many products today are sold over the Internet, which means you can work on your sales from your home office. Some of you may have weekday times available for moonlighting, or you may be able to adjust our schedule so that you gain access to a weekday time for your home-based business.

For those of you who want to transition into a position working for someone else, seek out opportunities that are in line with your career goals. Perhaps you have studied to be a copy writer, and you would like to begin to take on some clients. You can do this in the evening or on the weekends. The American Writers and Artists Institute has a great program on learning to be a copy writer for anyone interested! Or maybe you are a hospital nurse, and your ideal career is working with the elderly. Look for night staff positions in elder care facilities. Another example might be wanting to transition into working in Human Resources in an organization. If you are living in an area that has large box retail shops like Target or Wal-Mart, see whether they need any assistance in the evening or on weekends in their HR offices.

Coach Wisdom
Geri has been such a dedicated and hard working teacher of children who cannot function well in the traditional classroom. She has dedicated her life to working with these children in often very physically, emotionally, and mentally challenging circumstances. Along the way, she was introduced to a method of working with these children that represented a break-through for teachers and children. She decided to study this method in her spare time and is now teaching classes in this method on weekends throughout the year. Although this takes time away from her family, Geri is thinking about transitioning into more flexible work and work that is about teaching others to implement effective methods in working with her cherished children. Moonlighting has worked for Geri—and for her students and teachers.

Part-Time

Consider part-time work in your ideal career area as an advanced step in making the transition from the old to the new career. Being able to reduce your primary work to part-time allows most people to maintain benefits and a regular pay check. And, you can devote the other part-time to your ideal career. Again this is not without its drawbacks in terms of trying to juggle two jobs at the same time. You have to maintain clear goals and boundaries for each job, leaving enough time for other lifestyle needs.

What working part-time in your new field helps you to do is to begin to feel the solid ground under your feet in this new career. You begin to identify with being a medical billing specialist instead of a retail sales person. You get used to the terminology, the client needs, the product, the service, the working atmosphere.

Temporary Positions

The whole world of temporary positions has changed substantially over the past 10 years. The number of temporary workers and independent contractors has grown much faster than the number of permanent employees. The major reasons for organizations to use temporary workers are based on the need to have more staff to meet the demands in the industry and for short-term cover for staff that are out sick, on leave, or on vacation. If you are looking at a career move into a high career demand area, then you may be able to enter it through filling temporary positions.

Temporary positions are also a great way to obtain permanent employment because organizations are using temporary positions as a means to screen for full-time employment. More than 70 percent of temporary workers who are looking for permanent employment obtain it by working as a temporary employee. Although clerical and secretarial work is still the largest temp work category, technical and computing occupations are second. Independent contractors work in temporary positions as a way of life. Roberta is an HR specialist who works with small companies that do not have an HR function. She fulfills their HR needs on a temporary, case-by-case basis. So she works for a variety of companies on a temporary basis.

Temporary positions are a great way to move around to different organizations to see which ones match your work environment preferences the best.

Volunteer Work

Cathy is trying to make a transition from nursing to medical billing. She has taken some courses in medical billing and is planning on getting a certificate in this area. And she wants to leave nursing now. Without any experience in medical billing to put on her resumé, she is finding it difficult to get an interview. She decided to volunteer at a local hospital in the medical billing office for several hours a week. This way, she will be working in and learning about medical billing. And she will be building up her experience. This could also lead to a part-time or full-time position in the future as she demonstrates her knowledge and skills over time. She already has all the self-management skills she needs to work with the public.

Volunteer work has traditionally been a way for women to gain skills and experience as they think about re-entering the work force. There are so many organizations and opportunities for volunteer work. Just to list a few:

- Hospitals/Nursing Homes/Elder Care Facilities
- Schools
- Churches
- Human Service Organizations
- Community Services
- Day-Care
- Political Campaigns
- Social and Professional Organizations

- Small Businesses
- Family Business
- Recreational Activities/Centers
- Scouts and Other Service Organizations

The following are great websites that have volunteer opportunities:

- www.crossculturalsolutions.or. This is a not-for-profit international volunteer organization that operates volunteer programs in Brazil, China, Costa Rica, Ghana, Guatemala, India, Peru, Russia, Tanzania, and Thailand. Volunteers work with local people on locally designed projects.

- www.servenet.org. Users can enter their ZIP code, city, state, skills, interests, and availability and be matched with organizations in need of help. They have more than 5,700 registered nonprofit organizations and more than 35,000 volunteer opportunities. It provides the largest database of volunteer opportunities in America.

- www.peacecorps.gov. Opportunities to use your skills to help people in interested countries to meet their needs for trained men and women.

- www.volunteer.org.nz. Educational, environmental, and community aid volunteer work. They place volunteers in community projects in China, Ecuador, Ghana, Nepal, New Zealand, Romania, Russia, Thailand, and Uganda.

There are many, many more. Think about what you want to do and then make a list of the kinds of organizations and places that might want a volunteer. You can offer your volunteer services in almost any career area. It doesn't hurt to explore this possibility with any organization in which you want to work. Just be sure that you have thought out what you want to get out of this experience. This is a two-way street, and you are looking for opportunities to use your skills, grow, learn, and gain experience.

Internships

Internships are particularly great for college students and recent graduates. If you are still in college or about to graduate, speak to your career center about doing an internship in your field of study. Your academic department is also a great resource for having knowledge about places to do internships. Taking an internship in your field of study can add clout to your resumé and job hunting prospects. It can also lead to job offers in the organizations in which you do your internship. Almost every industry has some type of internship program. Some of them are paid, but most are not. Here are some resources for locating internships that match your career needs:

◆ www.quintcareers.com. Quintessential Careers has extensive information on internships for college grads.

◆ www.internshipprograms.com offers internship listings in the following areas: large corporations, advertising/marketing/PR companies, journalism and communications, government agencies, and sports.

◆ www.IdeaList.org. This website has public service information, volunteer jobs, and internship opportunities in 14,000 nonprofit or community organizations in 25 countries.

◆ www.RSInternships.org. Rising Star Internships has listings in many career fields.

◆ www.careeronestop.org. Career One Stop has an extensive resource list of internships across occupations. Look in the resource library by typing "internships"—that will take you where you want to go.

Insider Tips

Type "internships" and the "title" of your career area at an online search engine—for example, Google—and check out the list of sites that turn up.

Some professional fields require a post-doctoral internship in order to be able to practice in the profession. Information on these internships can be obtained from your academic department or the graduate school in your academic institution.

The Least You Need to Know

◆ Always think strategically about any job that you take during your transition into your new career. Remind yourself of your career goal and only take jobs that will get you closer to achieving your ideal job.

◆ The benefits of moonlighting, part-time work, temp work, volunteer work, and internships are on-the-job training, learning about different organizational cultures, finding ones that fit your work environment preferences, positioning yourself for full-time employment, giving yourself flexibility of work hours, and building your reputation in your field.

◆ Each of us is in our own unique situation of transitioning into our perfect career. It's important to look at the "try out a job" options in terms of our career goals and lifestyle needs.

26

Make a Plan of Action

In This Chapter

- ◆ Understand the beauty and productivity of a plan of action
- ◆ Create a mission statement to live by
- ◆ Set your goals
- ◆ Make a plan and stick to it

Well, you have made it all the way to the end of this book on how to find your perfect career. Guess what? This is not the end. In order to make sure that you continue your journey and secure your perfect career, you need to make a plan of action.

So many other things can come into play in our lives to take us off course. We get all excited (and, of course, you are right now) about our own future and goals. Then, the day-to-day happens, and in a month we can be back in our old routines. We don't forget about our goals, but they sure take much longer to implement without a *plan*. Don't worry, in this chapter you will write your plan and learn how to focus your energy on your high-priority goals.

Your Mission Statement

Before we get to the plan, let's make a mission statement. You already have your vision of what you want your life to be like in five years (your "Vision Summary" from Chapter 5). Your vision represents the inspiration of your long-term goal. It is just out of reach, but always alluring and inviting. Your mission is what is going to drive your behavior everyday. Following are the components of your mission statement. After you read through these, you will have a chance to use a worksheet to write down your components before you actually write your mission statement:

1. My essential nature. This part of your mission statement needs to capture the essence of what is important to you in your life and work. It is the context piece of your mission statement. In other words, you are stating who you are and what you want from your life and your work. Take a look at your Career Profile Map to review your lifestyle preferences and your work environment preferences. You may have other things to add to this, but these two categories can provide a focus for you. You want to create a very concise statement that captures the essence of you.

2. Values. These are the values you want to guide your behavior and decisions everyday in order to be able to live the life and do the work you love. You already have these identified in your Career Profile Map. You are going to want to create a concise statement of the core values (in your own words) that you believe will help you to be true to yourself.

   My contribution—this is the work you are doing or want to do. This is the place in your mission statement to identify your perfect career:

   ♦ What is the work you are doing or going to do?

   ♦ Why is this work important to you?

   ♦ How does this work make a difference to others?

Here is an example of a mission statement, using these guidelines:

"My life and work are balanced and intertwined with support and friendships, colleagues, time for family and time for self. I maintain a variety of exciting and interesting projects that I love and are a mix of independent and collaborative work. I work primarily from my home office where I enjoy the beauty of nature all around me.

Guidance in my life comes from my connection to the beauty of spirit in all things around me; my commitment to being trustworthy in the eyes of my family, friends, colleagues, and clients; approaching my work creatively; having fun and being happy; respecting myself; and making a contribution to people's lives and well being.

I enjoy my perfect career in the field of organization and personal development. The core of my career centers around leadership consulting, career coaching, and curriculum/workshop design. I am open to new ventures where I can build on my core to meet new, creative, and exciting challenges. Everything I do helps others to develop their potential and live an authentic and satisfying life."

Your mission statement may be shorter or longer. You can mix up the pieces and interchange values, work, and life as you go. This is your mission, so there are no rules! Here is a worksheet to get you started:

Components of My Mission	Notes to Myself
A. My Essential Nature	_____
Lifestyle preferences	_____
(Career Profile Map)	_____
_____	
_____	_____
_____	_____
_____	_____
Work environment preferences	_____
(Career Profile Map)	_____
_____	_____
_____	_____
_____	_____
Other thoughts	_____
_____	_____
_____	_____

continues

continued

Components of My Mission	Notes to Myself
B. Values	
How I want to live my life values	_____
(Career Profile Map)	_____
	_____
	_____
Day-to-day values	_____
(Career Profile Map)	_____
	_____
	_____
Other thoughts	_____
	_____
	_____
	_____
C. Contribution	
My perfect career choice	_____
(The work I want to or am doing)	_____
	_____
	_____
Why it's important I do this work	_____
	_____
	_____
Difference my work makes to others	_____
	_____
	_____

After you have filled this out, go ahead and write up your first draft of your mission statement. Sometimes it takes a while to get it just right. Don't worry about that. Post it where you can see it. Read it everyday. Then make changes as desired! In fact, your mission statement is probably going to change over time as you grow and develop. Remember early on when we mentioned having a "career check-up." Every once in a while (even yearly), you want to look over your Career Profile Map and see whether there are any changes based on the intervening time that brings new knowledge, experience, and insight.

Identifying Goals

This is the way it works: Vision—Mission—Goals—Plan of Action. You have the big picture and future plan in your vision, you have the day-to-day grounding in your mission, and now you need to identify the goals you want to accomplish moving forward.

First, take a few minutes to think about where you are on your perfect career journey. Some of you will be ready to step into your perfect career. Or you may now want to conduct a job search. Others will need to prepare with more education or experience. And some of you may still need to continue to research your perfect career choices to make sure which one you want to pursue. Wherever you are, you need to take the next step to help you to carry through and do what you need to do to reach your perfect career. Picture yourself in your perfect career right now. Take a minute to close your eyes and see yourself in your career. Now let's start to form some goals for moving you into that picture for real.

Goals help us to articulate exactly what we want to accomplish. They help us to visualize the outcome or the end state. As stated in Chapter 3, your goals need to be specific, measurable, attainable, realistic, and have time frames.

Long-Range Goals

Let's start with long-range goals. Look at where you are right now (college, moonlighting, job hunt, researching …), and estimate how long it is going to take you to reach your ultimate goal of being in your perfect career. Some of you may find yourself looking at a very short time to achieve your ultimate goal. Others might find themselves looking at 10 years down the road.

For instance, if you are now in college, studying to be a doctor, you have pretty clear long-range goals like:

1. Graduate college.

2. Apply for medical schools.

3. Graduate medical school.

4. Apply for internships.

If you are conducting a job hunt, your goals are going to look something like this:

1. Write a top-notch resumé.

2. Write an eye catching cover letter.

3. Get references.

4. Use my network to identify job possibilities.

Anything over two months is considered long range. Write down all the long-range goals you can think of right here.

Long-Range Goals	Rank Order by When Goal Needs To Be Accomplished
1. _____	_____
2. _____	_____
3. _____	_____
4. _____	_____
5. _____	_____
6. _____	_____
7. _____	_____
8. _____	_____
9. _____	_____
10. _____	_____
11. _____	_____
12. _____	_____
13. _____	_____
14. _____	_____
15. _____	_____

Go back through your long-range goals and rank order these goals in terms of what you need to accomplish first, second, third, and so on. Don't worry about goals that can be worked on at the same time—this is just a rough estimate of your time line for your goals.

Short-Range Actions

Take the long-range goals from your rank order list that you need to accomplish within the next year and write them down here. Now, think about what you need to accomplish in the next two months. Next to each goal, write all the actions you can think of that you need to take to reach this goal. You can add to these actions every day. As you know, one action leads to another action, so you will be adding to your list as you go along. You should be trying to focus on the present steps you need to take versus confusing yourself with too many long-range actions. Keeping your mind and attention focused on what you have to do right now will get you there much faster.

Long-Range Goals	Actions Needed
1. _____	_____
2. _____	_____
3. _____	_____
4. _____	_____
5. _____	_____

A wonderful resource to keep you focused on your top priorities on a day-to-day basis is Time Design. Go to www.timedesign.com to look at their products and their workshops. Great stuff!

Action Plan

Here is a simple action plan that you can post on your office wall, your refrigerator, in your day planner, on your ceiling—wherever it will get your attention and keep you focused.

Two-Month Plan of Action

Long-Range Goal #1
_____

Action Steps	**Check Off When Accomplished**
1. _____	❏
2. _____	❏
3. _____	❏
4. _____	❏
5. _____	❏
6. _____	❏
7. _____	❏
8. _____	❏
9. _____	❏

Obstacles to accomplishing this goal:

_____

_____

_____

_____

How I will overcome these obstacles:

_____

_____

_____

_____

Rewards for accomplishing this goal:

_____

_____

_____

Long-Range Goal #2

Action Steps	Check Off When Accomplished
1. _____	❑
2. _____	❑
3. _____	❑
4. _____	❑
5. _____	❑
6. _____	❑
7. _____	❑
8. _____	❑
9. _____	❑

Obstacles to accomplishing this goal:

_____

_____

_____

_____

How I will overcome these obstacles:

_____

_____

_____

_____

Rewards for accomplishing this goal:

_____

_____

_____

_____

Create this template on your computer—one for each goal.

Sticking to Your Plan

How do you stick with a plan and carry it through? Well, you have to develop habits that support you in working on your plan on a day-to-day basis. This is something new that you have to incorporate in your life, and it may require that you change your behavior. Here is something to think about in terms of the type of support you are looking for to change your behavior; this information is based on a study that was done in 1993 by Brigham Young University:

When a Person ...	Chances of Behavior Being Incorporated in One's Life Is ...
Says, "That's a good idea."	10%
Commits, "I'll do it."	25%
Says when they'll do it	40%
Plans how to do it	50%
Commits to someone else	60%
Sets a specific future time to share progress with person they committed to	95%

So, the next steps to changing your habits to follow through on your plan would be to share your long-range goal and two-month plan with someone in your support network. If you are working with a support group already, this is perfect. If not, write down the names of three people that are in your network whom you think will be helpful in supporting you in your goals. You might consider people who can give you ideas, encouragement, and feedback and challenge you to keep on track. Write down those three names here and when you will contact them to check-in about your goal accomplishments:

Name	Contact Information	When I will speak with them
1. _____	_____	_____
2. _____	_____	_____
3. _____	_____	_____

Another wonderful way to help you accomplish your goals is to create environments all around you that support your mission. Look around you at where you spend your time. Think about the spaces you spend time in like your office and your home. Consider whom you hang out with on a regular basis. Consider the types of events you attend and the papers and magazines you read—the information and ideas you focus on. Consider how you are treating your body—do you have energy, are you fit, are you healthy? If you think about all aspects of your life the way you did in your Wheel of Life in Chapter 5, you can begin to put your environments in this wheel and rate how well each environment supports your ability to reach your goal. For more information on this, you can take an online workshop at www.Coachville.com.

All the Best

We want to wish the best to all of you who are out there doing the exercises and assessments in this book. Finding your perfect career is hard work, and we know it is well worth your time and effort. You deserve to be happy in work and in life. Although our focus here has been mainly on the work you do, you definitely want to fill out your whole life profile. Go back to your Wheel of Life in Chapter 5 and remember there are a whole bunch of things that make up a perfect life. Although your career is a big piece of your life, there are so many other pieces that yearn for your time and attention, and those pieces are ready to give satisfaction back 10 times over. Life is a journey; you are on it; we support and cheer you. Be happy, be well, do what you love.

The Least You Need to Know

- Making a plan of action will help you to reach your goal of being in your perfect career at a much faster pace than doing without one.

- Your mission statement guides your everyday actions and decisions and is made up of a description of your essential nature—what is really important to you in life and work, the core values that guide your behavior, and the contribution you make through the work you do.

- Action planning begins with setting long-range goals, rank ordering which goals need to be addressed first, and focusing on a two-month plan of action steps to reach your highest ranked goals.

♦ You have a higher success rate if you make a plan, share your plan with someone in your support network, and check-in on a regular basis for updates with that person on your accomplishments.

♦ You can do this—you can follow your dreams, do what you love, and work in your perfect career.

Appendix

Career Profile Map

Your Career Profile Map is where you will capture and write down all the information you learn from all the assessments and exercises in this book. It serves as your record of information about your career and life-style preferences. And it acts as your touch stone or guidance in choosing a career that matches what you have said is important to you. You will be instructed throughout the text of this book, when to record your assessment results and responses to exercises in this Career Profile Map.

Chapter 5: Your Dream Career

The Wheel of Life Assessment. Record the specific numbers you circled on each 1 to 10 scale indicating your current level of satisfaction with each of the following:

Money: ___

Mind: ___

Career/Work: ___

Emotions: ___

Family and Friends: ___

Significant Other: ___

Health and Fitness: ___

Environments: ___

Spirit: ___

Fun and Recreation: ___

Vision Summary. Record your findings from your five years from now exercise here.

_____

_____

_____

Chapter 6: Your Values

Values Sort Assessment. Record your ranked values from both the life you want to live and day-to-day list.

The Life I Want to Live	My Day-To-Day Action
1. _____	1. _____
2. _____	2. _____
3. _____	3. _____
4. _____	4. _____
5. _____	5. _____

Career Implications (notes to yourself):

_____

_____

_____

Chapter 7: Your Temperament and Personality

Shorter Personality Sorter. Record the four letters you circled; these represent your personality type. Also record the descriptive temperament name that corresponds with your personality type.

Personality Type: _____

Temperament: _____

Career Implications (notes to yourself):

_____

_____

_____

Chapter 8: Your Motivation

The Four Boxes of Life Assessment. Record your score and rank order the motivators from highest to lowest.

Motivators	Total Checked Off	Rank
Security	_____	_____
Relationships	_____	_____
Recognition	_____	_____
Contribution	_____	_____

Career Implications (notes to yourself):

_____

_____

Chapter 9: Your Interests

Orientation Scales Assessment. Record the total number of activities of interest you listed for each orientation.

Orientation Interest	Total
Influencing	____
Organizing	____
Helping	____
Creating	____
Analyzing	____
Producing	____
Adventuring	____

Top Three Priority Orientations. Record in order of priority, your three highest totals:

1. _____

2. _____

3. _____

Top Five Interests. Record your five favorite interests from the Orientation Scales Assessment table:

1. _____
2. _____
3. _____
4. _____
5. _____

Career Implications (notes to yourself):

_____

_____

_____

Chapter 10: Your Skills

Top Ten Skills. Transfer the data from your Skills Chart according to your Data, Things, and People Skills.

Skills Chart

Data Skills

I Want to Use This Skill in My Work	I Need to Get or Develop This Skill	Rank Order
_____	_____	_____
_____	_____	_____
_____	_____	_____
_____	_____	_____
_____	_____	_____
_____	_____	_____
_____	_____	_____
_____	_____	_____

Things Skills

I Want to Use This Skill in My Work	I Need to Get or Develop This Skill	Rank Order
_____	_____	_____
_____	_____	_____
_____	_____	_____
_____	_____	_____
_____	_____	_____
_____	_____	_____
_____	_____	_____
_____	_____	_____

People Skills

I Want to Use This Skill in My Work	I Need to Get or Develop This Skill	Rank Order
_____	_____	_____
_____	_____	_____
_____	_____	_____
_____	_____	_____
_____	_____	_____
_____	_____	_____
_____	_____	_____
_____	_____	_____

Top Five Transferable Skills. Record the key transferable skills that you see as strengths for you and ones you want to be able to use in your work.

1. _____

2. _____

3. _____

4. _____

5. _____

Top Five Self-Management Skills. Record the top five self-management skills that best represent you.

1. _____

2. _____

3. _____

4. _____

5. _____

Talents. Record the skills you have highlighted in the "Top Seven Skills," "Transferable Skills," and "Self-Management Skills" sections that best represent your talents.

_____

_____

_____

Career Implications (notes to yourself):

_____

_____

_____

Chapter 11: Your Lifestyle

Lifestyle Preference Assessment. Record the percentage points you assigned to each lifestyle category.

Ideal Lifestyle

___% Career/Job/Work

___% Personal Relationships (Family/Friends/Life Partner)

___% Fitness/Health

___% Spiritual Endeavors

___% Fun/Entertainment

___% Growth/Learning

___% Community

___% Other _____

100% Total

Actual Lifestyle

___% Career/Job/Work

___% Personal Relationships (Family/Friends/Life Partner)

___% Fitness/Health

___% Spiritual Endeavors

___% Fun/Entertainment

___% Growth/Learning

___% Community

___% Other _____

100% Total

Top Seven Lifestyle Descriptors. Record the most important lifestyle descriptors.

1. _____

2. _____

3. _____

4. _____

5. _____

6. _____

7. _____

Career Implications (notes to yourself):

_____

_____

_____

Chapter 12: Summing It All Up

Career Ideas List. Combine and record the list of careers that you came up with that related to each of your different profiles.

_____

_____

_____

_____

_____

Five Years From Now. Record the statement that incorporates all the aspects of your life and work.

_____

_____

_____

_____

_____

Statement of Self. Record a more in-depth description of what you know about yourself. Start with, "This is a summary of what I have learned (or affirmed) about myself so far in terms of what is important to me in my career and how I want to live my life …" and continue below.

_____

_____

_____

_____

_____

_____

_____

_____

_____

_____

Feedback (Statement of Self):

_____

_____

_____

_____

_____

_____

_____

_____

Chapter 14: Your Preferred Work Environment

Ideal Work Environment. Record the top five must have's for your ideal work location and environment. Also record the work style that describes your approach to your work.

Top Five Must Have's for Location. These meet your needs for your ideal work environment.

1. _____

2. _____

3. _____

4. _____

5. _____

Top Five Must Have's for Work Environment. These describe your approach to your work.

1. _____

2. _____

3. _____

4. _____

5. _____

Work Style: _____

Career Implications (notes to yourself):

_____

_____

_____

Chapters 15, 16, and 17: Jobs for Your Temperament, Your Interests, and That Fit Your Skills

Career Ideas List. List all the jobs that you checked off for each specific chapter. In instances where you have checked the same job listing as you did under jobs for your temperament or your interests, place an additional check mark in front of the job listing.

Jobs for My Temperament (Chapter 15)	Jobs for My Interests (Chapter 16)	Jobs that Fit My Skills (Chapter 17)
_____	_____	_____
_____	_____	_____

Jobs for My Temperament (Chapter 15)	Jobs for My Interests (Chapter 16)	Jobs that Fit My Skills (Chapter 17)
_____	_____	_____
_____	_____	_____
_____	_____	_____
_____	_____	_____
_____	_____	_____
_____	_____	_____
_____	_____	_____

Top Two or Three Careers I Want to Learn More About. From the list of possible careers you selected, list a few that you would like to learn more about.

1. _____

2. _____

3. _____

My Perfect Career Is: _____

Chapter 20: Interviewing Job Holders

Everyone I know List. Transfer the information you wrote down on this list. Keep adding to the list as you think of new contacts or are given contacts from people on your list.

Name	How I Know Them	Contact Information
_____	_____	_____
_____	_____	_____
_____	_____	_____
_____	_____	_____

Appendix B

Glossary

achievement oriented   This means that you want to get things done. You want to accomplish your goals and see the results of your efforts. People who are achievement oriented are doers. They value being competent at what they do and able to meet and exceed expectations.

authentic self   This means your true self or your real self. During this process of looking at who you are, it is important that you be absolutely honest with yourself about your preferences and your likes and dislikes.

barter   This means that you are exchanging one good or service for another. No money changes hands; just the goods or services are exchanged. This is a great way for small business owners to get services that they need without paying precious money for them. An example of this would be from Rene who exchanged a coaching session to help Karen get more focused on her business goals and get moving for a lovely piece of jewelry that Karen made.

career check-up   This is similar to a yearly physical. It involves making an appointment with yourself to check your levels of satisfaction with your career. Are you satisfied with the goals you set for yourself? Is your career consistent with your values and interests? Are you using and learning desired skills and competencies? It also gives you the chance to set goals for the coming year.

Career Profile Map   This is in Appendix A and is the place where you will write down the results of your assessments and tests. It will give you a comprehensive picture of what is important to you. Your values, interests, talents and skills, attributes, motivations, preferred work environment, and lifestyle. This profile will be your guidepost to selecting career options that match who you really are!

core values   These are the big ones—the most important ones. These are the ones that really make a difference in how we behave and the directions we choose. We all have many values that are important to us, but we are looking for those that are at the core of defining who we are.

curriculum specialists   These are also known as instructional coordinators, staff development specialists, or directors of instructional material. They play a large role in improving the quality of education in the classroom. They develop instructional materials, train teachers, and assess educational programs. Income ranges from $35,000 to $72,000.

divergent and convergent   These represent two stages of the decision making process. Divergent means keeping your net thrown wide and generating possibilities. In this case, looking for your perfect career match requires seeing all the jobs out there that could be possible for you. Convergent means you narrow your focus and gather those nets in close. This is where you will bring your choice down to 2 or 3 career options and evaluate them based on criteria from your Career Profile Map. Staying in the Divergent mode right now is important. For those of you who have the Judging function, you are going to have to fight your tendency to reach closer very quickly.

elements   These are parts of a whole. Career elements are parts of you. Parts that are important to you—talents or skills you like to use, environments you like to be in, amount of adventure you want in your life, pieces of your personality you enjoy using in work ….

entrepreneurial   This is being willing to take risks to make a profit. Most entrepreneurs see opportunities and are willing to step out of their comfort zone to pursue the chance to make a profit.

environmental scientists   These folks use their knowledge of the physical makeup and history of the earth to protect the environment. They locate water, mineral, and energy resources; predict future geologic hazards; and offer advice on construction and land-use projects. Environmental scientists make $29,000 to $50,000 a year.

lifestyle   This is an important aspect of career decision making. It takes into account all those individual preferences that you have in life. Things like amount of time you spend relaxing versus working or traveling versus home and community. It encompasses parts of yourself that need to be taken into consideration in your career choice.

measurable goals   This is a way of demonstrating the kinds of results your goal is achieving. You will know whether you have been successful. Results can be seen in the difference in cost, time, quantity, or quality.

mentor   This person agrees to show you the ropes—to be your guide. That means your mentor has to know quite a bit about the area you want to learn about. Suppose that you decide you are interested in collecting stamps. You locate the owner of a stamp collector shop. The owner agrees to teach you how to be a collector. This might include the types of stamps to collect, where you can locate the stamps, how to evaluate their worth, and so on. This person guides you through the whole process and gives you a complete picture of stamp collecting. Mentors are common in organizations to help new employees to learn "how we do things here."

milestone   A milestone is an important event. In Career terms it indicates that you have reached a certain plateau in your journey to identifying your perfect career. Setting milestones is a way to break down your long-range goals into manageable pieces. A milestone is when you have accomplished a big chunk of your goal. It indicates specific results achieved along the road to goal accomplishment. Milestones need to be acknowledged and celebrated. Sometimes goals are so big that you get discouraged along the way. Milestones help you to recognize that you are truly making progress and motivate you to continue the journey.

motivation   This is an internal need or want that activates and energizes your behavior and gives it direction. Motivation can come from your need for security, for relationships, for recognition, or for making a contribution. Motivation sustains your performance and helps you to reach your goals.

multicultural   This promotes the value of different cultures coexisting within a single society. It is a vision of cultural diversity that is deliberately fostered and protected. Multiculturalism is also known as diversity or pluralism, which means that differences among people and groups are recognized, respected, and valued.

mutual benefit employment   This is between employee and employer, which has replaced loyalty. It used to be that employees would pretty much work for one company for their whole working lives. In exchange for their loyalty, they received the security of employment and often retirement benefits. In today's work world, the exchange is different. Employees are looking for opportunities to learn, to keep their skills up, to remain employable. Employers are looking for employees who have the skills they need right now. As long as the employee and employer are meeting one another's needs, you have mutual benefit. When you don't, there is a parting of the ways. Today, we find employees moving around to different organizations to get the experiences that will keep them employable and more satisfied.

network   These are people we know and can access to gather information, provide referrals or support, and so on. It's interesting how we sometimes limit ourselves because we think that our network has to be people who are our best friends and family. Our network is huge—made up of all the people we rely on and know in our lives. Sit down and make a list of everyone you come into contact with over a three-month period. That includes people who provide services for you such as your doctor, lawyer, dentist, auto mechanic, accountant, lawn maintenance person, yoga instructor, and so on. It also includes people you provide services to through your work or life tasks. All of these people have the potential to provide you with excellent information that will help you in your career search. You just need to let people know what you are looking for and see whether there is a way for them to help.

occupational clusters   This refers to groupings of occupations under one title. For instance, the sales and related occupations cluster encompasses the following jobs: cashiers, counter and rental clerks, demonstrators, product promoters, and models, insurance sales agents, real estate brokers and sales agents, and so on. It is a classification system that helps job seekers, employers, and job experts to display and communicate information. Changes to the titles and content of these clusters have recently been made by the U.S. Department of Labor and can be found on the O*Net site.

query   This is used in computer speak to mean the question you are posing to your search engine so that it can retrieve the appropriate information for you. What you put in your query is very important. You need to be specific, simple, and understand that the search engine needs your guidance in coming up with the right information. After all, they have robots working for them!

SBA   This refers to the Small Business Administration, which is a government agency established to strengthen the economy by aiding, counseling, assisting, and protecting the interests of small businesses. Small businesses can receive all kinds of information on how to start a business, finance a business, and decide on the legal status of a business for free or at a very low cost. It is a wonderful service for small businesses.

self-assessments   These are appraisals of your own personal qualities and traits that help you identify your strengths.

self-management skills   These are personal qualities you use in your work. Your sense of humor, your tenacity, or your sense of responsibility can set you apart from others applying for a position. In addition, self-management skills are about assets you use to get along with others. These can be tone setters that contribute to a work environment such as being friendly and honest in your communication.

solopreneurs   This is a new term—that's right, it's not even in the dictionary yet! This means you are a solo-entrepreneur, someone who is in business for themselves. Most solopreneurs work out of their homes. You can be a consultant, a coach, a decorator, a real estate investor, an artist, a crafter, an Internet businesses owner, and so on. There are thousands of possibilities, and more and more people are looking into this lifestyle.

spirit   This is another dimension of knowledge beyond the cognitive, the tangible, the concrete. It gives us access to inspiration, peace, and insight into ourselves. Ways to be in touch with spirit can come through meditation, yoga, walking, spiritual practices, contemplating spiritual writings, and more.

strategic thinking   This means that you keep your focus on your goals, and all your actions and decisions are ones that move you toward accomplishing those goals.

student affairs staff   This is found in colleges and universities and is comprised of staff that is focused on providing services and programs for students on the campus. This category of jobs is highly populated by people with a Helping Orientation. There are several jobs that range from working with students to help them plan programs in the student activities or campus activities office to being a head of residence in a residence hall where you are in charge of the administration and programming aspects of residence living. Other jobs are in recruiting and admissions, financial aid services, health services and programming, and career and personal counseling. The collegial environment of college campuses often draws people from the Helping Orientation to this setting.

trustworthy   Being a trustworthy person is a measure of your character. Character is the foundation of who you are and how you behave. Being trustworthy means that you can count on this person to follow-through, to do what they say they will do, to be honest and consistent in their behavior with you. Stephen Covey, the author of *Seven Habits of Highly Effective People*, reminded us that we had moved away from developing our character to becoming too focused on developing skills. Character is based on values that are important to us and we want to act upon. They are solid and dependable and build trustworthiness.

temperament   This is your disposition. It represents tendencies you were born with to have certain attitudes and to behave in certain ways. It is known as the core or driving force of your personality.

transferable skills   These are skills that you can take with you from one job to another, such as listening or speaking clearly.

veterinary technologists   They usually love animals and are found performing medical tests and treating and diagnosing medical conditions and diseases in animals, under the supervision of a veterinarian. They work in either private clinics, animal hospitals, or research facilities where the median salary is $22,950 a year. The salary spread is from $16,170 to $33,750. Generally there is a requirement for completing a 2–4 year veterinary technology program and passing a state examination. The outlook for veterinary technologists is expected to grow faster than the average for all occupations.

vision   This describes what we aspire to become, to achieve, to create. The first component of a vision is the stretch goal. This has a specific time frame—5 years from now. It states our future dream, hope, or aspiration. The second component of a vision provides a vivid description or visual image of the stretch goal. You want the words you use to be descriptive, upbeat, and exciting. This vision will be carried around in your head and keep you focused on where you want to go. An example of a vision statement might be, "In 2009, I am sitting on the deck of my newly renovated house looking into my beautiful office space. My consulting and coaching business is flourishing; I have been writing a follow-up book to *Finding Your Perfect Career*, and the pace of my life is just right for enjoying family, friends, and the work I love to do."

writers   These generally fall into one of three categories. Writers and authors develop original fiction and nonfiction for books, magazines, trade journals, online publications, company newsletters, radio and television broadcasts, motion pictures, and advertisements. Editors examine proposals and select material for publication or broadcast, and review and revise a writer's work in preparation for publication. The third area includes technical writers who develop technical materials such as equipment manuals, appendices, or operating and maintenance instructions. The growth of online publications and services are growing in number and sophistication, and that's good news for writers and editors. Check out the American Writers and Artists Institute website and learn more about copywriting and travel writing.

Index

X–Y–Z

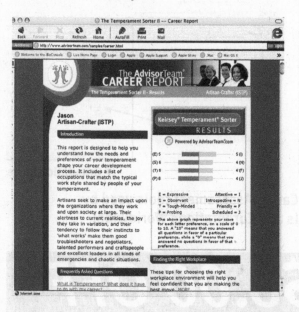
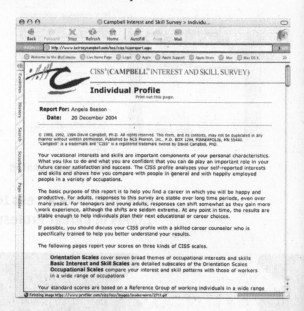

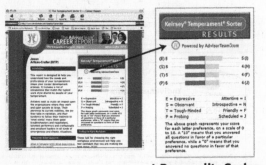
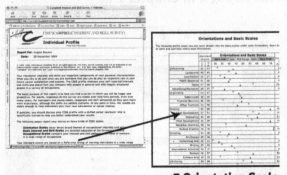